# TIDEWATER ON THE HALF SHELL
## F I N E · V I R G I N I A · R E C I P E S

Presented by
The Junior League of Norfolk–Virginia Beach, Inc.

The purpose of the Junior League is exclusively educational and charitable and is to promote voluntarism, to develop the potential of its members for voluntary participation in community affairs, and to demonstrate the effectiveness of trained volunteers.

Proceeds from the sale of **TIDEWATER ON THE HALF SHELL** will be used to support community projects sponsored by the Junior League of Norfolk-Virginia Beach, Inc.

For additional copies, use the order forms at the back of the book or write:

## TIDEWATER ON THE HALF SHELL

P.O. Box 956
Norfolk, Virginia 23501
Price $16.95 plus $3.00 shipping and handling. Virginia residents add 4.5% sales tax.

---

| First Printing | August, 1985 | 10,000 copies |
| Second Printing | November, 1985 | 15,000 copies |
| Third Printing | August, 1986 | 20,000 copies |
| Fourth Printing | April, 1987 | 30,000 copies |
| Fifth Printing | May, 1989 | 20,000 copies |
| Sixth Printing | July, 1991 | 25,000 copies |

Library of Congress Catalog Card Number 85-60705
ISBN 0-9614767-0-2

---

Cover Design and Graphics by
Barker, Campbell & Farley
Virginia Beach, Virginia

Creative portions of manuscript by
Margaret Graham Campbell

Printed by
S. C. Toof and Company
Memphis, Tennessee

# TIDEWATER ON THE HALF SHELL

The Tidewater region of Virginia was one of the first settled areas of the United States. New colonists arriving on Virginia shores were delighted to discover that, after their many travails, they had found safe harbor in this beautiful place. Of course, after their weeks at sea and their meager shipboard rations, the abundant fish and game they found was like paradise to them.

From these early beginnings came the centuries-old tradition of gracious living, bountiful hospitality, and sumptuous local cuisine which is still associated with Tidewater.

"On the half shell" is an idiomatic expression originally used to refer to the presentation of clams and oysters which are pried open and then served using the bottom shell as a dish. The implication is that the food is as fresh as it can possibly be. The expression is still used when serving oysters, but it has acquired a wider meaning. Serving something "on the half shell" implies that it is being presented in the most attractive, deluxe way—in a manner which is simple, but elegant.

The concept of simple elegance is one which strikes the right keynote for the recipes in TIDEWATER ON THE HALF SHELL . Cookbook users— and the lucky ones they cook for—have more sophisticated palates today than the colonial settlers of the past. They are more knowledgeable about food and have an almost infinite variety of ingredients available to them.

It takes a certain amount of confidence to return to simplicity in cooking. But the tradition of starting with the very best quality of food, then preparing and serving it simply, yet subtly enhancing its basic goodness with culinary skill—this is indeed a classic approach to food which will remain appealing for years to come.

# COOKBOOK BOARD

Susan Hathaway Gentry          Heather Laird Martin
**CQ-CHAIRMEN**

Sandra Dougan Laudenslager
**SECRETARY**

Susanne Boothby Councill
**MARKETING**

Martha Jacobs Goodman
**LEAGUE PRESIDENT**
**1984-85**

Sally Old Kitchin
**TREASURER**

Perry Wise Bussard
**TECHNICAL EDITOR**

Clara Bell Gurkin
**SUSTAINING ADVISOR**

Carolyn Miller Lammers
**FOOD EDITOR** ·

Kaye McPherson Taylor
**CREATIVE DESIGN**

Betty Howe Shannon
**SUSTAINING ADVISOR**

# COOKBOOK STAFF

Mary Lewis Ash
Anne Stall Burke
Mary Louis Stack Campbell
Meg Graham Campbell
Martha Gartrell Capshaw
Susan Gross Coe
Ann Reeves Farley

P.J. Hughes Forbes
Eleanor Magruder Harris
Elizabeth Wallin Hoey
Lida Kepner Hudson
Sally James Laster
Lucy Cunningham Lee
Melissa Kinsey Mathews

Diane Burrell Morris
Julie M. McCollum
Alice Milton Mountjoy
Ann Harrison Reichner
Page Camp Schoew
Wanda Buie Sellers
Nonie White Waller

# TESTING COMMITTEE

Andrea Harkness Bell
Betsy Fitch Benton
Joan Ward Birdsong
Sharon Callahan Connor
Sigrid Clark Couch
Ann Wray Cutchins
Cathy Ann Davis
Elizabeth Brichter DiPeppe

Pat Hamlin Hall
Nancy Rodenhizer Henderson
Paige Sommers Hood
Nancy Norman Huber
Catherine Taylor Koch
Kathy Farrell McNaughton
Karen Oetjen O'Brien

Susan Hodges Oldfield
Bev Muhlsteff Parker
Margaret Alley Richardson
Jane Rathbone Sanders
Elaine Smith Stephens
Carol Roberts Straeten
Mary Devine Timberlake
Jane Claytor Webster

# CONTINUING CHAIRMEN

Paige Gannon Romig
**1985-86**

Beth Urie Driscoll
Georgina Rawles Miller
**1988-89**

Sigrid Clark Couch
**1986-87**

Donna Houser Smith
**1989-90**

Nancy Bird Mills
**1987-88**

Nancy Holland Hodges
B. Paige Martin
**1990-91**

iv

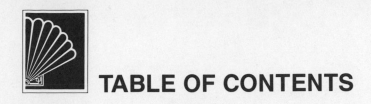

# TABLE OF CONTENTS

# DEDICATION

TIDEWATER ON THE HALF SHELL is dedicated to the long and out-
standing tradition of Junior League volunteer service in Tidewater.
Over the last 60 years, the Junior League of Norfolk-Virginia
Beach, Inc., has established an exemplary record of service to the
community. The organization has raised countless dollars and
contributed innumerable volunteer hours for community projects,
both alone and in conjunction with other groups. Junior League
volunteers have been leaders and catalysts in the arts, in educa-
tion, in health and in children's issues—in these areas and many
others they have served to enrich immeasurably the very special
quality of life in Tidewater. This book honors a 60-year commitment
made by the women of Tidewater, and with its proceeds, we hope
to insure the continuation of that commitment to community service through volunteerism.

# A Taste Of Tidewater

# A Taste Of Tidewater

# BED AND BREAKFAST

Orange Delight
Fresh Strawberries


Sunny-Side-Up Casserole
Applesauce Muffins        French Breakfast Puffs
English Muffin Loaf
Blueberry Jam

---

Banana Freeze
Cantaloupe


Baked Egg Casserole with Smithfield Ham
Blueberry Muffins        Oatmeal Spice Muffins
Biscuits Supreme
Delicious Fruit Marmalade


America's beginnings are all around us—from the shaded streets of Williamsburg and the silent battlefields of Yorktown to the cross where the first settlers landed near the Old Cape Henry Lighthouse in Virginia Beach. Visitors who come to explore the past or bask on the sunny beaches often begin their day with a light but sustaining breakfast.

# NEIGHBORHOOD COFFEE

Coffee        Spiced Tea
Sunshine Punch

Platter of Fresh Fruit with Fancy Fruit Spread
Rolls with Smithfield Ham Pâté
Vegetable Sandwiches
Sweet Potato Muffins        Fig Coffee Cake
Cinnamon-Pecan Nibbles

In Tidewater communities new faces appear every day, thanks to the Navy and other military bases. And new business growth continues at a remarkable rate, as the secret of Tidewater's mild climate, good schools, and delightfully relaxing lifestyle becomes better known. Last year's new Virginians greet this year's newcomers with a warm and sincere welcome. Next year, *they'll* be the hosts!

# HOLIDAY BRUNCH

Hospitable Grapes 'n Cheese Spread
Assorted Crackers
Tangy Bloody Marys          Orange-Ale Punch

Deviled Eggs and Shrimp Casserole
Savory Rice with Spinach
Tomato Aspic
Herb-Cheese Bread
Sweet Pickled Figs          Corn Relish
Dilled Okra

Applesauce Fruit Cake
Apricot Brandy Pound Cake

Colorful holiday celebrations take place throughout Tidewater. An annual tradition is the Christmas Illumination in Williamsburg. The James River plantations are an easy drive, and historic homes in Norfolk and Virginia Beach, open all year, are at their very best when sparkling with holiday cheer.

# LIGHT LUNCHEON

Champagne Sophisticate

Zesty Seafood Salad
Fresh Asparagus         Cheese Puff Ring

Luscious Lemon Dessert
Coffee

---

Orange Champagne Punch

Chicken Salad Pie
Spinach Tomatoes         Herb-Cheese Bread

Heavenly Snow Squares
Coffee

The season for outdoor sports goes on almost all year; even in mid-winter a sudden balmy day may fill the beaches. Tidewater tennis courts and golf courses are rarely deserted, and a lunch break provides a chance to relax and replenish energy.

# SPRING LUNCHEON

Azalea Punch
Cheese Wafers

Sausage-Zucchini Bake
Festive Fruit with Sherry Sauce
Tropical Salad
Great Grandmother's Sally Lunn Bread
Green Tomato Pickles
Lime Tea

Strawberry Forgotten Torte
Coffee

In Tidewater the sudden burst of springtime is heralded by a breath-taking show of forsythia and dogwood laced along the highways, and is highlighted by the yearly Azalea Festival where a queen is crowned amid the blooming meadows of the Gardens-by-the-Sea. Local homes are open during Garden Week when a light, elegant luncheon sustains each welcome guest.

# BUSMAN'S HOLIDAY

White Gazpacho

Salad Olé
Guacamole with Endive to dip
Celery and Carrot Sticks        Black Olives
Solar Tea with Fresh Mint

Carmelitas

---

Cold Zucchini Bisque

Salad Bowl Sandwich in Pita Pockets
Piquant Cheese on Endive
Old Church Watermelon Rind Pickles
Sparkling Cider

Pineapple Tote Cake

The pleasures of the casual life are irresistible. So many vacation-ers come to Tidewater that there's always a sense of holiday in the air. Day trips to the beach, adventuring in Williamsburg or Jamestown, tour-ing Virginia Beach and Norfolk—all call for picnic lunches to be enjoyed in a variety of scenic spots.

# BOATING PICNIC

Rainbow Brie       Shrimp Spread
Assorted Crackers

Chicken with Island Marinade
Cold Potato and Green Bean Salad
Fresh Fruit Mixture with Honey-Nut Dressing
French Bread
Dry Chenin Blanc or Sauvignon Blanc

Orange Chiffon Cake with White Chocolate Icing

The water is an intrinsic part of Tidewater living. Sailing out of Hampton Roads, one of the world's greatest natural harbors, you may see a catamaran bobbing next to a gigantic aircraft carrier. Long golden days afloat on the Chesapeake Bay are relaxing and exhilarating at the same time. Fresh breezes and sunlight sparkling on the water—days at sea can rouse the most lethargic appetite!

# OYSTER ROAST

Oysters on the Half Shell
Granny's Dipping Sauce
Roasted Oysters with Melted Butter
Easy Oyster Stew
Quick Snacking Crackers

Crowd-Pleaser Brunswick Stew
Overnight Cabbage Slaw     Cornbread
Trays of Fresh Vegetables
Green Goddess Dip     Spicy Vegetable Dip
Beer

Colossal Cookies

The delicate, slightly sweet taste of the Lynnhaven oyster is something that locals and visitors alike find absolutely delectable. Oyster roasts are a delightfully relaxed way to entertain. The fortunate guest who pops a freshly roasted oyster, dripping with seafood sauce, into his mouth can always find room for one more. And one more. . .

# FOURTH OF JULY COOKOUT

Easy Clam Dip     Bacon and Tomato Spread
Mild Crackers     Melba Rounds
Sundown Cooler

Grilled Steak/Red Wine Marinade
Snaps with Herbs     Fresh Corn on the Cob
Gazpacho Salad
Parmesan French Bread
California Napa Gamay Beaujolais

Pick-of-the-Peach Ice Cream
Best-Ever Butter Cookies

Beach weather brings outdoor cooking and all the delights of fresh produce. Whether plucked from your own backyard garden, or from the Farmer's Market which displays the year-round bounty of Tidewater farms, it's hard to believe food this good could be so easy. Nobody would ever guess you spent the whole day on the beach!

# COCKTAIL BUFFET

Open House Punch
White Pinot Noir

Chesapeake Crab Dip      Salmon Log
Assorted Mild Crackers
Marinated Eye of Round with Horseradish Sauce
Party Rolls
Caviar Crowned Mold      Jeweled Cheese Ball
Cold Antipasto
Shrimp Mini-Quiches      Chicken Nuggets

Sinful Chocolates      Lace Cookies
Sunny Island Bars

Hampton Roads Harbor cradled a fledgling Navy in the early days of our Republic—now it shelters the most powerful ships afloat. The dramatic Naval legacy of the Tidewater area is history that happens every day. Mark a special occasion such as a Change-of-Command with the casual sophistication of an elegant buffet. They'll all salute!

# NATO SMÖRGÅSBORD

Rum-Port Punch      Chardonnay

Greek Shrimp
Crustless Crab Quiche
Pasta Primavera
Flash un Kas      Country Pâté
Epicurean Eggplant
Mousse aux Concombres      Gazpacho Aspic
Chutney Dip with Assorted Fruit

Peaches and Cream Kuchen      Sherry Ice Cream Cake
Devonshire Apple Pie
Coffee

Tidewater is headquarters for NATO, the North Atlantic Treaty Organization, and thus also home—temporarily—for the delegations representing each of the NATO countries. A ceremonial flag-raising commemorates the flag day of each member country. On each nation's flag day, that country hosts a buffet featuring its native dishes and beverages.

# INFORMAL DINNER

Mushrooms Supreme

Chicken Spaghetti
Zucchini Squares          Winter Salad
White Zinfandel

Toffee Ice Cream Pie

---

Spicy Stuffed Brie
Thinly sliced French Bread

Seafood Gumbo with Rice
Spinach Salad Supreme with Oil and Vinegar Dressing
Beer Muffins
Gewürztraminer

Rum Cheesecake

Sport fishing is the passionate pastime of both tourists and locals. Black drum, channel bass, speckled trout, cobia, marlin, tarpon, dolphin—the list goes on and on. Twenty-three species of sport fish are caught from Virginia boats, piers and shores. And the eager fisherman always catches at least one thing—a hearty appetite!

# SUMMER EVENING REPAST

Shrimp and Artichoke Dip
Assorted Crackers
Red or White Sangria     Iced Tea Punch

Chilled Tomato Basil Soup
Hot Parmesan Puffs

Cold Chicken and Pasta
Cold Spiced Fruit
Spinach Bars

Black Bottom Ice Cream Pie
Coffee

Evenings on the dock at Waterside watching the sun go down and the gulls wheeling against the red sky—it's time to sail into the sunset yourself. Harbor cruises offer live entertainment, dancing, good food and a festive atmosphere—all of the elements of an ocean-going cruise, plus sightseeing: a gull's eye view of the world's largest natural harbor.

# NEW YEAR'S DAY DINNER

Cranberry Wine Punch
Herbed Nuts

New Year's Day Bean Soup

Smithfield Ham
Deviled Crab
Tantalizing Tomatoes and Artichokes
Apricot Casserole
Batter Bread
Festive Asparagus Salad
Best-Ever Bread and Butter Pickles
Beaujolais Villages or French Chablis

Chocolate on a Cloud
Coffee

Since earliest colonial days, setting an abundant table has been a point of pride in Tidewater. Bean soup brings in the New Year with a hearty helping of good luck in the traditional black-eyed peas. Today's sophisticated palates still relish the rich flavor of Smithfield ham—a delicious addition to any meal, its contribution to Tidewater dining has never been surpassed.

# FORMAL DINNER

Back Bay Duck Bits
Rosé of Cabernet Sauvignon

Potage Grand Luxe
Brut Champagne

Savory Scallops
French Muscadet

Kir Sorbet

Roast Spring Lamb
Old Fashioned Mint Sauce
Fresh Broccoli with Caper Sauce
Broiled Tomato Cups          Wild Rice
Nuits Saint Georges or other French Burgundy

Bibb Lettuce with Creamy French Dressing

Chilled Lemon Soufflé
Sauternes or other Dessert Wine

Choice of Liqueurs
or
Kahlúa-Amaretto Freeze

Relaxed elegance even in the most formal setting is a keynote of Tidewater sophistication. After all, hospitality means not only serving plentiful and delicious food but also putting your guests at their ease. From the colonial mansions of old Norfolk to the contemporary seaside homes of Virginia Beach, a warm and genuine welcome awaits those who come calling.

# MIDNIGHT MAGIC

Brut Rosé
or
Blanc de Blancs Champagne


Captain's Caviar          Smoked Salmon
Pumpernickel or Rye Slices          Toast Points
Shish-Kabob Pepper Chicken
Sliced Smithfield Ham in Biscuits Supreme
Chinese Meatballs
Creole Watercress Fritters          Marinated Mushrooms
Easy Broccoli Soufflé


Fruit Spectacular
Coconut Coffee


There's a cultural kaleidoscope in Tidewater. The Chrysler Museum is one of America's top 20 and has a stunning collection of Tiffany glass, as well as many other treasures. Restored colonial homes are open for the public to explore and the Gardens-by-the-Sea provide a pleasant stroll in any weather. There's an exciting array of constantly changing adventures in the arts—symphony, opera, stage and ballet. Tidewater's cherished traditions are being proudly maintained even as dynamic new ones take shape around us.

# APPETIZERS

# APPETIZERS

## COLD DIPS
Blue Cheese Dip 52
Chutney Dip 24
Easy Clam Dip 26
Green Goddess Dip 21
Guacamole 22
Herbed Vegetable Dip 21
Shrimp and Artichoke
  Dip 27
Smoked Oyster Dip 26
South-of-the-Border
  Platter 23
Spicy Vegetable Dip 21
Tex-Mex Dip 23
Zingy Chili Dip 22

## HOT DIPS
Chesapeake Crab Dip 24
Hot Crab Dip 25
Lobster Dip 24
Shrimp Fondue 25

## COLD SPREADS
Almond Pâté 29
Bacon and Tomato
  Spread 31
Captain's Caviar 36
Caviar Crowned Mold 37
Crabmeat Croatan 34
Fancy Fruit Spread 32
Ginger Cheese 33
Herb Cheese 30
Hospitable Grapes 'n
  Cheese Spread 32
Jeweled Cheese Ball 31
Liver Pâté 33
Piquant Cheese 30
Rainbow Brie 29
Salmon Log 34
Shrimp Spread 35
Smoked Oyster Pâté 33
Spicy Stuffed Brie 28

## HOT SPREADS
Chili Artichokes 37
Hot Cheese Appetizer 36
Mushroom Spread 27

## COLD APPETIZERS
Antipasto Mediterranean 38
Cold Antipasto 35
Country Pâté 39
Marinated Eye of Round with
  Horseradish Sauce 40
Marinated Mushrooms 28
Marinated Shrimp 41
Shrimp with Capers 41

## HOT APPETIZERS
Artichokes Continental 42
Asparagus-Ham
  Pinwheels 45
Back Bay Duck Bits 55
Buffalo Chicken Wings with
  Blue Cheese Dip 52
Chafing Dish Oysters 49
Cheese Squares 48
Chicken and Bacon Bits 53
Chicken Nuggets 54
Chinese Chicken Wings 53
Chinese Meatballs 55
Cocktail Pizzas 47
Flash un Kas 46
Gourmet Mushrooms 43
Hot Parmesan Puffs 48
Italian Toasts 45
Mushrooms Supreme 43
Oyster Spicies 50
Oysters Virginia Beach 49
Party Hors d'Oeuvres 46
Sausage Spinach Balls 47
Shish-Kabob Pepper
  Chicken 54
Shrimp Mini-Quiches 50
Sweet and Sour Meatballs 56
Taco Tarts 56
Zucchini Top Hats 44

## MISCELLANEOUS
Cheese Wafers 38
Herbed Nuts 51
Quick Snacking Crackers 40

# GREEN GODDESS DIP

Yields 2 cups

| | |
|---|---|
| 1 | cup mayonnaise |
| 1 | cup sour cream |
| ⅓ | cup chopped parsley |
| 2 | Tbsp. chopped chives |
| 1 | Tbsp. anchovy paste |
| 1 | Tbsp. tarragon vinegar |
| 1 | Tbsp. lemon juice |
| 1 | clove garlic, crushed |

• Combine ingredients and serve with fresh vegetables.

# HERBED VEGETABLE DIP

Yields 1 cup
Do ahead

| | |
|---|---|
| 1 | cup mayonnaise |
| 2 | tsp. tarragon vinegar |
| ⅛ | tsp. white pepper |
| ½ | tsp. salt |
| ⅛ | tsp. thyme |
| ½ | tsp. curry powder |
| 2 | Tbsp. chili sauce |
| 2 | Tbsp. grated onion |
| 1 | Tbsp. chopped chives |

• Mix ingredients. Chill several hours.
• Serve with fresh vegetables.

# SPICY VEGETABLE DIP

Yields 1 quart
Do ahead

| | |
|---|---|
| 2 | cups mayonnaise |
| 2 | cups small curd cottage cheese |
| ½ | cup grated onion |
| ½ | tsp. salt |
| 1 | clove garlic, finely minced |
| ½ | tsp. celery salt |
| 1 | tsp. dry mustard |
| 1 | tsp. pepper |
| ¼ | tsp. Tabasco sauce |

• Mix ingredients.
• Chill several hours before serving for best results.
• Serve with mushrooms, turnips, green peppers, carrots, kohlrabi—any raw vegetable assortment.

*Good way to get children to eat their "veggies".*

# GUACAMOLE

Yields 1 cup

| | |
|---|---|
| Pinch | + ¼ tsp. salt (reserve) |
| 1 | clove garlic, cut in 2 or 3 pieces |
| 1 | large ripe avocado, peeled and pitted |
| ¼ | tsp. chili powder |
| 1 | tsp. lemon juice |
| 2 | tsp. minced onion |
| | Mayonnaise |

- Sprinkle bowl with the pinch of salt and rub with garlic pieces. Remove garlic.
- Mash avocado in bowl, seasoning with the reserved salt, chili powder and lemon juice. Stir in the onion, mixing well.
- Cover with a thin layer of mayonnaise to keep dip from darkening; blend well just before serving.
- Serve in a large hollowed-out tomato with corn chips, or on a bed of lettuce as a salad.

*Sliced black olives make a nice garnish.*

# ZINGY CHILI DIP

Yields 1½ pints

| | |
|---|---|
| 1 | 28-ounce can tomatoes, drained and mashed |
| 2 | 4-ounce cans black olives, chopped |
| 1 | bunch green onions, chopped |
| 4 | ounces fresh mushrooms, chopped |
| 2 | Tbsp. vinegar |
| 1 | 4-ounce can diced green chilies, drained |
| 1 | 8-ounce can tomato sauce |
| 3 | Tbsp. olive oil |
| 1 | clove garlic, finely diced |
| ½ | tsp. salt |

- Re-drain tomatoes, removing as much juice as possible. Mix with all other ingredients.
- Allow to chill for several hours to blend flavors.
- Serve with tortilla chips.

*Will keep for up to two weeks in refrigerator if tightly covered.*

# TEX-MEX DIP

Serves 10-12
Do ahead

| | |
|---|---|
| 2 | 10½-ounce cans jalapeño bean dip |
| 3 | ripe, medium-sized avocados |
| | Juice of one lemon |
| | Salt and pepper to taste |
| 1 | cup sour cream |
| ½ | cup mayonnaise |
| 1 | package taco seasoning mix |
| ½ | cup chopped spring onions |
| 2 | medium tomatoes, peeled, drained and chopped |
| 1 | large can pitted black olives, sliced |
| 3 | cups (12 ounces) grated sharp Cheddar cheese |

- On large round or oval plate, layer as follows:
  Layer 1—jalapeño bean dip
  Layer 2—avocados, mashed with lemon juice, salt and pepper added
  Layer 3—mixture of sour cream, mayonnaise and taco seasoning
  Layer 4—spring onions
  Layer 5—tomatoes
  Layer 6—olives
  Layer 7—grated cheese
- Chill to allow flavors time to blend.
- Serve with corn chips.

# SOUTH-OF-THE-BORDER PLATTER

Serves 12

| | |
|---|---|
| 2 | large ripe avocados |
| 1 | clove garlic, finely minced |
| ¼ | tsp. salt |
| 1 | Tbsp. lemon juice |
| 2 | Tbsp. mayonnaise |
| 8 | ounces sour cream |
| 2 | 8-ounce jars picanté sauce |
| ¾ | cup chopped ripe olives |
| 3 | cups peeled and chopped tomatoes |
| 1½ | cups (6 ounces) grated sharp Cheddar cheese |

- Peel, seed and mash avocados. Stir in next four ingredients.
- Spread mixture on an attractive platter. Spread sour cream over avocado.
- Pour sauce over layers, according to taste.
- Top with layers of olives, tomatoes and cheese.
- Serve with corn chips.

## CHUTNEY DIP

Yields 2 cups

| | |
|---|---|
| 16 | ounces cream cheese, softened |
| 1 | tsp. seasoned salt |
| ½ | tsp. curry powder |
| ⅓ | cup chutney, chopped if in large chunks |
| ½-1 | cup sour cream |
| ¼ | cup dry Sherry |

- Beat cream cheese with blender or mixer to lighten. Add remaining ingredients.
- Chill until ready to use.
- Serve as dip for fresh fruit.

## LOBSTER DIP

Yields 1½ cups

| | |
|---|---|
| 8 | ounces cream cheese |
| ¼ | cup mayonnaise |
| 1 | clove garlic, finely diced |
| 1 | tsp. grated onion |
| 1 | tsp. mustard |
| 1 | tsp. sugar |
| 1 | tsp. salt |
| 1 | tsp. crushed red pepper |
| 5 | ounces lobster |
| 3 | Tbsp. white wine |

- Blend cheese and mayonnaise over heat. Add remaining ingredients.
- Serve in a chafing dish with mild crackers or croustades.

## CHESAPEAKE CRAB DIP

Yields 5 cups

| | |
|---|---|
| 24 | ounces cream cheese |
| 1 | pound backfin crabmeat |
| 1 | clove garlic, minced |
| ½ | cup mayonnaise |
| 2 | tsp. dry mustard |
| | Seasoned salt to taste |
| ¼ | cup dry white wine |
| ¼ | cup dry Sherry |

- Heat cream cheese gently in heavy saucepan; when soft, stir to blend and add next 5 ingredients. May be briefly set aside at this point.
- Before serving, add wine and Sherry.
- Pour into a chafing dish, allowing time to warm.
- Serve with melba toast rounds or bite-size pastry shells.

# HOT CRAB DIP

Yields 4 cups

16    ounces cream cheese,
      softened
8     ounces sour cream
4     Tbsp. mayonnaise
½     tsp. lemon juice
1     tsp. dry mustard
⅛     tsp. garlic salt, or 1 small
      clove garlic, finely minced
1     pound backfin crabmeat
4     ounces (1 cup) shredded
      Cheddar cheese
      Paprika

- Preheat oven to 325 degrees.
- Blend all ingredients except the crabmeat and
  ½ cup of the Cheddar cheese in a blender.
  Fold in the crabmeat and put into serving dish.
- Bake at 325 degrees for 45 minutes.
- Remove from oven, top with remaining cheese
  and sprinkle with paprika.
- Serve with *mild* crackers.

# SHRIMP FONDUE

Serves 12-15

2     5-ounce jars sharp cheese
      spread
16    ounces cream cheese
½     cup light cream
1     tsp. Worcestershire sauce
½     tsp. salt
¼     tsp. cayenne pepper
1     small clove garlic, minced
1     Tbsp. chopped chives
1     2-ounce jar pimientos,
      drained
1     pound fresh shrimp,
      cooked, peeled, chopped

- In top of double boiler, melt and blend first 3
  ingredients. Whisk in remaining ingredients
  except shrimp.
- When all ingredients are well mixed, add
  shrimp.
- Serve in chafing dish, spooning into small
  pastry shells or on small toast points.

*Garnish top with several whole shrimp and sprigs of dill.*

# EASY CLAM DIP

Yields 2 cups

| | |
|---|---|
| 1 | 6¾-ounce can minced clams |
| 8 | ounces cream cheese, softened |
| ¼ | tsp. salt |
| 2 | tsp. grated onion |
| 1 | tsp. Worcestershire sauce |
| 3 | drops Tabasco sauce |
| 2 | tsp. lemon juice |
| 1 | tsp. chopped parsley |

- Drain clams, reserving the juice.
- Combine all ingredients except clam juice and blend. Gradually add about ¼ cup of the juice and beat. Chill.
- Serve with crackers.

*May be served warm in chafing dish.*

# SMOKED OYSTER DIP

Yields 1 cup

| | |
|---|---|
| 1 | Tbsp. finely chopped onion |
| ⅓ | pound fresh mushrooms, chopped |
| 2 | Tbsp. butter |
| 3 | ounces cream cheese, softened |
| ½ | cup sour cream |
| 1 | 3½-ounce can smoked oysters, drained and chopped |
| 1 | Tbsp. seasoned salt |
| ½ | tsp. white pepper |
| | Dash Tabasco sauce |

- Sauté onions and mushrooms in butter in small skillet.
- Transfer mixture to medium size bowl and combine with remaining ingredients. Chill.
- To serve, hollow out interior of a purple cabbage and spoon dip into it. Surround with mild chips or crackers.

*May also be served warm in a decorative bowl.*

# SHRIMP AND ARTICHOKE DIP

Serves 25
Do ahead

1 pound medium or large shrimp, cooked, peeled, cleaned and cut in ½-inch pieces
1 14-ounce can artichoke hearts, drained and quartered
¾ cup sour cream
¾ cup mayonnaise
1 small bunch green onions, chopped
Juice of ½ small lemon
1 clove garlic, chopped
Salt and pepper to taste

- Mix all ingredients. Refrigerate overnight.
- Serve with mild crackers.


# MUSHROOM SPREAD

Yields 2½ cups

4 slices bacon
8 ounces (3 cups) fresh mushrooms, chopped
½ cup finely chopped onion
1 clove garlic, minced
2 Tbsp. flour
¼ tsp. salt
⅛ tsp. pepper
8 ounces cream cheese, cubed
2 tsp. Worcestershire sauce
1 tsp. soy sauce
½ cup sour cream

- In large skillet, cook bacon until crisp; drain, reserving 2 Tbsp. drippings. Crumble bacon and set aside.
- Cook mushrooms, onions and garlic in drippings until tender and most of liquid has evaporated. Stir in flour, salt and pepper. Add cheese, Worcestershire and soy sauce.
- Heat and stir until cheese is melted. Stir in sour cream and bacon. Heat through but *do not boil*.
- Serve in chafing dish with French bread or small pastry cups.

*Garnish with chopped parsley for additional eye appeal.*

## SPICY STUFFED BRIE

Serves 16

| | |
|---|---|
| 1 | 1-kilo Brie, semi-ripe, sliced in half horizontally by cheese shop, each layer individually wrapped |
| 1 | Tbsp. butter |
| 2 | cloves garlic, pressed |
| 1 | small sweet onion, finely chopped |
| 6-8 | large mushrooms, finely chopped |
| ½ | jar roasted red sweet peppers, chopped, remainder of jar reserved for garnish |
| 1 | 4-ounce can sliced black olives, drained and used to taste |
| 1 | Tbsp. dry Sherry |
| | Dash salt and pepper |

- In small skillet, sauté onion and garlic in butter until onion is translucent. Add mushrooms, peppers and olives. Sauté until done, about 3 minutes.
- Add Sherry and season to taste.
- Set aside or refrigerate until needed.
- Remove cheese layers from refrigerator at least 1 hour before serving. Remove plastic wrap and place first layer rind-side down on serving plate.
- Spread enough filling on Brie to cover the layer completely. Place second layer on top, rind-side up.
- Garnish with reserved red peppers, olives or parsley and serve with thinly sliced French bread.

*Easy but it looks like you've spent hours in the kitchen. Design a flower, a wreath, a valentine or any seasonal decoration to garnish the Brie.*

## MARINATED MUSHROOMS

Yields 2 pounds
Do ahead

| | |
|---|---|
| 1 | cup cider vinegar |
| ½ | cup salad or extra virgin olive oil |
| 1 | clove garlic |
| 1½ | Tbsp. salt |
| ½ | tsp. peppercorns |
| 1 | Tbsp. parsley, chopped |
| ½ | tsp. dried thyme |
| ½ | tsp. oregano |
| 1 | bay leaf |
| 1½ | cups water |
| 2 | pounds fresh mushrooms |

- Mix all ingredients, adding mushrooms last. Additional water may be added to cover mushrooms.
- Marinate in refrigerator at least 3 days before serving. Drain.
- Serve with cocktail toothpicks.

# RAINBOW BRIE

Serves 12-15

½    1-kilo ripe Brie

4    **Tbsp. sun-dried tomatoes, chopped**

3    **Tbsp. yellow sweet peppers or green salad peppers**

2    **Tbsp. stuffed baby eggplants, finely chopped**

- Arrange chopped vegetables in a rainbow pattern on top of Brie. Begin with tomatoes on outside rim; follow by placing peppers on next band and eggplants or other flavorful vegetable of your choice on next band. Small center half-circle may be left plain.

## FOR A CHEESE/DESSERT COURSE

½    **cup sweetened heavy cream, whipped**

½    **pint raspberries or strawberries**

6    **ounces apricots, peeled, chopped, patted dry**

4    **ounces green seedless grapes, sliced, or coarsely chopped kiwi fruit, patted dry**

- Spread a light layer of cream over Brie.
- Arrange fruit in rainbow pattern beginning on outer edge in a 1½-inch band with raspberries. Follow with apricots and then grapes.
- Chill until ready to serve. French bread, mild crackers or English biscuits are best accompaniments.

*Any combination of vegetables or fruits can be used as long as color and eye appeal are considered.*

# ALMOND PÂTÉ

8    **ounces ripe Brie, rind removed, softened**

¾    **cup butter (6 ounces), softened**

½    **cup slivered almonds, toasted**

2    **Tbsp. dry Sherry**

¼    **tsp. dried thyme**

- Whip all ingredients together; spoon mixture into a cheese crock.
- Cover and chill at least 2 hours, letting pâté stand for 1 hour before serving with crackers or crudities.

# PIQUANT CHEESE

Serves 25
Do ahead

| | |
|---|---|
| 16 | ounces cream cheese, softened |
| 2 | cups (8 ounces) grated sharp Cheddar cheese |
| 2 | tsp. Worcestershire sauce |
| 1 | small onion, finely minced |
| ½ | cup chopped walnuts or pecans |
| ¾ | cup finely chopped chipped beef |
| ¾ | cup finely chopped fresh parsley |

- Blend cheeses together, mixing well. Add next 2 ingredients, blending thoroughly.
- Stir in nuts and beef; form into one or two balls and roll in chopped parsley.
- Refrigerate at least 2 hours.

*May be used to stuff endive or celery.*

# HERB CHEESE

Serves 8
Do ahead

| | |
|---|---|
| 1 | large clove garlic, minced Tops of 4 parsley sprigs, chopped |
| 2 | tsp. dried dill |
| 4 | leaves fresh basil, chopped or 2 tsp. dried |
| 2 | tsp. chopped fresh chives |
| 1 | tsp. caraway seeds |
| 1 | Tbsp. lemon pepper |
| 12 | ounces cream cheese, softened |

- Using an electric mixer or food processor, blend well all ingredients except cheese.
- Add cheese, blending thoroughly.
- Refrigerate until 30 minutes before serving.
- Serve with crackers.

# BACON AND TOMATO SPREAD

Yields 1¼ cups

8 ounces cream cheese, softened
2 tsp. prepared mustard
½ tsp. celery salt
6 slices bacon, cooked crisp, drained, crumbled
1 medium tomato, peeled, seeded, drained, finely chopped
¼ cup finely chopped green pepper
Parsley to garnish

- Combine first 3 ingredients. Stir in bacon, tomato and green pepper.
- Cover and chill well.
- Serve in large hollowed-out tomato with toast points or melba rounds. Garnish with parsley.

# JEWELED CHEESE BALL

Yields 1 cheese ball

2 cups (8 ounces) shredded Cheddar cheese
1 cup chopped, pitted dates
¼ pound butter, softened
1 Tbsp. Brandy
½ cup toasted sliced almonds

- In medium bowl, beat together all ingredients except almonds until well blended.
- Shape mixture into large ball; roll in toasted almonds. Cover and refrigerate.
- Let stand at room temperature ½ hour before serving.
- Serve with assorted crackers.

*The lovely flavor of this cheese ball is predominately sweet. Good for dessert cheese course.*

# HOSPITABLE GRAPES 'N CHEESE SPREAD

Yields 2½ cups

| | |
|---|---|
| 16 | ounces cream cheese, softened |
| 3 | Tbsp. Brandy |
| ⅓ | cup finely chopped chutney |
| ¼ | cup finely chopped green onions |
| ¼ | cup chopped toasted almonds |
| ¼ | tsp. curry powder |
| 1 | cup green grapes, halved and seeded |
| | Green onion tops |
| | Grapes in clusters |

- In large bowl, mix first 6 ingredients until well blended. Chill.
- When firm, mound in oval shape on serving tray, covering surface with grape halves, cut-side down, to resemble a pineapple. Insert green onion tops at top of cheese mound.
- Surround with grape clusters and serve with crisp crackers.

*After cheese has been mounded, it can be refrigerated for up to 2 days before completing.*

# FANCY FRUIT SPREAD

Yields 1 cheese ball
Do ahead

| | |
|---|---|
| 16 | ounces cream cheese, softened |
| 2 | ounces butter, softened |
| 1 | cup sifted confectioners sugar |
| 2 | Tbsp. orange juice |
| 1 | Tbsp. grated orange rind |
| ½ | tsp. vanilla |
| 1 | cup finely chopped walnuts |
| | Rind of 1 orange, grated |

- Beat first 6 ingredients until smooth.
- Chill for ½ hour or more.
- Form into ball; garnish with walnuts and grated orange rind.
- Chill until ½ hour before serving.

*Fresh apple and pear slices, gingersnaps, shortbread or muffins are wonderful accompaniments, or surround spread with platter of fresh fruit or twisted orange slices.*

# GINGER CHEESE

Makes 1 cup
Do ahead

| | |
|---|---|
| 8 | ounces cream cheese |
| 2-3 | Tbsp. light cream |
| 3 | Tbsp. chopped preserved ginger |
| | Toasted almond slivers |

- Mix cream cheese with cream. Add bits of ginger. Sprinkle with almonds.
- Refrigerate until ½ hour before serving.

*Serve on English biscuits or fruit slices for unusual appetizer.*
*Good Oriental-style dessert served with apple and pear slices.*

# LIVER PÂTÉ

Makes 8 ounces
Do ahead

| | |
|---|---|
| 4-5 | turkey livers, or 10 chicken livers |
| 2-3 | onions, finely chopped |
| 2 | hard-boiled eggs, finely chopped |
| 4 | Tbsp. butter |
| | Salt and pepper to taste |
| | Pinch cayenne pepper |

- Boil livers until tender. Reserve cooking liquid and cool.
- Sauté onions in butter until translucent.
- For best texture, blend all ingredients in food processor until smooth. Add enough reserved cooking liquid to make pâté spreadable.
- Refrigerate in an airtight container for at least a day.
- Serve with celery sticks, French bread or mild crackers.

*Turkey livers available from butcher during holidays.*

# SMOKED OYSTER PÂTÉ

Serves 12
Do ahead

| | |
|---|---|
| 1 | 3¾-ounce can smoked oysters |
| 8 | ounces cream cheese |
| 2 | Tbsp. dry red wine |
| 1 | tsp. Dijon mustard |
| ½ | tsp. sage |
| ½ | cup chopped walnuts |
| ¼ | cup chopped fresh parsley |

- Drain oysters and purée in processor. Add cream cheese and process until smooth. Mix in next 3 ingredients. Form into a ball.
- Cover and chill overnight or until firm.
- Combine walnuts and parsley; roll pâté in the mixture to coat.
- Serve with crackers or French bread.

# SALMON LOG

Serves 8-12
Do ahead

| | |
|---|---|
| 1 | 15½-ounce can red sockeye salmon |
| 8 | ounces cream cheese, softened |
| 1 | Tbsp. lemon juice |
| 2 | tsp. grated onion |
| 1 | tsp. horseradish |
| ¼ | tsp. salt |
| ½ | cup chopped pecans |
| 3 | Tbsp. snipped parsley |

- Drain and flake salmon, removing all skin and bones. Combine with next 5 ingredients, mixing thoroughly.
- Chill several hours.
- Shape mixture into a log and roll in the combined pecans and parsley.
- Chill again.
- Serve with mild crackers.

*Freezes well.*

# CRABMEAT CROATAN

Serves 8

| | |
|---|---|
| 12 | ounces cream cheese, softened |
| 1 | small onion, grated |
| 2 | Tbsp. Worcestershire sauce |
| 2 | Tbsp. mayonnaise |
| 1 | Tbsp. lemon juice |
| 1 | small clove garlic, finely minced |
| ¼ | tsp. salt |
| ½ | cup chili sauce |
| 1 | pound backfin crabmeat Chopped fresh parsley |

- Combine first 7 ingredients. Beat until smooth, using an electric mixer. Spread mixture evenly on a 12-inch flat plate.
- Spread chili sauce evenly over mixture leaving a ¾-inch margin.
- Sprinkle crab over chili sauce.
- Garnish with parsley and serve with crackers.

## SHRIMP SPREAD

Serves 20

1    **pound medium shrimp, cooked, shelled and cut in half**
½    **cup mayonnaise**
8    **ounces cream cheese, softened**
½    **cup finely chopped onion**
½    **cup finely chopped celery**
3    **Tbsp. ketchup**
    **Juice of ½ lemon**
1    **small clove garlic, minced, or ¼ tsp. garlic powder**
1½   **tsp. Worcestershire sauce**
    **Seasoned salt to taste**
    **Pepper to taste**
    **Dill weed to taste**

- Combine all ingredients except dill weed. Chill.
- Sprinkle lightly with dill before serving.
- Serve with mild crackers.

*May be made a day ahead.*

## COLD ANTIPASTO

Serves 8-10
Do ahead

¼    **pound thinly sliced Genoa salami**
¼    **pound sliced Provolone cheese**
¼    **pound thinly sliced Prosciutto**
1    **large ripe tomato, thinly sliced**
2    **small onions, finely sliced**
    **Oregano to taste**
1    **clove garlic, finely minced**
½    **cup extra virgin olive oil**
½    **cup vinegar**
¼    **cup (1 ounce) freshly grated Parmesan cheese**

- Layer salami, Provolone and Prosciutto twice. Place tomato slices on top of layers; place onions on top of tomato. Sprinkle oregano and garlic over onions.
- After combining last 3 ingredients, pour over layers and marinate for up to 24 hours before serving.
- Serve antipasto on plates.

## CAPTAIN'S CAVIAR

Serves 30-40

| | |
|---|---|
| 1 | cup cottage cheese |
| 1 | cup sour cream |
| 1 | tsp. lemon juice |
| 1-2 | tsp. Worcestershire sauce |
| ½ | tsp. seasoned salt |
| 1 | tsp. fresh dill, finely chopped |
| 1 | envelope unflavored gelatin |
| ¼ | cup chilled dry white wine |
| 3 | red sweet peppers, chopped and sautéed in olive oil |
| 3 | hard-boiled eggs, finely chopped |
| 1 | 2-ounce jar red or black caviar (red has stronger flavor) |
| 3 | green onions, finely chopped |
| 3 | slices lemon |

- In food processor combine first 6 ingredients. Process until smooth.
- Sprinkle gelatin over wine and let soften for several minutes. Heat and stir until gelatin dissolves. Gradually stir dissolved gelatin into cheese mixture.
- Pour ½ of mixture into 9-inch springform pan. Refrigerate until lightly set. Layer with peppers. Add remaining cheese mixture and refrigerate until firm.
- Invert mold on platter. Spoon caviar in a 1-inch ring around outer edge of mold. Spoon eggs in 1½-inch ring inside caviar ring. Cover remaining surface with onions. Garnish center with lemon or lime slices and fresh dill sprigs.

*Good served on pumpernickel or rye.*

## HOT CHEESE APPETIZER

Serves 6-8

| | |
|---|---|
| 1 | cup diced onion |
| 1½ | cups (6 ounces) grated sharp Cheddar cheese |
| 1 | cup Duke's mayonnaise |

- Preheat oven to 450 degrees.
- Mix all ingredients together; place in small casserole.
- Bake at 450 degrees for 5 minutes or until hot and bubbly.
- Serve with crackers.

*May be made ahead and refrigerated until ready to bake.*

# CAVIAR CROWNED MOLD

Serves 16
Do ahead

| | |
|---|---|
| 6 | large eggs, hard-boiled and chopped |
| 1 | envelope unflavored gelatin |
| 2 | Tbsp. lemon juice |
| 2 | Tbsp. Sherry |
| 3 | Tbsp. finely chopped onion |
| 1 | cup mayonnaise |
| 1 | tsp. Worcestershire sauce |
| 2 | dashes seasoned salt |
| 6 | ounces lumpfish caviar, rinsed in fine sieve, then lightly blotted |
| 1 | Tbsp. finely minced parsley |

- Soften gelatin in lemon juice and put in top of double boiler with Sherry to dissolve.
- Mix eggs and onion.
- Combine gelatin mixture with the mayonnaise.
- Blend the two mixtures with the Worcestershire and salt. Fold in caviar *very carefully,* stirring no more than necessary to distribute evenly, or mold will turn gray.
- Spoon mixture into small greased mold and chill for several hours until firm.
- Unmold on lettuce, sprinkle fresh parsley over mold for color.
- Serve with crackers.

# CHILI ARTICHOKES

Serves 8

| | |
|---|---|
| 1 | 14-ounce can artichokes, drained and chopped |
| 2 | 4-ounce cans green chilies, drained and chopped |
| 2 | cups mayonnaise |
| 1½ | cups (6 ounces) fresh grated Parmesan cheese Paprika |

- Preheat oven to 350 degrees.
- Mix first 3 ingredients and pour into 9-inch pyrex or quiche dish. Sprinkle cheese over top and dust with paprika.
- Bake at 350 degrees for 25 minutes.
- Serve with crackers.

*Wonderful spooned over an omelet.*

# ANTIPASTO MEDITERRANEAN

Serves 10-12
Do ahead

8 ounces pepperoni, sliced

8 ounces salami, each slice quartered

7 ounces pitted green Spanish olives, drained

1 12-ounce can pitted black olives, drained

1 pound sharp Cheddar cheese, cubed

1 pound jalapeño Monterey Jack cheese, cubed

4 carrots, thinly sliced

3 celery ribs, thinly sliced

½ pound fresh mushrooms, sliced

1 cup blanched broccoli florets

1 cup blanched cauliflower florets

6 ounces small sweet gherkin pickles

1 bottle Italian dressing or your favorite recipe

- Pour dressing over combined ingredients.
- Marinate 12-24 hours refrigerated, tossing well from time to time.
- Serve with Italian bread.

# CHEESE WAFERS

Makes 150

2 cups (8 ounces) finely grated New York extra sharp Cheddar cheese, at room temperature

½ pound butter, softened

2 cups sifted flour

½ tsp. cayenne pepper
Dash Tabasco sauce
Salt

- Preheat oven to 350 degrees.
- Mix cheese and butter together. Gradually add 2 cups sifted flour to cheese mixture. Add seasonings.
- Using a floured rolling pin and board, roll out dough; cut with small cutter.
- Bake at 350 degrees for 8-10 minutes. Do not brown.

# COUNTRY PÂTÉ

Yields 2 loaves
Do ahead

| | |
|---|---|
| 1 | pound sliced bacon |
| 2 | Tbsp. butter |
| 2 | onions, chopped |
| 1 | pound ground beef |
| 2 | pounds bulk sausage |
| 1 | pound chicken livers, chopped |
| 3 | cloves garlic, crushed |
| ½ | tsp. allspice |
| ¼ | tsp. nutmeg |
| ¼ | tsp. ground cloves |
| 3 | eggs, slightly beaten |
| | Salt and pepper to taste |
| 1 | cup heavy cream |
| ¼ | cup Brandy or Bourbon |
| 2 | bay leaves |

- Preheat oven to 350 degrees.
- In a large pan of boiling water, parboil bacon for 10 minutes. Drain and pat dry.
- Line 2 loaf pans with bacon, reserving a few strips for the top.
- In a skillet, sauté the onions in butter until soft, but not brown.
- In a large mixing bowl, combine all ingredients except bay leaves and reserved bacon. Spread evenly into the loaf pans. Place remaining bacon across top. Place one bay leaf on top of each loaf. Cover each loaf pan with aluminum foil, sealing so that no air can enter.
- Place each loaf pan in baking pan half-filled with hot water. Cook 1¾-2 hours until a skewer inserted for ½ minute is hot to the touch when withdrawn.
- Drain each loaf pan with basting bulb. Place clean brick on top of each pan, leaving foil in place. Refrigerate overnight. Remove bricks and foil. Remove pâté from pans and allow to mature, covered, 3-7 days in refrigerator.
- Serve with sliced French bread. Garnish with curly endive or parsley.

*Needs to age 3-7 days.*
*Well worth the time and effort!*

# MARINATED EYE OF ROUND WITH HORSERADISH SAUCE

Serves 30-40
Do ahead

| | |
|---|---|
| 1 | 4-pound eye of round roast |

**MARINADE**

| | |
|---|---|
| 1 | cup soy sauce |
| ¼ | cup Gin |
| ½ | cup oil |
| 3 | cloves garlic, crushed |

- Combine ingredients and pour over roast which has been placed in pyrex dish. Cover with plastic wrap and marinate in refrigerator 24-48 hours, turning 3-4 times.
- Remove meat from marinade; towel dry and roast at 350 degrees for about 1 hour. Use meat thermometer and cook to medium-rare.
- Cool immediately in refrigerator; slice very thin for small sandwiches.
- Serve with Parker House rolls and Horseradish Sauce.

**HORSERADISH SAUCE**

Yields 2 cups

| | |
|---|---|
| 1 | cup heavy cream |
| 1 | cup mayonnaise |
| | Pinch of salt |
| ¼ | cup horseradish or to taste |

- Whip cream until soft peaks form.
- Beat in mayonnaise and salt until well mixed.
- Thoroughly blend in horseradish with spoon.
- Serve with roast beef sandwiches.
- For lighter sauce, omit the mayonnaise.

# QUICK SNACKING CRACKERS

Yields 4-6 cups
Do ahead

| | |
|---|---|
| ¾ | cup oil |
| 1 | 1-ounce package milk-base ranch dressing |
| ¼ | cup grated Parmesan cheese |
| 16 | ounces oyster crackers |

- Combine first 3 ingredients. Toss with crackers.
- Let stand for several hours, stirring occasionally.
- Store in tightly covered container.

*Fill jars full of crackers to use as gift items.*

# MARINATED SHRIMP

Serves 20-25
Do ahead

5   pounds shrimp, steamed and peeled
1   purple onion, sliced into rings
1   3½-ounce jar non-pareil capers

- Place shrimp, onion rings and capers in large shallow container.

**SAUCE**

1    cup salad oil
¾    cup vinegar
1½   Tbsp. Worcestershire sauce
1    Tbsp. Tabasco sauce
2    tsp. sugar
2    tsp. salt
½    tsp. pepper
     Chopped parsley for garnish

- Combine ingredients and pour over shrimp.
- Refrigerate for 24 hours, stirring occasionally.
- Remove to serving dish with slotted spoon. Some of the onion rings and capers may be sprinkled over the shrimp. Garnish with parsley.

*May be used as hot-weather entrée.*

# SHRIMP WITH CAPERS

Serves 6
Do ahead

1½   pounds medium shrimp
1    bay leaf
12   peppercorns
     Salt to taste
     Parsley, chopped
1    cup mayonnaise
     Juice of 1 lemon
1    onion, finely sliced
1    3½-ounce jar capers, drained

- Using a 2-quart saucepan, cover shrimp with water, adding the next 4 ingredients. Bring to a boil and simmer 1 minute, or until shrimp are just done.
- Drain, peel and devein shrimp, combining them with the remaining ingredients.
- Refrigerate overnight.
- Serve with buttered toast.

# ARTICHOKES CONTINENTAL

Serves 12
Do ahead

| | |
|---|---|
| 1½ | **cups chopped bacon** |
| 4 | **packages frozen artichoke hearts, thawed** |
| 2 | **cups (12 ounces) shredded Prosciutto** |
| 3 | **large Spanish onions, chopped** |
| 8 | **ounces dried shiitake mushrooms, soaked in warm water, drained and chopped** |
| 1⅓ | **cups finely chopped shallots** |
| 2 | **cups sliced carrots** |
| 1 | **stalk celery, chopped** |
| 6 | **cloves garlic, minced** |
| 1 | **bottle dry red wine (Beaujolais or Spanish red)** |
| 2 | **Tbsp. tomato purée** |
| 2 | **bay leaves** |
| 1 | **Tbsp. mixed herbs** |
| 2 | **Tbsp. chopped parsley** |
| | **Freshly ground pepper** |
| | **Salt to taste** |
| 8 | **ounces frozen beef concentrate or 1½ cups double-strength beef bouillon** |
| 1 | **tsp. sugar** |
| | **Olive oil for sautéeing** |
| ¼ | **cup Cognac** |
| 4 | **Tbsp. unsalted butter** |
| | **Handful minced parsley** |

- In a pan of cold water, bring bacon to a boil. Simmer 10 minutes and rinse with cool water. Pat dry.
- Put bacon in a medium skillet and lightly brown. Pour off any rendered fat. Add 3 or 4 artichoke hearts, the Prosciutto, onions, mushrooms, shallots, carrots, celery and garlic. Sauté for 5 minutes, stirring.
- Add ½ cup wine mixed with tomato purée. Bring to a boil; stir for several minutes. Add bay leaves, herbs, parsley, pepper, salt and remaining wine. Cover and simmer 2 hours.
- Stir in beef concentrate; simmer 10 minutes.
- Strain, removing as much juice as possible by pressing down on vegetables. Remove bay leaves and reserve.*
- Taste sauce; adjust seasonings, adding sugar if needed. If there is more than 2 cups of sauce, reduce.
- Sauté remaining artichoke hearts in large skillet in olive oil until lightly browned on edges. Add Cognac; toss gently until artichokes are glazed.
- Add wine sauce, simmer 10 minutes. Stir in butter.
- If sauce is still thin, add about 1 Tablespoon cornstarch to 2 Tablespoons of sauce. Pour into pan; sauce will thicken immediately.
- Sprinkle with parsley; serve in decorative bowl with toothpicks.

*To serve as a first course, spoon artichokes into pastry shells.
First 6 steps may be done a day ahead. Sauce is better if flavors marry.
*Prosciutto-vegetable mixture may be added to a basic tomato sauce and
served over pasta or added to soup stock or stew.*

# GOURMET MUSHROOMS

Serves 12-15
Do ahead

| | |
|---|---|
| 4 | **pounds mushrooms** |
| 1 | **pound butter** |
| 1 | **bottle Burgundy wine** |
| 1½ | **Tbsp. Worcestershire sauce** |
| 1 | **tsp. dill seed** |
| 1 | **tsp. ground pepper** |
| 2 | **small cloves garlic, minced** |
| 2 | **cups boiling water** |
| 3 | **beef bouillon cubes** |
| 3 | **chicken bouillon cubes** |

- Combine all ingredients in large pan. Bring to a slow boil on medium heat; reduce to simmer.
- Cook 5-6 hours with pot covered. Remove lid and cook another 3-5 hours until liquid barely covers mushrooms. Allow to cool.
- Serve hot in a chafing dish with toothpicks.

*Mushrooms remain firm but turn very dark; big hit with mushroom lovers!*

# MUSHROOMS SUPREME

Makes 36

| | |
|---|---|
| 36 | **medium-large mushrooms, cleaned and stemmed** |
| ¼ | **pound butter, melted** |
| 16 | **ounces whipped cream cheese with chives** |
| 8 | **slices bacon, fried and crumbled** |

- Preheat oven to 350 degrees.
- Brush outside of mushroom caps with butter.
- In small bowl, mix cheese and bacon. Spoon mixture into mushrooms, mounding slightly.
- Bake on cookie sheet at 350 degrees for 3-5 minutes, then broil 6 inches from heat for 3 minutes or until bubbling and lightly browned.
- Let cool slightly and serve.

*Mushrooms may be refrigerated for a couple of hours after filling if you do not mind them darkening slightly.*

# ZUCCHINI TOP HATS

Serves 12

| | |
|---|---|
| 4 | medium zucchini, not over 2 inches wide |
| | Salt |
| 2 | large tomatoes, skinned and seeded |
| 2 | medium Spanish onions, chopped |
| ½ | pound dried chanterelles, soaked in warm water and chopped |
| ½ | cup shredded carrots |
| 2 | Tbsp. extra virgin olive oil |
| ½ | tsp. ground white pepper |
| 1 | Tbsp. tomato purée |
| | Generous pinch saffron |
| 4 | egg whites |
| ¼ | cup grated Parmesan cheese |

- Wash zucchini, cutting into 1-inch segments. Hollow out insides of zucchini with a teaspoon, leaving a firm base and ⅛-inch sides. Salt zucchini and invert on a paper towel. Allow to drain for ½ hour.
- Heat olive oil in medium skillet and sauté vegetables until all liquid has evaporated. Remove from heat and add pepper, purée and saffron. Add salt to taste. Cool for 10 minutes.
- In a food processor or blender, mix vegetables and egg whites.
- Rinse zucchini and blanch for no more than 45 seconds in boiling water in a large stock pot. Remove and drain upside down on paper towels.
- When cool, place in buttered cake pans. Stuff each zucchini with a rounded teaspoonful of vegetable mixture. Top with Parmesan cheese.
- Bake at 400 degrees for 15-20 minutes or until lightly browned.
- Remove and serve after allowing a brief cooling period.

*Zucchini may be served as a main course vegetable by splitting zucchini lengthwise, hollowing and preparing according to appetizer instructions, dividing stuffing among eight pieces.*

# ASPARAGUS-HAM PINWHEELS

Yields 25-30

1    loaf very thin white bread
¼    pound butter, softened
1    1¾-ounce jar Smithfield
     ham spread
1    10-ounce can asparagus,
     well drained

- Remove crust from bread and flatten each slice with rolling pin.
- Butter one side of bread and sparingly spread other side with ham. Hold buttered bread in palm of hand to avoid sticking to counter.
- Place asparagus on one end of slice, trimming end of asparagus if too long. Roll up.
- Place on cookie sheet, rolled edge down.
- Bake at 350 degrees for 15-20 minutes or until heated through. If not brown enough after baking, place under broiler for a few seconds.

*May be made a day ahead and stored covered in refrigerator.*

# ITALIAN TOASTS

Serves 15-18

1    loaf French or Italian
     bread, in 36 slices
     Extra virgin olive oil
¼-⅓  cup Tapanade or Olivada
     (black olive spread)
1    pound Mozzarella cheese,
     thinly sliced
10   baby stuffed eggplants,
     chopped
18   sun-dried tomatoes, split
     in half
10   green silonica peppers
     (salad peppers), chopped
1    cup (4 ounces) grated
     Parmesan cheese
     Ground black pepper
     Chopped parsley

- Preheat oven to 350 degrees.
- Brush thin layer of olive oil over face of bread slices placed on cookie sheet.
- Spread light layer of Tapanade over bread, then add slice of Mozzarella, sprinkle of eggplants, slice of tomato, chopped pepper, layer of Parmesan; add a grind of black pepper.
- Bake at 350 degrees for 10 minutes, then broil 5 minutes more or until cheese melts and begins to brown.
- Remove immediately and let stand for 5 minutes or until cool enough to eat.
- Sprinkle with a little parsley before serving.

# FLASH UN KAS

Makes 60

**DOUGH**

| | |
|---|---|
| ½ | **pound butter, softened** |
| 8 | **ounces cream cheese, softened** |
| 2½ | **cups sifted flour** |

- Thoroughly cream butter and cheese. Add flour slowly, mixing until smooth.
- Chill well, up to 24 hours.
- Pinch off small amount of dough at a time; refrigerate remainder until needed.
- Roll dough to ⅛-inch thickness on a floured board. Cut out 2-inch rounds.
- Select one of the fillings.

**FILLINGS**

| | |
|---|---|
| 4½ | **ounces liver pâté** |
| 2 | **tsp. Worcestershire sauce** |
| 2 | **tsp. steak sauce** |
| | *or* |
| 4 | **ounces ground country ham** |
| 2 | **tsp. steak sauce** |
| 2 | **tsp. ketchup** |

- Mix filling ingredients.
- Spoon a rounded ¼ teaspoon of filling onto each round. Fold in half, pressing edges with a fork.
- Transfer to a cookie sheet.
- Bake at 400 degrees for 8-10 minutes until lightly browned.
- Serve hot.

*May be prepared ahead of time and placed unbaked on cookie sheets in freezer. When frozen, place in plastic bag and use as needed, allowing an extra few minutes of baking time.*

# PARTY HORS D'OEUVRES

Makes 36

| | |
|---|---|
| 2 | **cups (8 ounces) grated sharp Cheddar cheese** |
| 1 | **small can chopped black olives** |
| 2 | **Tbsp. minced onion** |
| 1 | **cup mayonnaise** |
| 4-5 | **strips of bacon, cooked and crumbled** |
| | **Party rye or pumpernickel bread slices** |

- Preheat oven to 300 degrees.
- Mix first four ingredients.
- Spread mixture on bread and top with bacon bits.
- Bake at 300 degrees for 10-15 minutes.
- Serve hot.

# COCKTAIL PIZZAS

Makes 60
Do ahead

| 1 | pound hot pork sausage |
| 1 | cup minced onions |
| ½ | cup (2 ounces) grated sharp Cheddar cheese |
| ½ | cup (2 ounces) grated Parmesan cheese |
| 1½ | tsp. oregano |
| 2 | cloves garlic, finely chopped |
| 10 | ounces tomato sauce |
| 4 | ounces tomato paste |
| | Salt to taste |
| 2 | cans refrigerated flaky biscuits (10-count) |

- Cook sausage, crumbling as it cooks. Drain well.
- In a large bowl, combine sausage with other ingredients except biscuits. Mix well.
- Separate each biscuit into 3 equal parts. Place rounds on ungreased cookie sheet.
- Place about 1-1½ Tablespoons of sausage mixture on each round. Freeze on cookie sheet. When frozen, transfer to plastic freezer bags.
- When needed, preheat oven to 425 degrees and bake for 8-10 minutes. Serve immediately.

# SAUSAGE SPINACH BALLS

Makes 48-60

| 2 | packages frozen chopped spinach, cooked and drained |
| 2 | cups seasoned stuffing |
| 4 | ounces (1 cup) grated Parmesan cheese |
| 2 | Tbsp. minced onion |
| 6 | eggs, well beaten |
| ¾ | cup (6 ounces) butter, melted |
| 2 | small cloves garlic, minced |
| 1½ | tsp. salt |
| ½ | tsp. pepper |
| 4 | ounces bulk sausage, cooked and drained |

- Preheat oven to 350 degrees.
- Combine all ingredients, mixing thoroughly.
- Form into small balls about the size of walnuts.
- Place on ungreased cookie sheet and bake at 350 degrees for 20 minutes or until browned.
- Serve immediately.

*May be prepared ahead and flash frozen on cookie sheet. Thaw before baking.*

# CHEESE SQUARES

Makes 72 pieces
Do ahead

| | |
|---|---|
| 1 | **loaf unsliced French bread** |
| 6 | **ounces cream cheese** |
| 2 | **cups (8 ounces) grated Cheddar cheese** |
| ½ | **pound butter** |
| 4 | **egg whites, stiffly beaten, but not dry** |

- Remove crust from bread, cutting 1-inch slices from loaf; cut slices into 1-inch squares. Makes 48-72 squares, depending on size of loaf.
- In double boiler over medium-low heat, melt cheeses and butter; when creamy, fold in beaten egg whites.
- Dip cubes in mixture and place on wax paper-lined cookie sheet and freeze. When frozen, transfer to air-tight plastic bags and store in freezer.
- To serve, bake at 450 degrees for 8 minutes, turning once.

*Squares keep in freezer for months.*

# HOT PARMESAN PUFFS

Makes 30

| | |
|---|---|
| 3 | **ounces cream cheese** |
| 1 | **cup mayonnaise** |
| 1½ | **tsp. grated onion** |
| ⅔ | **cup (2⅔ ounces) grated Parmesan cheese, half reserved for topping** |
| ⅛ | **tsp. cayenne pepper** |
| 1 | **loaf thinly sliced bread Paprika** |

- Preheat oven to 300 degrees.
- Mix first 5 ingredients. Set aside.
- Cut 2-inch bread rounds with cookie cutter and place on cookie sheet.
- Bake at 300 degrees for 5 minutes to harden.
- Generously spread cheese mixture on rounds and sprinkle with a pinch of the reserved Parmesan cheese and a dash of paprika.
- Broil until puffy and golden. Serve hot.

*The first 2 steps can be completed and set aside until last-minute finishing is desired.*

# OYSTERS VIRGINIA BEACH

Serves 6

| | |
|---|---|
| ½ | pound mushrooms, thinly sliced |
| 6 | Tbsp. butter |
| 3 | Tbsp. flour |
| 1-2 | dozen fresh oysters |
| ⅓ | cup dry Sherry |
| 3 | Tbsp. sliced green onions |
| 3 | Tbsp. chopped parsley |
| ¼ | tsp. salt |
| ⅛ | tsp. cayenne pepper |
| ⅛ | tsp. garlic powder |
| ½ | cup bread crumbs |

**OPTIONAL TOPPINGS**
Bacon, cooked and crumbled
Parmesan cheese

- Preheat oven to 350 degrees.
- Sauté mushrooms in 2 Tablespoons butter. Set aside.
- Melt remaining butter. Stir in flour; cook slightly.
- Add remaining ingredients except bread crumbs.
- Place in buttered 1½-quart casserole. Top with crumbs.
- Bake at 350 degrees for 15 minutes.
- Ladle into individual shells for serving, if desired, and add optional toppings.

# CHAFING DISH OYSTERS

Serves 6-8

| | |
|---|---|
| 1 | pint freshly shucked oysters with liquid |
| 2 | Tbsp. butter |
| 2 | Tbsp. flour |
| | Light cream |
| ½ | tsp. salt |
| ⅛ | tsp. paprika |
| 1 | cup chopped fresh mushrooms |
| 2 | Tbsp. dry Sherry |
| | Chopped parsley |

- Drain oysters, reserving liquid; cut each oyster in several pieces.
- In saucepan, melt butter; add flour and stir until blended.
- Measure oyster liquid and add enough cream to make 1 cup; add slowly to flour mixture. Blend well. Add salt and paprika. Cook, stirring constantly until sauce is smooth and thick; add oysters and mushrooms. Heat to boiling point but do not allow sauce to boil. Add Sherry and sprinkle with parsley.
- Keep warm in a chafing dish.
- Serve in patty shells or with melba toast rounds.

# OYSTER SPICIES

Oysters
Bacon, cut in thirds
Flour
Cayenne pepper
Vegetable oil for frying
Toothpicks

- Sprinkle flour in a pie plate, enough to coat the number of oysters you have. Reserve.
- Wrap oysters in bacon thirds and secure with a toothpick. Sprinkle with cayenne pepper to taste, then roll in flour.
- Fry in hot oil in a very heavy skillet or Dutch oven until golden brown.
- Serve hot.

*Best when spicy! Add more cayenne for super spicy.*

# SHRIMP MINI-QUICHES

Serves 30

**QUICHE SHELLS**

| 3 | ounces cream cheese, softened |
| ¼ | pound butter, softened |
| 1½ | cups flour |

- Preheat oven to 400 degrees.
- Combine cream cheese and butter, beating until smooth.
- Add flour and mix well. Shape dough into 30 1-inch balls.
- Place in lightly greased 1¾-inch muffin pans; shape into shells. Prick bottom and sides of pastry shells with fork.
- Bake at 400 degrees for 5 minutes. Let cool in pan on wire rack.

**QUICHE MIXTURE: SHRIMP**

| 30 | small fresh shrimp, steamed and peeled |
| 1 | extra large egg, beaten |
| ½ | cup heavy cream |
| 1½ | Tbsp. Brandy |
| ½ | tsp. salt |
| ½ | tsp. pepper |
| 1 | tsp. dried dill, or 1½ tsp. fresh dill |
| 1⅔ | ounces Gruyère or Swiss cheese |

- Preheat oven to 350 degrees.
- Place one shrimp in each shell.
- Combine egg, cream, Brandy, salt, pepper and dill, dividing evenly among shells, about 2 teaspoons each.
- Slice cheese into 30 small triangles and place one on each appetizer.
- Bake at 350 degrees for 20 minutes, or until set.
- Cool. Remove from tins; freeze in foil. To reheat, place frozen appetizers on baking sheet.
- Bake at 375 degrees for 7-10 minutes.

## QUICHE MIXTURE: CRAB

| | |
|---|---|
| 1 | cup backfin crabmeat |
| 1 | Tbsp. sliced green onion |
| 1 | cup (4 ounces) grated Swiss cheese |
| ½ | cup mayonnaise |
| 1 | tsp. lemon juice |
| ¼ | tsp. curry powder |
| 1 | 5-ounce can water chestnuts, drained and sliced |
| 2 | Tbsp. finely chopped parsley |

- Preheat oven to 350 degrees.
- Combine crab, green onion, cheese, mayonnaise, lemon juice and curry powder, mixing well.
- Spoon crab mixture into shells. Top each appetizer with a slice of water chestnut and some chopped parsley.
- Bake at 350 degrees for 20 minutes.

## QUICHE MIXTURE: BACON

| | |
|---|---|
| 1 | egg, beaten |
| ½ | cup milk |
| ¼ | tsp. salt |
| | Pinch of pepper |
| ½ | cup (2 ounces) shredded Cheddar cheese |
| 2 | slices bacon, cooked and crumbled |
| 2½ | Tbsp. minced onion |
| 1 | Tbsp. minced green onion |

- Preheat oven to 350 degrees.
- Combine ingredients; stir well and pour into prepared shells.
- Bake at 350 degrees for 20 minutes.

# HERBED NUTS

Yields 4 cups
Do ahead

| | |
|---|---|
| 3 | Tbsp. butter, melted |
| 3 | Tbsp. Worcestershire sauce |
| 1 | tsp. salt |
| ½ | tsp. cinnamon |
| ¼ | tsp. garlic powder |
| ¼ | tsp. cayenne pepper |
| | Dash Tabasco sauce |
| 1 | pound pecan halves |

- Preheat oven to 300 degrees.
- Mix all ingredients and add pecans. Toss until well coated.
- Place nuts in jelly roll pan and bake at 300 degrees for 20-25 minutes, stirring often.

# BUFFALO CHICKEN WINGS WITH BLUE CHEESE DIP

Serves 6-8
Do ahead

| | |
|---|---|
| 4 | pounds (24) chicken wings |
| | Salt and pepper |
| 4 | cups vegetable or peanut oil (or enough to cover) |
| 4 | Tbsp. butter |
| 2-5 | Tbsp. hot sauce (not Tabasco) |
| 1 | Tbsp. white vinegar |

- Cut chicken wings at joints, discarding smallest part of wing (the tip end). Salt and pepper wings.
- Heat oil and fry wings for 20-30 minutes or until crispy.
- Melt butter in saucepan; add hot sauce and vinegar. Pour mixture over wings. Toss to coat.
- Serve wings with Blue Cheese Dip and celery sticks on the side.

**BLUE CHEESE DIP**

| | |
|---|---|
| 1 | cup mayonnaise |
| 2 | Tbsp. chopped onion |
| 1 | clove garlic, finely chopped |
| ¼ | cup chopped fresh parsley |
| ½ | cup sour cream |
| 1 | Tbsp. lemon juice |
| 1 | Tbsp. white vinegar |
| ¼ | cup crumbled Blue cheese |
| | Dash cayenne pepper |
| | Salt and pepper |

- Mix all ingredients. Cover and chill for at least one hour.

*Have plenty of napkins ready for this one.*
*Dip may also be used as a salad dressing or vegetable dip.*

# CHINESE CHICKEN WINGS

Makes 16 pieces
Do ahead

2   **pounds chicken wings**
½   **cup soy sauce**
½   **cup dry Sherry**
¼   **cup sugar**
3   **cloves garlic, crushed**
1   **Tbsp. grated fresh ginger root**
    **Dash crushed red pepper**

- Cut chicken wings at joints discarding smallest piece (tip of the wings).
- Mix remaining ingredients in large bowl.
- Add chicken and marinate for at least 1 hour, 3 hours is better.
- Place wings in oblong pan and bake at 375 degrees for 50 minutes, turning oven up to 475 degrees during the last 10 minutes of baking time to make wings crispy.

*No marinade should be put on wings while cooking or chicken will be sticky.*

# CHICKEN AND BACON BITS

Makes 30 pieces

4   **large skinned and boned chicken breasts, cut into 30 small pieces**
10   **thin slices bacon, cut into thirds**
1   **egg, beaten**
1   **cup flour**
1   **Tbsp. cornstarch**
1   **Tbsp. sugar**
2   **tsp. salt**
1½   **tsp. baking powder**
½   **cup milk**
½   **cup water**
    **Oil for frying**

- Wrap each piece of chicken in a bacon piece and secure with toothpick.
- Add dry ingredients, one at a time, to egg, stirring until smooth. Add milk and water to mixture and blend well.
- Pour a 2-inch depth of oil into a deep saucepan and heat to 375 degrees on a deep-fat frying thermometer.
- Dip bacon rolls into batter and fry a few at a time until brown.
- Drain on paper towels.
- Serve hot with Sweet and Sour Sauce.

**SWEET AND SOUR SAUCE**
1   **cup apricot preserves**
2   **Tbsp. white vinegar**

- Mix ingredients; pour into bowl.

*May be frozen and reheated in a 425 degree oven until hot.*

# CHICKEN NUGGETS

Makes 60 pieces

| 4-6 | boned, skinned chicken breasts, cut into bite-size chunks |
| ½ | cup dry bread crumbs |
| ¼ | cup (1 ounce) grated Parmesan cheese |
| 1 | tsp. salt |
| 1 | tsp. dried thyme |
| 1 | tsp. dried basil |
| ¼ | pound butter, melted |

- Preheat oven to 400 degrees.
- Combine crumbs with next 4 ingredients.
- Dip chicken chunks into butter. Roll in crumb mixture. Place in a single layer, not touching each other, on a foil-lined baking sheet.
- Bake at 400 degrees for 10 minutes.
- Serve with toothpicks.

# SHISH-KABOB PEPPER CHICKEN

Makes 16 skewers
Do ahead

| 4 | large skinned and boned chicken breasts, cut into 32 ¾-inch cubes |

- Place chicken in covered dish.

**MARINADE**

| ½ | cup oil |
| 1 | 4-ounce jar of pimientos, drained and puréed |
| 2 | Tbsp. red wine vinegar |
| 2 | large shallots, minced |
| 1½ | tsp. salt |
| ½ | tsp. dried red pepper flakes |

- Combine ingredients for marinade and mix thoroughly. Add to chicken and cover tightly.
- Marinate the chicken for 2 days in the refrigerator.

**KABOBS**

| 2 | large green peppers, cut into 32 pieces |
| 16 | 3-inch wooden skewers |

- Preheat broiler.
- Alternate chicken and pepper cubes on skewers. Place in shallow pan.
- Broil 6 minutes each on opposite sides, longer if necessary.
- Serve immediately with any remaining sauce which has been heated to a boil. Drizzle sauce over skewers.

# BACK BAY DUCK BITS

**Duck breast fillets, skinned**
**Seasoned salt**
**Freshly ground pepper**
**Bacon slices, cut in quarters**

- Preheat oven to broil.
- Slice fillets across the grain ½ inch wide. Sprinkle with seasonings.
- Wrap each piece in ¼ bacon slice.
- Secure with toothpicks, arranging on a cookie sheet so that they do not touch.
- Broil on low rack until bacon is crisp. Drain and serve immediately.

# CHINESE MEATBALLS

Serves 8-12
Do ahead

## MEATBALLS

| | |
|---|---|
| 1 | **pound ground beef** |
| ¾ | **cup minced celery** |
| ¼ | **cup finely chopped almonds** |
| 1 | **clove garlic, crushed** |
| 1 | **tsp. salt** |
| ½ | **cup bread crumbs** |
| 1 | **Tbsp. soy sauce** |
| 2 | **eggs, beaten** |

- Preheat oven to 350 degrees.
- Combine first 5 ingredients; mix well.
- Add crumbs, soy sauce and eggs. Mix well. Shape into walnut-sized balls.
- Brown meatballs in a foil-lined pan at 350 degrees for 20 minutes, turning once. Drain on paper towels. Refrigerate until needed.
- Place in a chafing dish and cover with pineapple sauce.

## PINEAPPLE SAUCE

| | |
|---|---|
| ½ | **cup sugar** |
| 3 | **Tbsp. cornstarch** |
| 1 | **cup chicken broth** |
| ½ | **cup white vinegar** |
| 2 | **Tbsp. soy sauce** |
| ½ | **cup pineapple juice** |
| ½ | **medium green pepper, cut into fine strips** |
| 1 | **cup pineapple chunks** |

- In a medium saucepan, combine sugar and cornstarch. Stir in broth, vinegar and soy sauce until smooth.
- Stir in pineapple juice and cook over medium heat *stirring constantly* until thickened and *clear*.
- Add green pepper and pineapple chunks. Simmer for 2 minutes.
- Serve over meatballs in a chafing dish. Spear with toothpicks.

*May be served as an entrée with rice.*

# SWEET AND SOUR MEATBALLS

Serves 8-10
Do ahead

### MEATBALLS
½    pound hot sausage
½    pound mild sausage
½    cup fine bread crumbs
1    egg

- Preheat oven to 350 degrees.
- Mix and form balls in 1-inch spheres.
- Bake at 350 degrees for 15 minutes, turning once.
- Drain and refrigerate until needed.

### SAUCE
½    cup ketchup
1    Tbsp. cider vinegar
4    Tbsp. brown sugar
1    Tbsp. soy sauce

- Blend ingredients.
- Add meatballs to sauce and simmer 20 minutes.
- Serve in chafing dish.

# TACO TARTS

Makes 80
Do ahead

### FILLING
2    cups sour cream
4    Tbsp. taco sauce
4    ounces chopped ripe olives
1½    cups coarsely crushed tortilla chips

- Preheat oven to 425 degrees.
- Mix filling ingredients. Set aside.

### BEEF SHELLS
2    pounds extra lean ground beef
4    Tbsp. taco seasoning mix
4    Tbsp. cold water

### TOPPING
2    cups (8 ounces) shredded Cheddar cheese

- Mix ingredients. Press one level Tablespoon of mixture into bottom and sides of miniature muffin tins, forming a shell.
- Place a heaping ½ Tablespoon of filling into each shell. Sprinkle 1 teaspoon of Cheddar cheese on top of each tart.
- Bake for 9 minutes at 425 degrees.
- Remove tarts from pan and place on paper towels to drain for a minute. May be served immediately or frozen on an uncovered cookie sheet and then transferred to airtight plastic bags or foil. Thaw, then reheat in 375 degree oven for 10-15 minutes.

# BEVERAGES

# BEVERAGES

**COLD, NON-ALCOHOLIC**

**COLD, ALCOHOLIC**

**HOT, NON-ALCOHOLIC**

**HOT, ALCOHOLIC**

# SUNSHINE PUNCH

Makes 24 punch cups
Do ahead

½  cup sugar
½  cup hot water
1  46-ounce can pineapple juice
1  6-ounce can frozen orange juice concentrate
1  6-ounce can frozen lemonade concentrate
1  quart ginger ale, chilled

- Dissolve sugar in hot water. Add remaining ingredients except ginger ale; chill.
- Just before serving, add ginger ale. Serve as punch over ice ring or in tall glasses.

# ORANGE-ALE PUNCH

Makes 10 punch cups

3½  cups chilled ginger ale
1  6-ounce can frozen orange juice concentrate
⅓  cup light corn syrup
Orange slices, optional
Whole strawberries, optional

- Combine ingredients. Pour over ice or ice ring in small punch bowl. Garnish with orange slices and strawberries.

# BANANA FREEZE

Makes 5 quarts
Do ahead

3  bananas
1  6-ounce can frozen lemonade concentrate
3  quarts lemon-lime soda
1  12-ounce can frozen orange juice concentrate
3  cups pineapple juice
3  cups water
2  cups sugar

- Combine bananas and lemonade concentrate in container of electric blender; process until smooth.
- Add remaining ingredients; mix well. Pour into plastic freezer containers; freeze 3-4 hours or until slushy.
- To serve, spoon into chilled glasses. Garnish with a piece of fruit.

*Refreshing drink for hot summer nights.*

# ORANGE DELIGHT

Serves 4-6

| | |
|---|---|
| 1 | 6-ounce can frozen orange juice concentrate |
| 1 | cup milk |
| 1 | cup water |
| ½ | cup sugar |
| 1 | tsp. vanilla |
| 8-10 | ice cubes |

• Combine all ingredients in blender container. Blend 30 seconds.
• Serve immediately.

# LIME TEA

Serves 8-10

| | |
|---|---|
| 5 | cups boiling water |
| 5 | tea bags |
| 1 | 6-ounce can frozen limeade concentrate |
| 1 | cup sugar |
| 5 | cups water |
| | Fresh lime |
| | Fresh mint |

• Steep tea in boiling water for 5 minutes. Remove tea bags. Add limeade and sugar; stir well.
• Add remaining water. Serve cold garnished with fresh mint and lime slices.

# ICED TEA PUNCH

Serves 8-10

| | |
|---|---|
| ½ | gallon strong tea |
| | Sugar to taste, approximately ½ cup |
| 1 | 6-ounce can lemonade concentrate |
| 2 | 12-ounce bottles ginger ale, chilled |

• Mix sugar with tea; chill.
• Add remaining ingredients just before serving.

# COFFEE PUNCH

Serves 30
Do ahead

½   gallon milk
5   Tbsp. instant coffee
½   gallon vanilla ice cream
2   cups heavy cream,
     whipped, optional

- Combine coffee and milk. Let stand refrigerated overnight.
- About 1 hour before serving, place ice cream in punch bowl. When ready to serve, pour coffee milk over ice cream; stir well.
- Whipped cream may be folded in, if desired.

*Good for summer brunch or coffee.*
*Coffee ice cream could be substituted for a stronger coffee taste.*

# TANGY BLOODY MARYS

Makes 90 6-ounce servings

8    46-ounce cans V-8 juice
1    gallon Vodka
2½   cups lemon juice
1¾   cups Worcestershire
     sauce
3    Tbsp. salt
2    tsp. Tabasco sauce
2    tsp. pepper
     Celery sticks

- Mix in a 5-gallon container and chill. May be stored for a week in refrigerator.
- Serve by the pitcher or in a punch bowl. Garnish with a celery stick in each glass.

*Great drink for a large brunch but is easily halved for a smaller crowd.*

# CHAMPAGNE SOPHISTICATE

Makes 20 6-ounce servings

1    46-ounce can
     unsweetened pineapple
     juice, chilled
1    6-ounce can frozen
     lemonade concentrate
2    fifths extra dry
     Champagne, chilled

- Combine juice and lemonade concentrate. Pour over ice ring in punch bowl.
- Add Champagne. Serve immediately. Garnish with fruit in or around bowl.

*Nice light taste for a summer bridal shower.*

# ORANGE CHAMPAGNE PUNCH

*Makes 20 punch cups*

| | |
|---|---|
| 1 | lemon, sliced |
| 1 | lime, sliced |
| 1 | orange, sliced |
| 1 | 12-ounce can frozen orange juice concentrate |
| 2 | fifths Champagne, chilled |
| 1 | cup Triple Sec |

- Freeze fruit slices in water to make ice ring.
- Combine remaining ingredients; pour over ring in punch bowl.

# AZALEA PUNCH

*Makes 20 6-ounce servings*

| | |
|---|---|
| 4 | 6-ounce cans orange juice concentrate |
| 6 | cups cold water |
| 1 | cup sugar |
| ¾ | cup Grenadine |
| ¼ | tsp. salt |
| 2 | fifths pink Champagne, chilled |

- Combine all ingredients except Champagne. Chill.
- When ready to serve, mix with Champagne. Serve over ice; garnish with mint, orange slices or lime slices.
- Cost and strength may be cut by using only one bottle of Champagne.

*A very pretty punch for a ladies luncheon.*

# REFRESHING CRANBERRY COCKTAIL

*Makes 1 large drink*

| | |
|---|---|
| ½ | cup cranberry juice |
| ½ | cup orange juice |
| 1 | ounce Grand Marnier or Cointreau |
| 1 | ounce Vodka |
| | Maraschino cherry |
| | Orange slice |

- Combine all ingredients. Pour over ice. Garnish with cherry and orange slice.

# CRANBERRY WINE PUNCH

Makes 10 6-ounce servings
Do ahead

| | |
|---|---|
| 3 | cups cranberry juice |
| 2 | cups dry red wine |
| ½ | cup bottled lime juice |
| ½ | cup orange juice |
| ½ | cup sugar |
| ¼ | cup bottled lemon juice |
| 10 | ounces club soda, chilled |
| | Orange slices |
| | Mint sprigs |

- Combine first 6 ingredients; chill well.
- When ready to serve, add club soda, orange slices and mint sprigs. Serve over ice.

# SUNDOWN COOLER

Makes 16 punch cups
Do ahead

| | |
|---|---|
| 34 | ounces lemon-lime soda |
| 1 | 1-litre bottle *dry* white wine |
| 1 | lemon, thinly sliced |
| 1 | lime, thinly sliced |
| 1 | tray ice cubes |

- Chill ingredients. Pour over ice and sliced fruit in punch bowl or pitcher.
- Serve in chilled glasses with lemon slice garnish.

# RED OR WHITE SANGRIA

Serves 10-12
Do ahead

### RED SANGRIA

½    cup sugar
    ¼-inch lemon slices
    ¼-inch orange slices
    Apple wedges
1    fifth red wine
¼    cup Brandy or Rum
24    ounces ginger ale
    Diced bananas

### WHITE SANGRIA

½    cup sugar
    ¼-inch lime slices
    Cherries
    Strawberries
    ¼-inch lemon slices,
    optional
1    fifth white wine
¼    cup white Rum
24    ounces lemon-lime soda

- Combine sugar and fruit except bananas in large pitcher.
- Add liquor, refrigerate.
- Before serving, add ginger ale and bananas for red sangria; add lemon-lime soda for white sangria.

# RUM-PORT PUNCH

Serves 12-16
Do ahead

½    gallon *white* Port
10-12    ounces Rum
    Juice of 3 lemons

- Mix ingredients.
- Serve well-chilled.

*Small portions should be served to avoid overnight guests.*

# VIRGINIA BEACH PUNCH

Makes 8 punch cups
Do ahead

| 3 | lemons, quartered |
| ½-¾ | cup sugar |
| 1½ | cups water |
| 2 | cups Bourbon |
| 1 | tsp. Rum |

- In saucepan, combine first 3 ingredients. Bring to a boil; cool.
- Add liquor and place all ingredients in a jar. Let stand overnight.
- Next day, remove lemons, squeezing well. Refrigerate. Serve over ice.
- Cherries and orange slices make a nice garnish.

*Great for holiday parties, multiplies easily.*

# WHISKEY SOURS

Makes 25 6-ounce servings
Do ahead

| 64 | ounces Bourbon |
| 36 | ounces frozen lemonade concentrate |
| 24 | ounces water |
| 18 | ounces frozen unsweetened lemon juice |
| 18 | ounces frozen orange juice concentrate |

- Combine all ingredients. Chill, serve over ice.

# OPEN HOUSE PUNCH

Makes 36 punch cups
Do ahead

| 1 | fifth Southern Comfort |
| 6 | ounces fresh lemon juice |
| 1 | 6-ounce can frozen orange juice concentrate |
| 1 | 6-ounce can frozen lemonade concentrate |
| 3 | quarts 7-Up |

- Chill ingredients. Mix in punch bowl, adding 7-Up last. Drop of red food coloring may be added, if desired. Stir.
- Float block of ice, ice ring or ice cubes; add orange and lemon slices.

## STRAWBERRY-BANANA DAIQUIRI

Serves 4

| | |
|---|---|
| 1 | **6-ounce can frozen limeade concentrate** |
| 1 | **10-ounce package frozen strawberries** |
| ¾ | **cup Rum** |
| ⅓ | **cup blended whiskey** |
| 1 | **ripe banana** |
| 6 | **ice cubes, or more as needed** |

• Blend all ingredients with ice in electric blender.
• Serve immediately or store in freezer for short periods of time while serving.

## HOLIDAY EGG NOG

Makes 40-50 punch cups
Do ahead

| | |
|---|---|
| 12 | **eggs, separated** |
| 1 | **cup sugar** |
| 1 | **cup Bourbon** |
| 1 | **cup Cognac** |
| ½ | **tsp. salt** |
| 6 | **cups heavy cream, whipped** |
| | **Nutmeg** |

• Beat yolks with sugar until thick. Add Bourbon and Cognac slowly. Chill several hours.
• Beat whites with salt until stiff.
• Add whites and cream to yolk mixture. Chill 1 hour or more. Sprinkle with nutmeg.

## OVERBOARD EGG NOG

Makes 40-50 punch cups
Do ahead

| | |
|---|---|
| 12 | **eggs, separated** |
| 1 | **cup sugar** |
| 4 | **cups milk** |
| 4 | **cups heavy cream** |
| 1½ | **cups blended whiskey** |
| 1 | **cup Rum** |
| | **Nutmeg** |

• Beat yolks until light. Using mixer, slowly add sugar, then milk and cream.
• Pour in whiskey in a thin stream. Add Rum.
• Beat whites until stiff. Fold into mixture. Serve ice cold. Sprinkle with nutmeg before serving.

## KAHLÚA VELVET FROSTY

Serves 6

1    **cup Kahlúa**
1    **pint vanilla ice cream**
1    **cup light cream**
⅛    **tsp. almond extract**
1½    **cups crushed ice**

- Mix all ingredients in blender container. Blend until smooth.

*Wonderful on a hot summer day.*

## KAHLÚA-AMARETTO FREEZE

Serves 8-10
Do ahead

1    **quart chocolate ice cream**
2    **cups light cream**
¼    **cup Amaretto**
¾    **cup Kahlúa**

- Mix all ingredients in blender (it may be necessary to divide and make 2 batches).
- Store in freezer until ½ hour before serving time. Serve in Champagne glasses with fancy cookies.

*Marvelous way to serve dessert and after-dinner drink all at once.*

## HOT APPLE CIDER

Yields 1½ gallons

1½    **gallons apple cider**
½    **cup brown sugar**
10    **whole cloves**
6-7    **cinnamon sticks**
1    **orange, thinly sliced**

- Simmer all ingredients in a large pot for ½ hour or until oranges are translucent.
- If it is to be stored, strain spices. Serve warm.

## CRAN-APPLE PUNCH

Makes 28 punch cups

2    **quarts apple cider**
1½    **quarts cranberry juice**
4    **3-inch cinnamon sticks**
1½    **tsp. whole cloves**

- In a large pot, bring all ingredients to a slight boil. Reduce heat and simmer for 15-20 minutes. Strain and serve.

# SPICED TEA

Yields 2 quarts

| | |
|---|---|
| 1 | quart water |
| 1 | stick cinnamon |
| ⅔ | tsp. whole cloves |
| 3 | tea bags |
| ½-¾ | cup sugar |
| 1½ | cups unsweetened pineapple juice |
| 2 | cups unsweetened orange juice |

- Bring water to a boil, add spices. Simmer 10 minutes.
- Remove spices, add tea. Allow to steep for 10 minutes. Remove tea bags.
- Add sugar and juices. Serve warm. May be refrigerated but do not boil when reheating.

# MULLED WINE

Makes 24 6-ounce servings
Do ahead

| | |
|---|---|
| | Peel of 3 oranges |
| | Peel of 3 lemons |
| 3 | cinnamon sticks, crushed |
| 3 | nutmegs, crushed |
| 33 | whole cloves |
| 4 | fifths dry red wine |
| ½ | fifth Brandy |
| 4 | Tbsp. honey |

- Place first 5 ingredients in cheesecloth bag.
- In large saucepan, combine wine, Brandy, honey and cheesecloth bag.
- Simmer for several hours. Serve piping hot.

# HOT WINE MIX

Yields 6 cups mix

| | |
|---|---|
| 6 | cups sugar |
| 2 | Tbsp. ground cinnamon |
| 2 | Tbsp. ground cloves |
| 1 | Tbsp. ground allspice |
| ¾ | tsp. ground nutmeg |

- Combine ingredients; mix well. Store in airtight container.

*Directions For Use:*
Add 2 teaspoons of mix to ½ cup water; bring to boil.
- Reduce heat and add 1 cup Burgundy wine. Heat thoroughly but do not boil. Make as much or as little as you want from time to time.

*Add "Directions-for-Use" card to a small jar of mix for Christmas gift giving.*

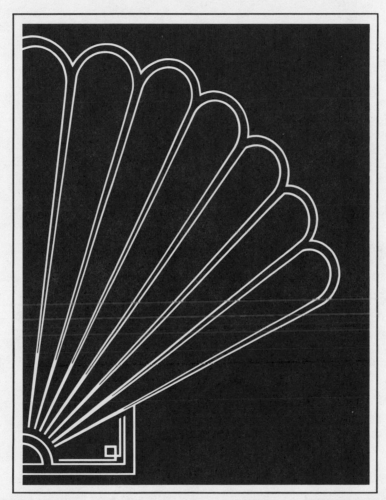

# EGGS, CHEESE AND PASTA

# EGGS, CHEESE AND PASTA

# MARY JANE EGGS

Serves 6-8

| | |
|---|---|
| 4 | eggs, beaten |
| 1 | cup flour |
| 1 | cup milk |
| ¼ | pound butter |
| 1 | cup fresh blueberries, washed and drained |
| ⅓ | cup powdered sugar |

- Preheat oven to 350 degrees.
- Beat together eggs, flour and milk.
- Melt butter in 13 x 9-inch dish. Add ½ tsp. melted butter to egg mixture. Mix, then pour egg mixture into butter in dish. *Do not stir.*
- Bake at 350 degrees for 35 minutes. Immediately after removing from oven, pour blueberries over eggs and sprinkle with powdered sugar. Serve immediately.

*Easy, delicious and wonderful for breakfast or brunch.*

# EGGS LOUIS

Serves 4-6

| | |
|---|---|
| 2 | cups grated sharp Cheddar cheese |
| 1½ | cups seasoned croutons, crumbled |
| 6 | eggs |

- Preheat oven to 350 degrees.
- Grease a 9-inch square dish.
- In bottom of dish, spread half of the grated cheese.
- Spread half of the croutons over the cheese.
- Arrange 6 "nests" in dish; break an egg into "nest".
- Cover ingredients with remaining croutons and cheese.
- Bake at 350 degrees for 15-20 minutes.

## SUNRISE SPECIAL

Serves 6

⅔ cup mayonnaise
¼ tsp. salt
⅛ tsp. pepper
1 tsp. Worcestershire sauce
¼ cup milk
1 cup grated Cheddar cheese
6 eggs
3 Tbsp. grated Parmesan cheese

- Preheat oven to 350 degrees.
- Combine first four ingredients in a small pan. Add milk gradually while stirring ingredients over medium heat. Add Cheddar cheese. Turn heat to low and beat with a wire whisk until thick, about 5 minutes.
- Put 2 Tablespoons of mixture in each of 6 custard cups. Break an egg into each dish being careful not to break yolk. Top with remaining sauce. Sprinkle with Parmesan.
- Set cups in shallow pan of water.
- Bake at 350 degrees for 25 minutes.

## BAKED EGG CASSEROLE WITH SMITHFIELD HAM

Serves 8

¼ pound Smithfield ham, sliced, or 8 slices Canadian bacon
½ pound Swiss cheese, sliced
8 eggs
1 cup cream
⅓ cup grated Parmesan cheese

- Preheat oven to 450 degrees.
- Line a 13 x 9-inch casserole with either ham or bacon.
- Top with a layer of Swiss cheese.
- Break eggs onto cheese, being careful not to break the yolks. Drizzle cream over the egg white until the yolk peeks through.
- Bake at 450 degrees for 10 minutes. Sprinkle with Parmesan cheese and bake for 10 minutes more. Cut into squares to serve.

# SUNNY-SIDE-UP CASSEROLE

Serves 8-10

| | |
|---|---|
| ¾ | **pound sharp Cheddar cheese** |
| ½ | **tsp. dry mustard** |
| ½ | **tsp. paprika** |
| 1 | **tsp. salt, or to taste** |
| ¾ | **cup sour cream** |
| 1 | **pound sausage, cooked and drained** |
| 10 | **eggs** |

- Slice half of cheese to cover bottom of 11 x 7-inch baking dish. Grate other half and set aside.
- Mix seasonings with sour cream. Pour half of mixture over cheese.
- Layer crumbled sausage over sour cream.
- Break whole eggs on top of sausage.
- Spread on remaining sour cream (dollop, without breaking eggs).
- Top with remaining grated cheese.
- Bake at 325 degrees for 25-30 minutes, or until set.

*May be prepared ahead, refrigerated and brought to room temperature before baking.*

# CHEESE CLOUD BREAKFAST CASSEROLE

Serves 8
Do ahead

| | |
|---|---|
| 8 | **slices bread, crusts removed, buttered on one side** |
| ½ | **pound sharp Cheddar cheese, grated** |
| 1 | **pound hot sausage, browned and crumbled** |
| 1 | **pound mild sausage, browned and crumbled** |
| 7 | **eggs** |
| 2¾ | **cups milk** |
| 1 | **tsp. dry mustard** |
| 1 | **tsp. salt** |

- Cut bread into 1½-inch squares. Place half of bread squares in buttered 13 x 9-inch casserole dish.
- Layer half of cheese on top of bread.
- Layer half of each kind of sausage on top of cheese.
- Repeat layers of bread, cheese and sausage.
- Beat eggs with milk, mustard and salt. Pour over mixture.
- Cover and chill overnight.
- Bake at 350 degrees for 45 minutes. Let stand a few minutes before serving.

## RISE 'N SHINE SAUSAGE AND EGGS

Serves 4

| | |
|---|---|
| 1 | pound hot sausage |
| 4 | eggs |
| ⅓ | cup milk |
| ¼ | tsp. dry mustard |
| 1 | 4-ounce can sliced mushrooms, drained |
| 1 | small onion, coarsely chopped |
| ⅓ | cup chopped green olives |

- Preheat oven to 350 degrees.
- Cook and *thoroughly* drain sausage; set aside.
- Beat eggs; add milk and dry mustard. Combine last 3 ingredients with sausage and egg mixture; mix well. Pour into 2-quart casserole.
- Bake at 350 degrees for 45 minutes or until edges brown.

*A salad topped with Curry Dressing for Fruit is a good accompaniment.*

## OVEN OMELET

Serves 8-10

| | |
|---|---|
| 8 | slices bacon |
| 4 | green onions, thinly sliced |
| 8 | eggs |
| 1 | cup milk |
| ½ | tsp. salt |
| 2½ | cups shredded Monterey Jack cheese (Swiss or Cheddar may be substituted) |

- Preheat oven to 350 degrees.
- Fry bacon until crisp; drain and coarsely chop. Reserve small amount of grease and sauté onions until limp.
- Beat eggs with milk and salt. Stir in bacon, onions and 2 cups of cheese. Pour into greased, shallow 2-quart baking dish.
- Bake at 350 degrees for 35-40 minutes, or until mixture is set and top is lightly browned. Sprinkle with remaining cheese. Return to oven until cheese melts. Serve immediately.

# DEVILED EGGS AND SHRIMP CASSEROLE

Serves 6-8

## SHRIMP MIXTURE

| | |
|---|---|
| 6 | eggs, hard-boiled |
| ½ | tsp. salt |
| 1 | tsp. dry mustard |
| ¼ | tsp. Worcestershire sauce |
| ½ | tsp. cayenne pepper |
| 1½ | tsp. vinegar |
| 2 | Tbsp. butter, melted |
| 1½ | pounds shrimp, cooked and peeled |
| ½ | pound mushrooms, sliced |
| 2 | Tbsp. butter |
| 1 | Tbsp. lemon juice |

- Preheat oven to 300 degrees.
- Devil eggs, using next 6 ingredients. When yolks are mixed with seasonings, stuff halved whites with mixture and cut halves once again to form quartered deviled eggs. Layer eggs in bottom of buttered 13 x 9-inch casserole. Add cooked shrimp.
- Sauté mushrooms in butter, adding lemon juice to keep from browning. Add to casserole.
- May be prepared to this point and refrigerated until time to make sauce.

## SAUCE

| | |
|---|---|
| ¼ | pound butter |
| 4½ | Tbsp. flour |
| 1½ | cups milk |
| 1½ | tsp. prepared mustard |
| 1 | Tbsp. Worcestershire sauce |
| ½ | pound sharp Cheddar cheese, grated |
| 1½ | tsp. onion juice |
| | Generous dashes of cayenne pepper, paprika and Tabasco sauce |

- Melt butter; add flour and whisk well over medium heat. Add milk and stir until smooth. Stir in remaining ingredients, mixing until cheese is melted and sauce is smooth.
- Pour over casserole and bake at 300 degrees for 20-30 minutes or until sauce bubbles and begins to brown around edges.

# CHILI RELLENOS CASSEROLE

Serves 8
Do ahead

| | |
|---|---|
| 4 | 4-ounce cans whole green chilies, drained, patted dry and set aside |
| 8 | ounces hot pepper cheese, sliced to fit inside chilies |
| 1 | 28-ounce can Italian style tomatoes, seeded, chopped and juice strained and set aside |
| 1 | large onion |
| 3 | cloves garlic |
| 1½ | tsp. cumin |
| 1 | tsp. cinnamon |
| ½ | tsp. cilantro |
| ¼ | cup lard |
| | Bouquet garni of 2 bay leaves, 4 whole cloves and 1 tsp. peppercorns |
| | Salt to taste |
| 1 | tsp. sugar |
| | Freshly ground black pepper |
| 6-8 | ounces Mozzarella or Monterey Jack cheese |
| 8 | extra large eggs, beaten until thick and light |
| ½ | tsp. thyme |
| 1 | tsp. savory |
| ½ | tsp. cinnamon |
| 1½ | tsp. Tabasco sauce |

- Two hours before baking, gently stuff chilies with pepper cheese. Refrigerate.
- In a food processor, coarsely chop tomatoes with juice, onion, garlic, cumin, cinnamon and cilantro (Chinese parsley).
- In large skillet, render lard, removing browned fat. Pour tomato mixture into skillet, stirring to prevent sticking; simmer for 4 minutes over medium heat. Add bouquet garni; lower heat and cook for another 10 minutes. Add salt, sugar and pepper to taste. Keep sauce warm.
- Layer half of Mozzarella on bottom of 13 x 9-inch casserole or 2 decorative quiche dishes.
- Add remaining herbs and spices to eggs. Pour egg mixture over cheese. Gently arrange chilies in eggs. They will sink. Top with remaining cheese.
- Spoon a bit of tomato sauce over eggs in an appealing pattern.
- Bake at 350 degrees for 35-40 minutes until cheese melts and eggs are set and lightly browned.
- Serve hot with remaining sauce.
- Garnish with fresh parsley or cilantro.

*As a first course for 12-14 persons, sauce recipe may be doubled and casserole served cut in smaller pieces on a bed of sauce.*

# CHILIES RELLENOS

Serves 6

| | |
|---|---|
| 2 | 4-ounce cans whole green chilies |
| ½ | pound Monterey Jack cheese, sliced into ⅛-¼-inch slices |
| 2 | eggs, slightly beaten |
| ⅔ | cup flour |
| 1½ | cups milk |
| 1 | tsp. salt |

- Preheat oven to 350 degrees.
- Remove seeds from chilies.
- Alternate one layer of chilies with one layer of cheese slices in a soufflé dish or deep casserole. Add flour, salt and milk to eggs. Mix well. Pour over chilies and cheese.
- Bake at 350 degrees for 50 minutes or bake at 400 degrees for 30 minutes.
- Serve immediately.

*Will puff up like a soufflé.*

# ARTICHOKE QUICHE

Serves 8-12

| | |
|---|---|
| 2 | 6-ounce jars marinated artichoke hearts |
| 1 | clove garlic, minced |
| 1 | small onion, chopped |
| 4 | eggs |
| ¼ | cup dry bread crumbs |
| ¼ | tsp. salt |
| ⅛ | tsp. pepper |
| ⅛ | tsp. oregano |
| ⅛ | tsp. Tabasco sauce |
| 1 | Tbsp. parsley |
| ½ | cup grated sharp Cheddar cheese |

- Preheat oven to 325 degrees.
- Drain artichoke hearts, saving marinade from one jar. Chop hearts and set aside.
- Sauté onion and garlic in reserved marinade until translucent. Drain and set aside.
- Beat eggs until frothy; add all ingredients; stir well.
- Pour into greased 9-inch pie plate or quiche dish.
- Bake at 325 degrees for 30 minutes until firm and golden brown.
- May be prepared ahead and reheated at 300 degrees for about 15 minutes.

*To serve as an hors d'oeuvre, bake in an 11 x 7-inch casserole and cut into squares.*

# SPINACH PIE

Serves 4-6

1    10-ounce package frozen chopped spinach, cooked
1    pound Ricotta cheese
1    cup grated Cheddar cheese
1    Tbsp. oil
1    tsp. garlic salt
½    tsp. black pepper
1    egg, beaten with fork
1    Tbsp. butter, cut into pieces

- Preheat oven to 350 degrees.
- Drain and squeeze as much water out of spinach as possible.
- Combine all ingredients except butter. Mix well.
- Place mixture in a 9-inch pie plate. Top with butter.
- Bake at 350 degrees for 40 minutes.

*Wonderful meatless entrée.*

# SPINACH QUICHE

Serves 6

1    9-inch pie shell, baked and cooled
1    10-ounce package frozen chopped spinach, thawed
2    Tbsp. butter, melted
1    cup cottage cheese
3    eggs, beaten
½    cup milk
½    cup grated Parmesan cheese
     Pinch nutmeg
¼    tsp. salt
⅛    tsp. pepper
¼    tsp. sugar

- Drain and squeeze spinach. Set aside.
- Blend melted butter, cottage cheese, eggs and milk. Add Parmesan cheese, nutmeg. salt, pepper and sugar. Mix well. Blend in spinach. Pour into pie shell.
- Bake at 375 degrees for 50 minutes or until filling is set. Let stand 5 minutes before cutting.

# CRUSTLESS ZUCCHINI QUICHE

Serves 6-8

| | |
|---|---|
| 1½ | pounds zucchini, shredded |
| 1½ | tsp. salt |
| 4 | eggs, beaten |
| 2 | cups shredded Monterey Jack cheese |
| ¼ | tsp. pepper |
| ¼ | cup chopped green onion |
| 1 | small clove garlic, minced |
| 1 | tsp. dried basil |
| 1 | tomato, sliced |

- Preheat oven to 350 degrees.
- Sprinkle salt over shredded zucchini in a colander; let stand until moisture is drawn out (½ hour). With a tea towel, wring out water. Place dry zucchini in a bowl.
- Mix half the cheese and remaining ingredients, except tomato, with the zucchini. Pour into lightly greased pan. Lay sliced tomato on top. Sprinkle with remaining cheese.
- Bake at 350 degrees for 30 minutes.

*Great for light lunch or served as a vegetable.*

# CRUSTLESS CRAB QUICHE

Serves 6-8

| | |
|---|---|
| ½ | pound fresh mushrooms, thinly sliced |
| 2 | Tbsp. butter |
| 4 | eggs |
| 1 | cup sour cream |
| 1 | cup small curd cottage cheese |
| ½ | cup grated Parmesan cheese |
| 4 | Tbsp. flour |
| 1 | tsp. onion powder |
| ¼ | tsp. salt |
| 4 | drops Tabasco sauce |
| 2 | cups shredded Monterey Jack cheese |
| 16 | ounces fresh backfin crabmeat |

- Preheat oven to 350 degrees.
- Sauté mushrooms in butter. Drain on paper towels.
- In blender, combine remaining ingredients except Monterey Jack cheese and crabmeat. Blend until thoroughly mixed.
- Pour mixture into large bowl. Stir in mushrooms, cheese and crabmeat.
- Pour into 9 or 10-inch quiche dish or 10-inch pie plate.
- Bake at 350 degrees for 45 minutes or until knife comes out clean. Let stand 5 minutes before cutting.
- May be prepared ahead and brought to room temperature before baking.
- One-half pound slivered ham may be substituted for crab.

*Serve with salad and crusty French Bread.*

# PIZZA RUSTICA

Serves 10

**PASTRY**

| | |
|---|---|
| 3 | **eggs** |
| 2 | **Tbsp. salad oil** |
| 2 | **Tbsp. water** |
| 2 | **cups flour** |
| 1 | **tsp. baking powder** |
| ½ | **tsp. salt** |

- In a small bowl, beat together first 3 ingredients.
- Sift flour, baking powder and salt into a medium bowl. Make a well in center and pour in egg mixture. Stir with fork until well blended.
- Turn dough onto lightly floured pastry cloth or board. Cover dough with bowl to rest for 10 minutes. Knead until smooth (about 3 minutes).
- Shape pastry into a ball; wrap in waxed paper; refrigerate until ready to use.
- Preheat oven to 400 degrees.
- Lightly grease a 10-inch flan pan (with removable bottom) or 10-inch pie plate.

**FILLING**

| | |
|---|---|
| 1 | **Tbsp. salad oil** |
| ½ | **pound Italian sweet sausages** |
| 3 | **eggs** |
| 1½ | **pounds Ricotta cheese** |
| ½ | **pound Mozzarella cheese, grated** |
| ¼ | **cup grated Parmesan cheese** |
| ½ | **pound Prosciutto ham, coarsley chopped** |
| ¼ | **cup chopped parsley Dash pepper** |
| 6 | **eggs, hard-boiled and peeled** |
| 1 | **egg yolk** |
| 1 | **Tbsp. water** |

- In hot oil in skillet, sauté sausages until browned on all sides. Discard fat. Slice sausages ¼ inch thick. In large bowl, beat eggs until blended. Add Ricotta, Mozzarella, Parmesan, Prosciutto, parsley, pepper and sausage; mix well.
- On floured board, roll half of pastry into a 13-inch circle. Trim edge; reserve trimmings.
- Fold rolled pastry in half; transfer to prepared pan. Make sure fold is in center; unfold, carefully fitting into bottom of pan.
- Add filling and place whole eggs in 6 indentations made with spoon; cover eggs with filling.
- Roll trimmings ⅛ inch thick; with cookie cutter or knife, cut out 8 leaves. Set aside.
- Roll remaining pastry into 12-inch circle; trim edge. Place pastry on top of filling. Fold edge of top crust under bottom. Press together to seal; crimp.
- Make slits near center for steam vents; arrange leaves on top. Brush with egg yolk beaten with 1 Tablespoon water.
- Bake at 400 degrees for 35-40 minutes, or until crust is golden brown. Serve warm.

# PROVINCIAL PIE

Serves 4

| | |
|---|---|
| 1 | **pound Monterey Jack cheese, grated** |
| ½ | **cup mayonnaise** |
| 1 | **9-inch pie shell, baked and cooled** |
| 1 | **large ripe tomato, peeled and thinly sliced** |
| ½ | **pound sweet Italian sausage, lightly browned and crumbled** |
| ½ | **tsp. salt** |
| ¼ | **tsp. pepper** |
| 1 | **tsp. sweet basil** |
| ¼ | **cup grated Parmesan cheese** |

- Preheat oven to 375 degrees.
- Mix Monterey Jack cheese with mayonnaise and place half of mixture in bottom of pie shell.
- Next, layer sausage, the remaining cheese mixture, and tomato slices on pie. Sprinkle with salt, pepper, basil and Parmesan cheese.
- Bake at 375 degrees for 25 minutes.

*More like a pizza than a quiche; a family favorite.*

# FETTUCCINI CARBONARA

Serves 8

| | |
|---|---|
| 1 | **pound bacon** |
| 1 | **pound hot fettuccini, slightly undercooked and drained** |
| 4 | **Tbsp. butter, slivered** |
| 3 | **cups heavy cream** |
| 1 | **cup grated Parmesan cheese** |
| | **Pepper** |
| 4 | **egg yolks** |

- Cut bacon into 1-inch pieces and fry in large skillet until firm, but not crisp. Pour off all but 3 Tablespoons of grease.
- Add fettuccini and butter bits to skillet. Toss until butter begins to melt. Add about 2½ cups of cream and toss again.
- When cream begins to bubble, add cheese and stir to distribute evenly. Continue tossing until sauce begins to thicken. Add generous grind of pepper.
- Beat egg yolks with remaining cream and pour into skillet. Toss to coat evenly. Remove from heat and serve immediately.

*Very rich! A wonderful appetizer or entrée.*

# LINGUINI WITH RED CLAM SAUCE

Serves 6

⅓  cup olive oil
1  large garlic clove, minced
3½  cups (28-ounce can) stewed tomatoes
1  6-ounce can tomato paste
¼  cup red wine
1  tsp. salt
¼  tsp. black pepper
2  pinches thyme
2  pinches oregano
3  dozen fresh clams, chopped or 2 6½-ounce cans chopped clams
10  large sprigs parsley, chopped
1  pound linguini or thin spaghetti, cooked and drained

- In deep skillet, sauté garlic in oil until slightly brown. Add next 7 ingredients and bring to a boil.
- Add clams and parsley. Reduce heat; simmer for 3-5 minutes.
- Pour over platter of linguini or thin spaghetti.

# TRIPLE CHEESE PUDDING

Serves 6-8

6  eggs
1  cup milk
½  cup flour
1  tsp. baking powder
¼  pound butter, melted
10  ounces Monterey Jack cheese, grated
3  ounces cream cheese with chives
12  ounces cottage cheese
½  tsp. salt

- Preheat oven to 350 degrees.
- Beat eggs; add remaining ingredients and mix well.
- Pour mixture into a 13 x 9-inch buttered pan and bake at 350 degrees for 1 hour.

*Good for brunch or dinner with Regal Mushrooms,*
*Broiled Tomato Cups and salad.*

# LINGUINI WITH TOMATO-SHRIMP SAUCE

Serves 4-6

## LIGHT TOMATO SAUCE

| | |
|---|---|
| 1 | 28-ounce can tomatoes in purée |
| 2 | small onions, sliced |
| ½ | tsp. salt |
| | Fresh-ground black pepper to taste |
| 1 | tsp. dried basil |
| 4 | Tbsp. butter |

• Cook sauce ingredients except butter over medium low heat for 20 minutes, stirring frequently. Add butter; cook until melted.
• May be frozen until needed.

## LINGUINI WITH SHRIMP

| | |
|---|---|
| | Light Tomato Sauce |
| ½ | pound raw, peeled shrimp |
| 2 | cloves garlic, minced |
| 3 | Tbsp. chopped parsley |
| 2 | Tbsp. olive oil |
| | Hot pepper sauce or crushed red pepper to taste |
| 1 | pound linguini, cooked and drained |

• Heat tomato sauce; add shrimp and all other ingredients except linguini. Cover and simmer 3-5 minutes. Serve over hot linguini.

# TOMATO AND BASIL FETTUCCINI

Serves 4-6

| | |
|---|---|
| ¼ | cup chopped onion |
| 1 | clove garlic, minced |
| ¼ | cup olive oil |
| 3½ | cups tomatoes, chopped or 28-ounce can peeled tomatoes, chopped, liquid reserved |
| 6 | fresh basil leaves, chopped or 1 Tbsp. dried |
| 1 | tsp. salt |
| ½ | tsp. pepper |
| 1 | 12-ounce package fettuccini |
| | Grated Parmesan cheese |

- Sauté onion and garlic in oil until onion is tender but not brown.
- Add tomatoes, liquid and seasonings. Bring to a boil over medium heat. Reduce heat and simmer uncovered 15-20 minutes, stirring occasionally.
- Cook fettuccini according to package directions; drain well. Immediately toss hot fettuccini with tomato mixture in serving dish.
- Garnish with Parmesan cheese.

*Good side dish for dinner or luncheon entrée.*

# PASTA WITH CREAMY HERB SAUCE

Serves 4-6

| | |
|---|---|
| 1½ | cups heavy cream |
| 4 | Tbsp. unsalted butter |
| ½ | tsp. salt |
| ⅛ | tsp. grated nutmeg |
| | Pinch cayenne pepper |
| ¼ | cup freshly grated Parmesan cheese |
| 1 | cup finely chopped mixed fresh herbs (basil, mint, watercress, chives, parsley) If using dried herbs, try ⅓ cup, then add to taste |
| 1 | pound angel hair pasta, cooked and drained |

- Combine first 5 ingredients in heavy saucepan and simmer 15 minutes until slightly thickened.
- Whisk in cheese and herbs and simmer for 5 minutes longer. Taste and correct seasonings. Serve immediately over cooked pasta.

# PASTA PRIMAVERA

Serves 6

| | |
|---|---|
| ¼ | pound unsalted butter |
| 1 | medium onion, chopped |
| 1-2 | large cloves garlic, minced |
| 1 | pound thin asparagus, cut in 1-inch pieces |
| ½ | pound mushrooms, sliced |
| 6 | ounces cauliflower, cut in bite-size pieces |
| 1 | medium zucchini, thinly sliced |
| 1 | carrot, halved lengthwise and thinly sliced |
| 1 | cup whipping cream |
| ½ | cup chicken broth |
| 2 | tsp. sweet basil |
| 1 | cup frozen tiny peas, thawed |
| 5 | green onions, chopped |
| | Salt and pepper to taste |
| 1 | pound linguini, fettuccini or vermicelli (broken into 2-inch pieces if desired), cooked and drained |
| 1 | cup grated Parmesan cheese |
| | Cooked shrimp or diced ham (optional) |

- Heat wok or large deep skillet over medium heat. Melt butter, sauté onion and garlic 2 minutes.
- Add all vegetables except peas and green onions; stir-fry 2 minutes.
- Increase heat to high. Add cream, broth and basil; let boil 3 minutes. Stir in peas and green onions. Cook 1 minute.
- Adjust seasonings and toss with pasta, cheese and optional shrimp or ham. Serve immediately.

*Other vegetables may be added as desired.*

# VEGETARIAN LASAGNA

Serves 4-6

| | |
|---|---|
| 5 | lasagna noodles, cooked and drained |
| 1 | 10-ounce package frozen chopped spinach, cooked |
| ¼ | cup chopped onions |
| 2 | tsp. oil |
| ½ | cup grated carrots |
| 1 | cup sliced mushrooms |
| 1 | 8-ounce can tomato sauce |
| 1 | 6-ounce can tomato paste |
| ½ | cup chopped black olives |
| ¾ | tsp. oregano |
| 1 | cup cottage cheese |
| 4 | ounces sliced Monterey Jack cheese |
| ¼ | cup grated Parmesan cheese |

- Sauté onions in oil until soft; add carrots and mushrooms. Cook until tender. Stir in tomato sauce, tomato paste, olives and oregano.
- Grease casserole dish. Layer half each of noodles, cottage cheese, spinach and sauce mixture. Add ⅓ of Monterey cheese. Repeat. Place remaining Monterey and the Parmesan cheese on top.
- Bake at 375 degrees for 30 minutes. Allow to cool 10 minutes before cutting.

# LINGUINI WITH ARTICHOKE SAUCE

Serves 2-4

| | |
|---|---|
| ¼ | cup olive oil |
| 4 | Tbsp. butter |
| 1 | Tbsp. flour |
| 1 | cup chicken stock or broth |
| 2 | garlic cloves, crushed |
| 2 | tsp. lemon juice |
| 1 | tsp. minced parsley |
| 1 | 14-ounce can artichoke hearts, packed in water |
| 2 | Tbsp. grated Parmesan cheese |
| 1 | tsp. drained capers |
| ½ | pound linguini or other thin pasta |

- Heat oil in large skillet; add butter and melt. Add flour and cook, stirring, for 3 minutes over medium heat.
- Slowly stir in chicken stock; increase heat and cook 1 minute.
- Add garlic, lemon juice and parsley and cook uncovered over low heat for about 5 minutes. Recipe can be held at this point for up to 2 hours.
- Drain and quarter artichokes. Add to prepared mixture with cheese and capers. Cook uncovered, basting artichokes, for about 8 minutes.
- Meanwhile, cook pasta according to package directions. Drain and toss with hot sauce. Serve with more cheese and chopped parsley.

*Wonderful meatless entrée or serve as first course.*

# SOUPS AND SANDWICHES

# Soups and Sandwiches

## COLD SOUPS

Carrot Vichyssoise  90
Chilled Mushroom Soup  92
Chilled Tomato Basil
   Soup  92
Chilly Dilly Soup  89
Cold Zucchini Bisque  93
Senegalese  90
Speedy Gazpacho  91
Vichyssoise  89
White Gazpacho  91

## HOT SOUPS

Broccoli and Oyster
   Soup  94
Broccoli Bisque  93
Chesapeake Bay Crab
   Soup  96
Clam Chowder  94
Elegant Zucchini Soup  98
French Onion Soup  97
Mushroom Chowder  97
Outer Banks Clam
   Chowder  95
Potage Grand Luxe  96
Vegetable Soup  98
Virginia Clam Chowder  95

## HEARTY SOUPS AND STEWS

Basil Soup  99
Brunswick Stew  104
Company Beef Stew  101
Crowd-Pleaser Brunswick
   Stew  105
Easy Oyster Stew  106
Greek Beef Stew  102
New Year's Day Bean
   Soup  100
Oyster Stew  106
Savory Cabbage Soup with
   Cheese  103
Seafood Gumbo  107
Symphony Chili  99
Vegetable-Cheese
   Chowder  101

## SANDWICHES

Baked Turkey
   Sandwiches  108
Cheese Puff Sandwiches  102
Clam Sandwich Norfolk  110
Crab Burgers  111
Hot Crab Sandwich  110
Quesadillas  108
Salad Bowl Sandwich  112
Tidewater Crab Rolls  100
Vegetable Sandwiches  109

## SANDWICH SPREADS

Cheddar Pecan Spread  109
Cucumber Spread  103
Pimiento Cheese  111
Smithfield Ham Pâté  105
Spicy Cheese Spread  112

# CHILLY DILLY SOUP

Serves 4-6
Do ahead

1    **large ripe avocado, peeled and sliced**
1    **10¾-ounce can beef consommé**
1    **cup milk**
⅓    **cup cottage cheese**
¼    **tsp. cayenne pepper**
2    **kosher dill pickle spears, chopped**
¼    **cup chopped cucumber**

- Place all ingredients except cucumber in blender or food processor, blend until smooth. Refrigerate 1-2 hours until cold.
- Serve garnished with cucumbers.

*Serve as appetizer for summer dinner or with sandwiches for luncheon.*

# VICHYSSOISE

Serves 4-6

2    **medium onions, thinly sliced**
3    **stalks celery, thinly sliced**
3    **Tbsp. butter**
4    **medium potatoes, pared and diced**
4    **cups chicken stock**
2    **cups light cream**
   **Salt and pepper to taste**
   **Chives or parsley garnish**

- Cook onions and celery in covered pan with butter until translucent and tender. Do not brown. Add potatoes and broth. Cook until potatoes are tender.
- Purée in blender or food processor. Add cream. Season to taste. Chill.

*Delicious cold or hot.*

# CARROT VICHYSSOISE

Serves 4
Do ahead

| | |
|---|---|
| 2 | Tbsp. butter |
| 2 | bunches scallions, sliced |
| 2 | cups chicken broth |
| 2 | cups cooked sliced carrots |
| ½ | tsp. salt |
| ⅛ | tsp. pepper |
| ½ | cup heavy cream |
| 1 | Tbsp. snipped chives or dill weed to garnish |

- Melt butter in saucepan; add scallions and cook for 5 minutes.
- Add 1 cup of broth; cover and simmer over low heat 15 minutes or until tender.
- Place in blender. Add remaining broth, carrots, salt and pepper. Blend until smooth.
- Pour into bowl, stir in cream. Chill thoroughly. Serve topped with garnish.

*May be served hot.*

# SENEGALESE

Serves 4-6

| | |
|---|---|
| 1 | medium mild onion, chopped |
| 1 | medium cucumber, peeled and cubed |
| ¾ | cup chicken broth |
| 1 | 10¾-ounce can cream of chicken soup |
| 1 | cup sour cream |
| 6 | dashes Tabasco sauce |
| 6 | dashes Worcestershire sauce |
| ¼ | tsp. celery salt |
| ⅛-¼ | tsp. curry powder |
| | Chopped chives, slivered cucumbers, or parsley to garnish |

- Place all ingredients except seasonings in food processor or blender. May need to do in 2 portions. Blend until smooth.
- Add seasonings and blend a few seconds. Chill overnight.
- Garnish to taste.

# SPEEDY GAZPACHO

Serves 8-10
Do ahead

| | |
|---|---|
| 32 | ounces tomato juice |
| 1 | cucumber, peeled, seeded and chopped |
| 1 | green pepper, seeded and chopped |
| 3 | stalks celery, chopped |
| ¼ | cup red wine vinegar |
| 1 | Tbsp. Worcestershire sauce |
| 1 | Tbsp. chopped fresh parsley |
| 1 | tsp. instant beef bouillon |
| ½ | tsp. onion salt |
| ¼ | tsp. white pepper |
| ¼ | tsp. garlic powder |

- Place all ingredients in blender. May need to do in 2 batches. Blend until smooth.
- Pour into large bowl or pitcher. Chill.

# WHITE GAZPACHO

Makes 7-8 cups
Do ahead

| | |
|---|---|
| 2 | medium cucumbers, peeled and diced |
| 1 | clove garlic |
| 3 | cups chicken broth |
| 2 | cups sour cream |
| 1 | cup plain yogurt |
| 3 | Tbsp. white vinegar |
| 2 | tsp. salt |
| ½ | tsp. pepper |
| | Chopped green onions or chopped tomatoes to garnish |

- In blender or food processor, place cucumbers, garlic and 1 cup of broth. Purée.
- Add remaining broth. Slowly add remaining ingredients, except garnish, blend well. Chill thoroughly.
- Garnish with chopped green onions or chopped tomatoes if desired.

# CHILLED MUSHROOM SOUP

Serves 4
Do ahead

| | |
|---|---|
| 2 | Tbsp. butter, melted |
| 1 | small onion, chopped |
| ½ | cup chopped tender celery |
| 8 | ounces fresh mushrooms, sliced |
| 2 | cups water |
| 2 | tsp. chicken bouillon granules |
| | Shake of nutmeg |
| 2 | parsley sprigs |
| | Squeeze of lemon to taste |
| 1 | cup milk |
| 1 | cup Ricotta cheese |
| | Chopped fresh chives |

- Sauté onion, celery and mushrooms in butter. Add water, bouillon, nutmeg and parsley. Simmer 20 minutes.
- Add lemon juice, milk and Ricotta. Blend until smooth.
- Chill and serve. Garnish with chives.

# CHILLED TOMATO BASIL SOUP

Serves 6
Do ahead

| | |
|---|---|
| 2 | Tbsp. butter, melted |
| 2 | cups chopped onion |
| 2 | cups peeled, seeded, cubed cucumbers |
| 3 | cups peeled, cored, cubed tomatoes |
| 3 | basil leaves or 1 tsp. dried basil |
| 2 | cups chicken broth |
| 2 | cups yogurt |
| | Salt to taste |
| 1 | tsp. chopped fresh mint |

- Sauté onions in butter for 10 minutes. Add cucumbers, tomatoes, basil and broth. Cook for 30 minutes, stirring frequently. Cool.
- Place cooked mixture in blender, purée.
- Pour into bowl, blend in yogurt and salt. Chill thoroughly. Garnish with mint.

# COLD ZUCCHINI BISQUE

Serves 8
Do ahead

| | |
|---|---|
| 6 | cups thinly sliced zucchini |
| 1 | medium onion, sliced |
| 2 | Tbsp. butter |
| 2 | Tbsp. oil |
| 2 | 10½-ounce cans chicken broth, undiluted |
| ¾ | cup milk |
| 1 | tsp. salt |
| ¼ | tsp. pepper |

- Heat butter and oil in a Dutch oven. Add vegetables and sauté until limp. Add chicken broth, cover and simmer 15 minutes or until tender.
- Cool slightly, then pour into blender and purée until smooth. The mixture may be puréed in batches.
- Add milk and seasonings. Refrigerate until well chilled.

# BROCCOLI BISQUE

Serves 6-8

| | |
|---|---|
| 1 | head broccoli; cut florets into small pieces and chop stalks |
| ¼ | pound butter |
| 4 | medium potatoes, peeled and sliced |
| 4 | stalks celery, diced |
| 1 | medium onion, sliced |
| 4 | cups chicken stock |
| | Salt and pepper to taste |
| | Nutmeg |
| | Sour cream |

- Place florets in ice water. Soak.
- Melt butter in large pot. Add broccoli stalks, potatoes, celery and onions. Cook until translucent. Add stock. Cook, loosely covered, for 30 minutes.
- Remove from heat and purée in batches. Return to heat and add drained florets. Simmer, uncovered, for 10 minutes.
- Serve with dollop of sour cream and sprinkle with nutmeg.

# BROCCOLI AND OYSTER SOUP

Serves 4

½    **cup light cream**
1    **Tbsp. flour**
1    **cup chicken broth**
1    **cup milk**
2    **Tbsp. butter, melted**
     **Pepper to taste**
1    **10-ounce package broccoli or spinach, cooked**
½    **small onion, sliced**
1    **Tbsp. chicken bouillon granules**
     **Pinch marjoram**
     **Pinch rosemary**
     **Dash of garlic powder**
8    **ounces oysters, drained**
2    **Tbsp. butter**

- Blend cream and flour in blender until smooth. Add broth, milk, butter and pepper; blend.
- Add vegetables and seasonings; blend until smooth. Pour into saucepan and heat.
- Sauté oysters in butter over low heat until just beginning to curl. Add to saucepan; heat through.

# CLAM CHOWDER

Yields 1 quart

5    **slices bacon, drippings reserved**
½    **cup chopped onion**
½    **cup chopped green pepper**
2    **cloves garlic, minced**
2    **cups chopped clams, liquid reserved (2 cans or 3 dozen fresh)**
1    **16-ounce can stewed tomatoes**
1    **cup cooked rice**
½    **tsp. thyme**
½    **tsp. oregano**
     **Salt and pepper to taste**

- Fry bacon, remove and crumble. Set aside.
- Sauté onion, pepper and garlic in bacon drippings. Add clam liquid, tomatoes, rice and seasonings. Simmer 10 minutes.
- Add clams, bring to boil. Sprinkle with bacon. Serve immediately.

## VIRGINIA CLAM CHOWDER

Serves 8-10

| | |
|---|---|
| 2 | dozen shucked clams, chopped, liquid reserved |
| 2 | cups chopped potatoes |
| 1 | cup chopped celery |
| 1 | cup chopped onion |
| ¾ | cup butter |
| ¾ | cup flour |
| 4 | cups light cream |
| | Salt and pepper |

- In large pot, place potatoes, celery and onions. Pour reserved clam juice over vegetables. Add enough water to cover. Cook until potatoes are tender.
- In large pot, melt butter. Whisk in flour until smooth. Cook for 1-2 minutes. Add cream, undrained vegetables and clams. Heat through. Season.

## OUTER BANKS CLAM CHOWDER

Makes 3 quarts

| | |
|---|---|
| 8 | slices bacon, fried and cut up |
| 2 | tsp. reserved bacon drippings |
| 1 | onion, chopped |
| 6 | medium potatoes, peeled and diced |
| 5 | cups water |
| 2 | 8-ounce bottles clam juice |
| 1 | tsp. salt to taste |
| ¼ | tsp. pepper |
| | Several dashes cracked pepper |
| 1 | pint fresh clams with juice, chopped |

- In large soup kettle, sauté onions in bacon drippings. Add remaining ingredients.
- Bring to a boil; reduce heat. Cover and simmer for 1 hour or until potatoes are done.

*Clam broth base makes this different from the usual New England or Manhattan chowders.*

# CHESAPEAKE BAY CRAB SOUP

Serves 4

| | |
|---|---|
| 4 | Tbsp. butter, melted |
| 1 | small onion, finely chopped |
| 3 | Tbsp. flour |
| 2 | cups light cream |
| 2 | cups milk |
| 1 | pound backfin crabmeat |
| 2 | Tbsp. Sherry |
| | Salt and red pepper to taste |

- Sauté onion in butter until translucent. Stir in flour. Add cream and milk; simmer 5 minutes over medium heat.
- Add crabmeat, Sherry and seasonings. Heat through.

# POTAGE GRAND LUXE

Serves 10-12

| | |
|---|---|
| ½ | pound unsalted butter |
| ½ | cup flour |
| 2 | quarts seafood stock or oyster juice |
| 5 | cups heavy cream |
| 1½ | tsp. cayenne pepper |
| 1½ | pounds ripe Brie, rind removed |
| 2½ | cups Brut Champagne |
| 48 | oysters |
| 1 | cup finely chopped green scallions |
| 2 | Tbsp. finely chopped shallots |
| 1 | Tbsp. clarified butter |
| | Salt and white pepper to taste |

**OPTIONAL GARNISH**
Chopped chives
Golden caviar

- In large saucepan, melt butter. Add flour to form roux, stirring constantly until mixture is thick.
- Add stock in a slow, steady stream, whisking constantly until it is well blended. Bring to a boil, lower heat and simmer for 10 minutes.
- Add cream and simmer for 5 minutes, stirring constantly.
- Add pepper and diced Brie. Stir until smooth.
- Add Champagne, oysters and scallions. Blend, cover and turn off heat. Let stand 10 minutes.
- Sauté shallots in clarified butter until translucent. Add to soup and adjust seasoning.
- Serve in small soup cups garnished with freshly cut chives and a spoonful of golden caviar.

# MUSHROOM CHOWDER

Serves 6-8

½   cup chopped onion
½   cup butter
1   pound sliced mushrooms
1   cup diced potatoes
1   cup chopped celery
½   cup chopped carrot
1   tsp. salt
¼   tsp. pepper
1   Tbsp. flour
2   Tbsp. water
3   cups beef or chicken stock
1   cup milk
    Parmesan cheese

- Sauté onions in butter in large pot until golden brown.
- Add vegetables, salt and pepper. Cook 15 minutes.
- Mix remaining ingredients. Add to vegetables. Heat through, do not boil. Top each serving with Parmesan cheese.

# FRENCH ONION SOUP

Serves 4

3   Tbsp. butter
5   cups sliced onions
¼   tsp. crushed peppercorns
1   Tbsp. flour
3   10¾-ounce cans condensed beef broth
1½   cups water
½   cup dry Sherry
1   8-ounce can mushrooms, drained
1   bay leaf
4   slices French bread toast
½   cup grated Swiss cheese
½   cup grated Mozzarella cheese

- Melt butter in heavy soup pot and sauté onions over medium heat. Stir in peppercorns. When onions are golden, add flour and cook 1 minute, stirring constantly.
- Add broth, water, Sherry, mushrooms and bay leaf. Simmer 45 minutes.
- Ladle broth into 4 ovenproof soup crocks. Top with toast and cheeses.
- Broil until cheese is golden brown.

# VEGETABLE SOUP

Serves 6-8

Beef soup bone
Salt to taste
3-4 medium potatoes, chopped
1 large onion, chopped
1 stalk celery, chopped
1 carrot, grated
3-4 okra pods, sliced
1 28-ounce can tomatoes
½ cup frozen corn
⅛ cup barley
Crushed red pepper flakes to taste

- Cook soup bone in water to cover, with salt for 2-3 hours. Skim surface occasionally.
- Remove bone, add remaining ingredients. Simmer 1 hour.

# ELEGANT ZUCCHINI SOUP

Yields 2 quarts

2 pounds zucchini, sliced
1½ cups thinly sliced onion
½ green pepper, slivered
2 Tbsp. butter
¼ cup water
1½ cloves garlic, crushed
1 bay leaf
Salt and pepper to taste
½ cup parsley sprigs
1 chicken bouillon cube
1 cup boiling water
⅔ cup evaporated milk
½ cup dry white wine

- Sauté zucchini, onion and green pepper in butter. Add water, garlic and bay leaf. Cook until tender. Remove bay leaf. Add seasonings and parsley.
- Place in blender, purée until smooth. May be frozen at this point.
- When ready to continue preparation, combine purée with bouillon cube in boiling water until hot.
- Add milk, blend; add wine. Do not boil. Adjust seasonings.
- To serve, garnish with parsley or onion.

*One-half cup contains only 38 calories.*
*Make purée and freeze while zucchini is abundant.*

# BASIL SOUP

Serves 6-8

| | |
|---|---|
| 2 | cups firmly packed fresh spinach, stems removed |
| 1 | cup firmly packed fresh parsley sprigs |
| 8 | cups chicken broth |
| ¾ | cup fresh basil, or ¼ cup dried basil |
| ¼ | cup chopped walnuts |
| 1 | garlic clove, minced |
| ¼ | cup olive oil |
| 1 | cup orzo noodles |
| 1 | egg |
| ½ | cup water |
| 2 | cups shredded Parmesan cheese |

- In blender, purée spinach, parsley and 1 cup broth. Add basil, walnuts and garlic. Blend until smooth, about 2 minutes. Add olive oil. Blend again.
- Pour into large pot. Stir in remaining broth. Heat to boiling, add noodles, return to boil. Reduce heat; simmer covered 15 minutes.
- Beat egg in water. Stir in 1¾ cups cheese. Gradually add 1 cup of hot soup. Blend well.
- Gradually stir cheese mixture into soup. Garnish with remaining cheese.

*A meal in itself.*

# SYMPHONY CHILI

Yields 1 gallon

| | |
|---|---|
| 4 | large onions, chopped |
| 1 | clove garlic, chopped |
| ⅓ | cup olive oil |
| 2 | pounds ground round |
| 2 | large green peppers, chopped |
| 2 | 16-ounce cans light red kidney beans, drained |
| 1 | 28-ounce can tomatoes, chopped |
| 5 | Tbsp. chili powder |
| 2 | tsp. salt |
| ¼ | tsp. cayenne pepper |
| 2 | cups water |
| 4 | bay leaves |

- Sauté onions and garlic in oil until translucent.
- In 5-quart pot, brown beef and drain. Mix in green peppers and steam for 2 minutes.
- Add all ingredients to beef, mix well.
- Cook on low heat for 3 hours. Serve over rice.

# NEW YEAR'S DAY BEAN SOUP

Serves 6-8
Do ahead

| | |
|---|---|
| ¼ | cup dried black-eyed peas |
| ¼ | cup dried great northern beans |
| ¼ | cup dried kidney beans |
| ¼ | cup dried lentils |
| ¼ | cup dried lima beans |
| ¼ | cup dried navy beans |
| ¼ | cup dried pinto beans |
| ¼ | cup dried split green peas |
| 2 | Tbsp. salt |
| 1 | ham hock with ham shreds |
| 1 | 28-ounce can tomatoes, undrained |
| 2 | medium onions, quartered |
| 2 | Tbsp. lemon juice |
| 1½ | tsp. chili powder |
| 1 | tsp. black pepper |

- Wash and drain dried beans. Place in large pot; cover with water. Add salt. Soak overnight.
- In morning, drain beans. Add 2 quarts water and ham hock with ham shreds. Bring to boil, lower heat; cover and simmer slowly for 3 hours.
- Cut ham off bone, return meat to pot. Add remaining ingredients. Simmer 30 minutes more.
- As a holiday gift, layer beans in a clear container attaching recipe.

# TIDEWATER CRAB ROLLS

Serves 4

**ROLLS**

| | |
|---|---|
| 1 | 8-ounce can refrigerated crescent rolls |
| 4 | slices natural Swiss cheese |
| 8 | ounces backfin crabmeat |
| 2 | Tbsp. mayonnaise |
| 1 | Tbsp. finely chopped green pepper |
| ¼ | tsp. salt |

- Preheat oven to 375 degrees.
- Separate crescent rolls into 8 triangles. Place ½ slice of cheese on each roll.
- Combine remaining ingredients and spoon onto dough. Roll up.
- Bake at 375 degrees for 18 minutes or until rolls are brown.

**SAUCE**

| | |
|---|---|
| 1 | Tbsp. butter |
| 1 | cup sour cream |
| 1 | tsp. curry powder |
| | Salt and pepper to taste |

- Melt butter and add remaining ingredients. Heat but do *not* boil.
- Spoon over crab rolls.

# COMPANY BEEF STEW

Serves 6-8

| | |
|---|---|
| ¼ | cup oil |
| 3 | pounds stewing beef, cut into 1-inch cubes |
| 2 | cups chopped onions |
| 1 | clove garlic, crushed |
| 1 | cup red wine |
| 3 | cups water |
| 2 | beef bouillon cubes |
| ½ | cup chopped fresh parsley |
| 2 | bay leaves |
| 1 | Tbsp. salt |
| ½ | tsp. pepper |
| 6 | potatoes, peeled and cubed |
| 6 | carrots, peeled and cut into 1-inch pieces |
| 18 | small white onions, peeled |
| ½ | cup water |
| ¼ | cup cornstarch |

- In large heavy saucepan, heat oil; brown beef. Add onions and garlic; cook until golden.
- Add next 7 ingredients. Bring to a boil, reduce heat. Cover and simmer 1½-2 hours.
- Add vegetables, simmer 1-1½ hours or until tender.
- Mix water and cornstarch until smooth. Stir into stew, stirring constantly, until thickened.

# VEGETABLE-CHEESE CHOWDER

Serves 8

| | |
|---|---|
| 1 | cup chopped potatoes |
| ½ | cup chopped carrots |
| ½ | cup chopped celery |
| ½ | cup chopped onion |
| ½ | cup chopped green pepper |
| 4 | Tbsp. butter |
| 3 | cups chicken broth |
| | Salt and pepper to taste |
| 2 | cups milk |
| ½ | cup flour |
| 3 | cups shredded sharp cheese |
| 1 | Tbsp. minced parsley |

- In large soup kettle, sauté vegetables in butter. Stir in broth, salt and pepper. Simmer uncovered for 30 minutes.
- Blend flour and milk. Stir into broth. Add cheese and parsley. Cook, stirring frequently, until thick and bubbly. Correct seasoning, if needed. Serve hot.

# GREEK BEEF STEW

Serves 4-6

| | |
|---|---|
| 1 | **cup minced fresh parsley** |
| 1 | **6-ounce can tomato paste** |
| ½ | **cup white wine** |
| ¼ | **cup red wine vinegar** |
| 1 | **tsp. ground cumin** |
| 1 | **tsp. ground cinnamon** |
| 1 | **tsp. oregano** |
| ½ | **tsp. sugar** |
| | **Salt and pepper to taste** |
| 3 | **pounds boneless chuck, cut in 1-inch cubes** |
| 2 | **pounds small white onions, peeled or regular onions cut in eighths** |
| 1 | **bay leaf** |

- Preheat oven to 325 degrees.
- In a large bowl combine parsley, tomato paste, wine, vinegar, cumin, cinnamon, oregano, sugar, salt and pepper.
- Add chuck, onions and bay leaf. Combine mixture well.
- Transfer mixture to Dutch oven; heat over moderate heat, stirring until hot.
- Bake covered at 325 degrees for 1¾ hours or until meat is very tender.
- Transfer to serving dish and top with Feta cheese and walnut mixture.

### OPTIONAL TOPPING

| | |
|---|---|
| ½ | **pound Feta cheese, crumbled** |
| 1 | **cup walnuts** |

- Combine ingredients.

*Good buffet dish served over rice. No knives needed!*

# CHEESE PUFF SANDWICHES

Makes 10-12 sandwiches
Do ahead

| | |
|---|---|
| ½ | **pound sharp Cheddar cheese, cubed** |
| ¼ | **pound butter, softened** |
| ¼ | **pound margarine, softened** |
| 1 | **egg** |
| 1½ | **loaves sandwich bread** |

- In processor, cream cheese, butter and margarine until smooth. Add egg and mix well.
- Spread mixture on each slice of bread. Make each sandwich with 3 layers. Place on cookie sheet and freeze about 30 minutes.
- Remove from freezer; slice off crusts. Spread remaining cheese mixture on sides (not bottom) of sandwiches. Wrap individually and freeze.
- To serve, unwrap frozen sandwich, cut in half diagonally, place on cookie sheet and bake at 350 degrees for 15 minutes.

# SAVORY CABBAGE SOUP WITH CHEESE

Serves 4-6

| | |
|---|---|
| 8 | slices lean bacon, coarsely chopped |
| 1 | medium onion, coarsely chopped |
| 1 | bunch scallions, chopped |
| 1 | pound cabbage (½ head), coarsely chopped |
| 1 | pound potatoes, peeled and coarsely chopped |
| 5 | cups chicken stock |
| | Salt and fresh pepper to taste |
| 1½ | tsp. mixed herbs |
| 1 | cup grated Gruyère cheese |
| ½ | cup grated Crème de Polder or other Gouda cheese |
| ¾ | cup heavy cream |
| ½ | tsp. dried dill or 1 tsp. fresh |
| ½-1 | tsp. cayenne pepper |

- In a Dutch oven or other large range-top pan, sauté bacon over medium heat until crisp.
- Add onions, scallions and cabbage to pan. Sauté for 7 minutes or until onion is translucent but not brown.
- Add potatoes to mixture and stir briefly; pour in chicken stock, adding salt and pepper. Bring to a boil, turn down heat and simmer 45-50 minutes. If a smooth soup is desired, pour soup into processor, purée and then strain before continuing.
- Over medium heat, add cheeses a little at a time, stirring until melted. Do not boil.
- Immediately before serving, add remaining ingredients. Adjust seasonings.
- Serve with hot bread and salad for a hearty main course.

# CUCUMBER SPREAD

Yields 1 cup

| | |
|---|---|
| 8 | ounces cream cheese, softened |
| ⅔ | cup grated, peeled cucumber |
| 1 | tsp. chives |
| ⅛ | tsp. onion salt |
| ⅛ | tsp. salt |
| ⅛ | tsp. pepper |

- Combine all ingredients. Beat until fluffy.
- Refrigerate, covered, until ready to use as sandwich spread.

# BRUNSWICK STEW

Serves 10-12

1    **large chicken, cut up**
1    **quart water**
2    **slices bacon, cut into 2-inch pieces**
1    **large onion, sliced**
1    **tsp. salt**
1    **28-ounce can whole tomatoes or 3 large fresh tomatoes, peeled**
2    **large potatoes, cubed**
1    **10-ounce package frozen butterbeans, or 1 cup fresh butterbeans**
½    **tsp. sugar**
2    **tsp. salt**
½    **tsp. pepper**
    **Dash red pepper**
1    **16-ounce package frozen corn or cut from 3 large ears**
2    **Tbsp. butter, melted**
2    **Tbsp. flour**

- In 5-quart heavy pot, stew chicken, water, bacon, onion and salt for 2 hours over medium-low heat.
- Remove chicken, cool; skin and remove meat from bones. Cut into medium-size pieces. Return to pot.
- Add remaining ingredients except corn, butter and flour. Cook ½ hour. Add corn, cook another ½ hour. Mix butter and flour. Add to stew and simmer ½ hour.

*Serve with hot rolls and a green salad.*

# CROWD-PLEASER BRUNSWICK STEW

Makes 2 gallons
Do ahead

| | |
|---|---|
| 4-5 | pound stewing chicken |
| 1½ | pounds pork chops, fat trimmed |
| 4 | quarts water |
| | Salt and pepper |
| 8 | tsp. chicken bouillon granules |
| 2 | stalks celery |
| 2 | 28-ounce cans tomatoes, chopped |
| 1 | 14½-ounce can tomato wedges, chopped |
| 1 | 15-ounce can tomato sauce |
| 1 | 24-ounce can tomato juice |
| 2 | cups chopped onions |
| 2½-3 | cups potatoes, peeled and cubed |
| 1 | 16-ounce package frozen baby lima beans |
| 1 | 16-ounce package frozen small peas |
| 1 | 17-ounce can white shoepeg corn, drained |
| | Tabasco sauce to taste |
| | Salt and pepper to taste |

- Combine first 6 ingredients. Cook until meat is done. Remove meat from bones in small pieces. Refrigerate until ready to use. Strain and reserve 4 quarts stock. Remove fat from surface.
- Add all tomato ingredients and onions to stock. Cook 15 minutes.
- Add potatoes and meat. Cook 30 minutes. Add beans, peas and corn.
- Add seasonings to taste. Cook for 10-15 minutes more.
- Best made a day ahead, chilled and reheated.

*Freezes beautifully.*

# SMITHFIELD HAM PÂTÉ

Makes 1½ cups

| | |
|---|---|
| ½ | pound Smithfield ham, ground |
| ½ | cup mayonnaise |
| 2 | Tbsp. prepared mustard |
| 2 | Tbsp. butter, softened |

- Combine ingredients; store in refrigerator.
- Use as a sandwich spread or serve on small rolls.
- Rolls may be prepared ahead and heated in foil before serving.

# EASY OYSTER STEW

Serves 8

1   quart select oysters or 48-60 freshly shucked oysters
½   pound butter
1   pint heavy cream
1   pint light cream
2   tsp. Worcestershire sauce
2   tsp. Tabasco sauce
2   tsp. celery salt
    Paprika

- In a large, heavy pan, quickly sauté oysters in their liquor with the butter. Cook just until edges of oysters begin to curl.
- Add rest of ingredients except the paprika.
- Pour into mugs and garnish with a sprinkle of paprika.
- When cooking for a crowd, add 2 cups of milk for more servings.

# OYSTER STEW

Serves 4-6

4   Tbsp. butter
2   stalks celery, diced
1   medium onion, diced
1   4-ounce can sliced mushrooms
¼   cup flour
1   cup white wine
1   cup reserved oyster liquid
2   tsp. chicken bouillon granules
2   Tbsp. chopped fresh parsley
    Pinch thyme, nutmeg and pepper
    Fresh lemon juice, to taste
½   cup whipping cream
2   Tbsp. grated Parmesan cheese
1   quart fresh shucked oysters, drained

- Sauté celery and onion in butter. Add mushrooms, cook gently.
- Stir in flour. Add wine, oyster liquid and bouillon granules. Bring to a boil, stirring well.
- Reduce heat, add seasonings, cream and cheese; blend well. Add oysters, cook until edges curl. DO NOT BOIL.
- Serve as a hearty stew or main course over rice.

# SEAFOOD GUMBO

Serves 16

| | |
|---|---|
| 6 | slices bacon |
| ½ | cup reserved bacon drippings |
| 6 | Tbsp. flour |
| 2 | large onions, chopped |
| 1 | large green pepper, chopped |
| 2 | stalks celery, chopped |
| 3 | cloves garlic, pressed or minced |
| 3 | 16-ounce cans tomatoes |
| 4 | cups tomato juice or V-8 juice |
| 4 | cups water |
| 10 | bay leaves |
| 3 | Tbsp. Worcestershire sauce |
| 1½ | Tbsp. Sherry Peppers Sauce |
| 4 | cups sliced okra |
| | Salt and pepper to taste |
| ½ | cup chopped parsley |
| 1 | quart oysters, drained |
| 2 | pounds backfin crabmeat |
| 3 | pounds shrimp, shelled and deveined |
| 1 | Tbsp. gumbo filé, optional |
| 6-8 | cups cooked rice |

- In large pot, cook bacon; remove and measure drippings.
- Make roux from flour and bacon drippings. Stir over medium heat constantly for 15 minutes or until darkened. Add onions, pepper, celery, garlic and stir. Cook about 15 minutes.
- Mix tomatoes, juice, water, bay leaves, Worcestershire, pepper sauce, okra, salt, pepper and parsley. Blend well.
- Gradually add to roux, stirring constantly. Simmer 1½ hours, stirring often.
- Bring to a boil, reduce heat and add seafood. Simmer gently, uncovered, for 5 minutes. Add filé to thicken if desired.
- Serve in deep bowl over rice.

*Gumbo may be done ahead up to the point of adding seafood.*

# BAKED TURKEY SANDWICHES

Serves 8

| | |
|---|---|
| 16 | slices white bread, crusts removed |
| ¼ | pound butter (for bread) |
| ¼ | pound fresh mushrooms |
| 2 | Tbsp. butter |
| 2 | cups cooked turkey, sliced |
| 3 | hard-boiled eggs, chopped |
| ¾ | cup mayonnaise |
| ⅓ | cup sliced ripe olives |
| 2 | Tbsp. chopped onion |
| | Salt |
| | Lemon juice |
| | Paprika |
| 1 | 10¾-ounce can cream of chicken soup |
| 1 | cup sour cream |
| 2 | Tbsp. Sherry |

- Preheat oven to 325 degrees.
- Butter both sides of bread, place 8 slices in a 13 x 9-inch baking dish.
- Sauté mushrooms in 2 Tablespoons butter. Combine turkey, eggs, mayonnaise, olives and onions. Add mushrooms, salt, lemon juice and paprika to taste.
- Spread mixture over bread and top with remaining bread slices.
- Combine soup, sour cream and Sherry. Pour over sandwiches.
- Bake at 325 degrees for 30 minutes.

*Great light supper for Sunday evening.*

# QUESADILLAS

Serves 6
Do ahead

| | |
|---|---|
| 1 | 14½-ounce can stewed tomatoes |
| 1 | small onion, diced |
| 1 | 4-ounce can green chili peppers, diced |
| ½ | pound Monterey Jack cheese, grated |
| ½ | pound Cheddar cheese, grated |
| 1 | 12-count package flour tortillas |
| | Bacon grease to cover bottom of skillet |
| | Sour cream for topping |

- Mix tomatoes, onions and peppers together. Cover mixture and refrigerate overnight.
- Before preparing tortillas, begin heating tomato mixture.
- Place equal amounts of each cheese on half of tortilla. Fold tortilla over and fry in bacon grease. Fry until both sides are golden and cheese melts. Place on serving plates.
- Spoon heated tomato mixture over tortillas and top with a spoonful of sour cream.

# VEGETABLE SANDWICHES

Makes 100 small sandwiches
Do ahead

| | |
|---|---|
| 1 | envelope unflavored gelatin |
| ¼ | cup cold water |
| 2 | cups mayonnaise |
| 1 | cup finely chopped celery |
| 2 | cucumbers, peeled, seeded and finely diced |
| 1 | onion, finely chopped |
| 2 | small carrots, grated |
| ½ | green pepper, finely diced |
| 1 | tsp. salt |

- Soften gelatin in cold water. Dissolve in top of double boiler over boiling water.
- Add mayonnaise; mix. Add remaining ingredients, mixing well. Chill. Use as sandwich spread.
- For tea sandwiches, trim crusts from bread and cut into shapes.

OPTIONAL
   Dash pepper
   Dash Worcestershire sauce
   Dash Tabasco sauce

*Will keep in refrigerator for several weeks.*

# CHEDDAR PECAN SPREAD

Yields 1½ cups

| | |
|---|---|
| 1 | cup shredded sharp Cheddar cheese |
| 1 | Tbsp. finely chopped onion |
| ½ | cup Hellmann's mayonnaise |
| ¼ | cup chopped pecans |
| 2 | strips well-cooked bacon, crumbled |

- Blend ingredients and chill in covered container.
- Serve as a sandwich spread or with sesame or wheat crackers.

*So easy, but such unusual taste.*

# CLAM SANDWICH NORFOLK

Serves 8

1    pound Monterey Jack cheese, grated
3    6½-ounce cans chopped clams, drained
2    Tbsp. finely chopped parsley
2    Tbsp. chopped chives
2    Tbsp. finely minced onion
     Dash of pepper
8    slices pumpernickel bread

- Combine all ingredients except bread.
- Place slices of bread in individual ovenproof dishes.
- Top with clam mixture divided among the dishes.
- Broil until golden and bubbly.

*Could be adapted to serve as an hors d'oeuvre on crackers or melba toast, adding cooked and crumbled bacon topping.*

# HOT CRAB SANDWICH

Serves 6
Do ahead

     Juice of ½ lemon
     Salt to taste
     Cayenne pepper to taste
1    pound backfin crabmeat
12   slices whole wheat bread, crusts removed
     Butter
12   slices sharp Cheddar cheese
4    eggs
2    cups light cream
4-6  Tbsp. dry Sherry

- Add lemon juice, salt and pepper to crabmeat.
- Butter bread slices on one side. Place 6 slices buttered side *down* in a 13 x 9-inch baking dish. Top each slice with 1 slice of cheese, ⅙ of crab mixture, another slice of cheese and another slice of bread, buttered side *up*.
- Mix eggs and cream, beating slightly. Add Sherry. Pour over sandwiches. Cover with foil and refrigerate overnight.
- Before baking, allow to stand at room temperature for 1 hour.
- Remove foil and bake at 325 degrees for 50-60 minutes or until lightly browned.

# CRAB BURGERS

Serves 4

1  cup backfin crabmeat
¼  cup diced celery
2  Tbsp. chopped onion
½  cup shredded Cheddar cheese
½  cup mayonnaise
4  English muffins

- Preheat oven to broil.
- Combine all ingredients except muffins.
- Lightly butter muffins and barely toast halves under broiler.
- Spread crab mixture on muffins and broil until bubbly and lightly browned.
- Serve with a fruit salad.

*Tuna or salmon may be substituted for crabmeat.*

# PIMIENTO CHEESE

Yields 2 quarts

2  pounds sharp Cheddar cheese, coarsely grated
3  hard-boiled eggs, coarsely grated
1  large white onion, coarsely grated
3  4-ounce jars diced pimientos with juice
1  pint mayonnaise
3  Tbsp. prepared mustard
3  Tbsp. Worcestershire sauce
2  tsp. salt
¼-½  tsp. each:
       coarsely ground pepper
       paprika
       onion powder
       garlic powder
       celery salt

- Combine ingredients until just well mixed. Do not mash or pack down.
- Chill in covered container. Use to stuff celery or to spread on crackers or sandwiches.

*Keeps up to 3 weeks in refrigerator.*

# SALAD BOWL SANDWICH

Serves 6

| | |
|---|---|
| 1-2 | **7-ounce cans tuna, drained and flaked** |
| 1 | **cup cherry tomatoes, halved** |
| 1 | **medium green pepper, diced** |
| ¼ | **cup diced red onion** |
| ½ | **cup sliced black olives** |
| 8 | **ounces Mozzarella cheese, shredded** |
| ½ | **cup oil and vinegar dressing** |
| 2 | **tsp. crushed basil** |
| 6 | **whole wheat or white pita bread** |

- Combine all ingredients except bread; toss.
- To serve, open pocket of pita bread and stuff with tuna mixture.

# SPICY CHEESE SPREAD

Yields 1 cup

| | |
|---|---|
| 8 | **ounces sharp Cheddar cheese, grated** |
| 2 | **Tbsp. finely chopped onion** |
| ¼ | **tsp. salt** |
| 2 | **Tbsp. ketchup** |
| ¼ | **cup salad dressing** |
| 1 | **tsp. sugar** |
| 1 | **Tbsp. vinegar** |
| | **Worcestershire sauce to taste** |
| | **Tabasco sauce to taste** |
| 2 | **Tbsp. pimiento** |
| ¼ | **cup finely diced green pepper** |

- Combine cheese with remaining ingredients. Store in covered container in refrigerator.
- Serve on crackers or use as sandwich spread.

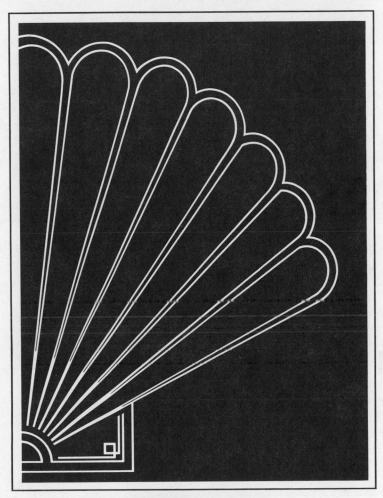

# BREADS

# BREADS

# OVERNIGHT COFFEE CAKE

Serves 12
Do ahead

| | |
|---|---|
| ¾ | cup butter, softened |
| 1 | cup sugar |
| 2 | eggs |
| 8 | ounces sour cream |
| 2 | cups flour |
| 1 | tsp. baking powder |
| 1 | tsp. nutmeg |
| ½ | tsp. salt |
| 1 | tsp. baking soda |
| ¾ | cup packed light brown sugar |
| ½ | cup chopped pecans |
| 1 | tsp. cinnamon |

- Combine butter and sugar; cream until light and fluffy. Add eggs and sour cream; mix well.
- Combine next 5 dry ingredients; add to batter and mix well. Pour into greased and floured 13 x 9-inch pan.
- Combine brown sugar, pecans and cinnamon; mix well and sprinkle evenly over batter.
- Cover and chill overnight. Uncover and bake at 350 degrees for 30-35 minutes.

## GLAZE

| | |
|---|---|
| 1 | cup sifted confectioners sugar |
| 1 | Tbsp. plus 1 tsp. water |
| ½ | tsp. vanilla |

- Combine ingredients and drizzle over warm cake.

*Whole berry cranberry sauce may be spooned over batter before sprinkling brown sugar mixture on top.*

# CINNAMON-PECAN NIBBLES

Serves 8-10

| | |
|---|---|
| ½ | cup butter |
| 1 | cup brown sugar |
| 2 | tsp. water |
| 1 | cup chopped pecans |
| 1 | Tbsp. cinnamon |
| 2 | cans refrigerator biscuits (10 count), cut into quarters |

- Preheat oven to 400 degrees.
- Melt butter in saucepan. Add remaining ingredients except biscuits. Heat until mixture *begins* to boil. Remove from heat. Add biscuits and stir.
- Pour mixture into a greased tube cake pan.
- Bake at 400 degrees for 15 minutes. Unmold on serving platter immediately.

# FIG COFFEE CAKE

Serves 9

| | |
|---|---|
| ½ | cup brown sugar |
| 2 | Tbsp. butter, softened |
| ½ | tsp. ground cinnamon |
| 12 | fig-filled bar cookies, crumbled |
| 2 | eggs |
| ¾ | cup sugar |
| ⅓ | cup butter, melted |
| 1½ | cups sifted flour |
| 1½ | tsp. baking powder |
| ½ | tsp. salt |
| ½ | cup milk |
| 1 | tsp. vanilla |

- Preheat oven to 350 degrees.
- Combine the first 4 ingredients; mix well and set aside.
- Beat eggs in a large bowl; add sugar and butter, beating well.
- Combine flour, baking powder and salt. Add to egg mixture alternately with milk, mixing well. Stir in vanilla.
- Pour half of batter into a greased and floured 8-inch square pan; top with half of the fig mixture. Pour remaining batter on top. Spoon remaining fig mixture on top in a lattice pattern.
- Bake at 350 degrees for 30-40 minutes.

*Very attractive looking coffee cake.*

# ALMOND CRESCENTS

Makes 16-20

**ROLLS**

| | |
|---|---|
| 8 | ounces almond paste |
| ¼ | pound butter, softened |
| 1 | Tbsp. grated lemon rind |
| 2 | Tbsp. lemon juice |
| 2 | 8-ounce packages refrigerated crescent rolls (8-10 count) |

- Preheat oven to 350 degrees.
- Combine all ingredients except rolls; mix well.
- Separate rolls and spread each with 1 Tablespoon almond mixture. Roll up crescent as shown on package and place 2 inches apart on ungreased cookie sheet.
- Bake at 350 degrees for 10-15 minutes or until golden.

**ICING**

| | |
|---|---|
| 1 | cup confectioners sugar |
| 2 | Tbsp. butter |
| 1 | Tbsp. milk |
| 1 | 2½-ounce package sliced almonds |

- Combine all ingredients except almonds; mix until smooth.
- Spread icing on top of rolls and sprinkle with almonds.
- Serve warm.

*Can be made ahead and frozen; reheat covered loosely with foil.*

# APPLESAUCE MUFFINS

Makes 48

½  pound butter
2  cups sugar
2  eggs
4  cups flour
3  tsp. cinnamon
2  tsp. ground cloves
2  tsp. allspice
2  tsp. baking soda
2  cups applesauce
1  cup chopped pecans
1  cup raisins

- Preheat oven to 400 degrees.
- Cream butter and sugar in large bowl. Add eggs and mix well.
- Sift all dry ingredients together and add to creamed mixture alternately with applesauce.
- Add pecans and raisins if desired.
- Fill greased muffin tins ⅔ full and bake at 400 degrees for 15 minutes.
- Batter may be stored in refrigerator for up to 6 weeks.

*Wonderful for breakfast—children love them.*

# BLUEBERRY MUFFINS

Makes 12

2  cups cake flour, or 1¾ cups flour, sifted twice
⅓  cup sugar
3  tsp. baking powder
4  Tbsp. butter, melted
2  eggs, beaten
¾  cup milk
3  Tbsp. grated lemon or orange rind
1  cup fresh blueberries, lightly floured

- Preheat oven to 400 degrees.
- Mix first 3 ingredients in large bowl.
- Mix butter, eggs, milk and rind together; add to dry ingredients. Mix well. Fold in blueberries.
- Fill greased muffin tins ¾ full and bake at 400 degrees for 15-20 minutes.

# BAY BRIDGE BRAN MUFFINS

Makes 36

| | |
|---|---|
| 2 | cups All-Bran cereal |
| 1 | cup Bran Buds cereal |
| 1 | cup boiling water |
| 1½ | cups sugar |
| ½ | cup vegetable shortening |
| 2 | eggs |
| ½ | tsp. vanilla |
| 2½ | cups flour |
| 2½ | tsp. baking soda |
| ½ | tsp. salt |
| 2 | cups buttermilk |
| ⅔ | cup raisins |

- Preheat oven to 400 degrees.
- Combine cereals and water; mix well and let cool.
- Cream sugar, shortening, eggs and vanilla.
- Sift flour, soda and salt together. Add to creamed mixture alternately with buttermilk. Add bran mixture.
- Fill greased muffin tins ⅔ full and bake at 400 degrees for 15-20 minutes.
- Batter may be stored in refrigerator for up to 6 weeks.

*Make fresh hot muffins daily, or bake large batch, freeze and reheat.*

# FRENCH BREAKFAST PUFFS

Makes 24

| | |
|---|---|
| ½ | cup sugar |
| ⅓ | cup shortening (part butter) |
| 1 | egg |
| 1½ | cups flour |
| 1½ | tsp. baking powder |
| ½ | tsp. salt |
| ¼ | tsp. nutmeg |
| ½ | cup milk |
| ½ | cup sugar |
| 1 | tsp. cinnamon |
| 6 | Tbsp. butter, melted |

- Preheat oven to 350 degrees.
- Cream sugar, shortening and egg.
- Sift together flour, baking powder, salt and nutmeg. Add to creamed mixture alternately with milk, beating well after each addition.
- Fill greased miniature muffin tins ⅔ full.
- Bake at 350 degrees for 12-15 minutes.
- Combine sugar and cinnamon. Remove muffins from pans immediately, dip in butter and roll in sugar mixture until coated.
- Serve warm.

*May be prepared ahead, frozen and wrapped in foil to reheat.*

# OATMEAL SPICE MUFFINS

Makes 18

| | |
|---|---|
| 1 | cup oatmeal, uncooked |
| 1 | cup buttermilk |
| 1 | cup light brown sugar |
| 1 | egg, slightly beaten |
| 1¾ | cups flour |
| 1 | tsp. baking powder |
| 1 | tsp. baking soda |
| 1 | tsp. salt |
| ½ | tsp. ground cinnamon |
| ¼ | tsp. ground cloves |
| ½ | cup vegetable oil |
| ½ | cup raisins |

- In large bowl, combine oatmeal and buttermilk; let stand for 1 hour. Add brown sugar and egg; mix well.
- Combine flour, baking powder, soda, salt, cinnamon and cloves. Stir into oatmeal mixture. Stir in oil and raisins.
- Spoon into greased muffin tins, filling ½ full.
- Bake at 400 degrees for 15-20 minutes.

*Delicious, moist muffins.*

# SWEET POTATO MUFFINS

Makes 24

| | |
|---|---|
| ¼ | pound butter, softened |
| 1 | cup sugar |
| 1¼ | cups cooked, mashed sweet potatoes |
| 2 | eggs |
| 2¼ | cups flour |
| 1½ | Tbsp. baking powder |
| 1 | tsp. nutmeg |
| 1 | tsp. salt |
| ½ | tsp. cinnamon |
| 1¼ | cups milk |
| ½ | cup finely chopped pecans |
| 1½ | tsp. lemon extract |

**TOPPING**

| | |
|---|---|
| ¼ | cup sugar |
| 1 | Tbsp. cinnamon |

- Preheat oven to 400 degrees.
- In a large bowl, cream butter and sugar until light and fluffy. Stir in sweet potatoes. Add eggs one at a time, stirring well.
- Sift together flour, baking powder, nutmeg, salt and cinnamon.
- Alternately add dry ingredients and milk to sweet potato mixture, stirring well after each addition. Stir in pecans and lemon extract.
- Fill greased muffin tins ⅔ full.
- Mix topping ingredients together; sprinkle evenly on batter.
- Bake at 400 degrees for 20-25 minutes.

*for sugar*

# APPLE MUFFINS

Makes 12-18

| | |
|---|---|
| 2 | cups flour |
| 3½ | tsp. baking powder |
| ¼ | tsp. nutmeg |
| ½ | tsp. ground cinnamon |
| 4 | Tbsp. butter |
| ½ | cup sugar |
| 1 | egg, well beaten |
| 1 | cup milk |
| 1½ | cups chopped apples |
| | Confectioners sugar |
| | Melted butter |

- Preheat oven to 400 degrees.
- Mix flour and baking powder; add nutmeg and cinnamon.
- Cream butter and sugar in large bowl until soft and fluffy. Add egg. Alternately add the dry mixture with milk, blending after each addition. Fold in apples.
- Fill greased muffin tins ½ full. Sprinkle with confectioners sugar.
- Bake at 400 degrees for 15 minutes.
- Sprinkle again with sugar and drizzle with melted butter. Return to oven for 1 minute.
- Serve hot.

# SOUR CREAM MUFFINS

Makes 12-16

| | |
|---|---|
| 2 | cups buttermilk baking mix |
| ¼ | pound butter, melted |
| 1 | cup sour cream |

- Preheat oven to 400 degrees.
- Mix all ingredients in medium bowl.
- Fill greased muffin tins ⅔ full.
- Bake at 400 degrees for 10-12 minutes until light brown. Serve immediately. No butter needed.

# BEER MUFFINS

Makes 12

| | |
|---|---|
| 2 | cups buttermilk baking mix |
| 1 | cup beer |
| 3 | Tbsp. sugar |

- Preheat oven to 350 degrees.
- Mix all ingredients.
- Spoon into greased muffin tins.
- Bake at 350 degrees for 10-15 minutes.

# APPLESAUCE NUT BREAD

Makes 1 loaf

**BATTER**

| | |
|---|---|
| 1 | cup sugar |
| ⅓ | cup vegetable oil |
| 1 | cup applesauce |
| 2 | eggs |
| 3 | Tbsp. milk |
| 2 | cups flour |
| 1 | tsp. baking soda |
| ½ | tsp. baking powder |
| ½ | tsp. cinnamon |
| ¼ | tsp. salt |
| ¼ | tsp. nutmeg |
| ¾ | cup chopped pecans |

- Preheat oven to 350 degrees.
- Combine first 5 ingredients; mix well. Combine dry ingredients; add to applesauce mixture. Mix well; stir in nuts.
- Spoon batter into greased 8-cup loaf pan.
- Bake at 350 degrees for 30 minutes. While loaf is baking, prepare topping mixture.

**TOPPING**

| | |
|---|---|
| ¼ | cup packed light brown sugar |
| ½ | tsp. cinnamon |
| ¼ | cup finely chopped pecans |

- Combine ingredients; mix well.
- Spoon topping on top of loaf and cover loosely with foil.
- Bake *additional* 30 minutes.

# APPLE-BANANA BREAD

Makes 2 loaves

| | |
|---|---|
| 3-4 | apples, peeled and finely chopped |
| | Lemon juice |
| 3 | large bananas, mashed |
| ¼ | pound butter |
| 2 | cups sugar |
| 2 | large eggs |
| 3 | cups flour |
| 1½ | tsp. baking powder |
| 1½ | tsp. baking soda |
| ½ | tsp. salt |
| 1 | tsp. vanilla |

- Preheat oven to 350 degrees.
- Sprinkle apples with lemon juice; add bananas and set aside.
- Cream butter; add sugar, continuing to beat. Add eggs, beating well after each addition. Stir in fruit.
- Sift and mix all dry ingredients. Stir in fruit mixture. Add vanilla.
- Spoon batter into 2 loaf pans.
- Bake at 350 degrees for 45-60 minutes or until golden brown.

# NUTTY BANANA BREAD

Makes 1 loaf

| | |
|---|---|
| 1½ | cups flour |
| 1 | tsp. baking soda |
| ½ | tsp. salt |
| 1 | egg, beaten |
| 1 | cup sugar |
| 4 | Tbsp. butter, melted |
| 3 | ripe medium bananas, mashed |
| 1 | cup chopped nuts |

- Preheat oven to 325 degrees.
- Combine flour, soda and salt in medium bowl.
- Mix egg, sugar and butter. Add bananas and combine with flour mixture. Add nuts.
- Pour into greased 6-cup loaf pan.
- Bake at 325 degrees for 60-75 minutes.
- Batter may be used to make muffins. Fill muffin tins ⅔ full. Bake at 350 degrees for 25-30 minutes.

# BANANA-OATMEAL BREAD

Makes 1 loaf

| | |
|---|---|
| 4 | Tbsp. vegetable shortening |
| ½ | cup sugar |
| 2 | eggs, beaten |
| 2 | Tbsp. water |
| 4 | ripe bananas, mashed |
| 1½ | cups sifted flour |
| 2 | tsp. baking powder |
| ½ | tsp. salt |
| ½ | tsp. baking soda |
| 1 | tsp. vanilla |
| ¾ | cup regular or quick oatmeal |
| ½ | cup chopped nuts |

- Cream shortening and sugar; add eggs.
- Mix water with bananas.
- Combine flour, baking powder, salt and soda. Alternately add dry mixture and bananas to shortening mixture, blending well after each addition. Add vanilla, oatmeal and nuts.
- Pour into greased 8-cup loaf pan. Let stand for 30 minutes.
- Preheat oven to 350 degrees and bake for 45-60 minutes.

# SENSATIONAL STRAWBERRY BREAD

Makes 1 loaf
Do ahead

| | |
|---|---|
| 1½ | cups flour |
| ½ | tsp. salt |
| ½ | tsp. baking soda |
| ½ | tsp. cinnamon |
| ½ | cup sugar |
| 1 | egg |
| ½ | cup oil |
| 1 | 10-ounce package frozen strawberries, thawed and drained |
| ½ | cup chopped pecans |

- Preheat oven to 350 degrees.
- Mix dry ingredients. Add egg and oil; mix thoroughly.
- Fold in berries and nuts and pour into greased 8-cup loaf pan.
- Bake at 350 degrees for 55-60 minutes.
- Let loaf stand overnight before slicing.

*Very moist bread; good toasted.*

# BUTTERMILK-RAISIN BREAD

Makes 4 small loaves

| | |
|---|---|
| 2 | cups whole bran cereal |
| 2 | cups buttermilk |
| 2 | tsp. baking soda |
| 2 | eggs, beaten |
| 2¼ | cups flour |
| ¼ | tsp. salt |
| 1 | cup chopped pecans |
| 1 | cup raisins |
| 1 | cup packed dark brown sugar |
| 4 | empty 1-pound cans |

- Preheat oven to 350 degrees.
- Mix cereal, buttermilk and soda in large bowl. Let batter stand until liquid is absorbed, about 5 minutes.
- Stir in remaining ingredients; mix until moistened.
- Divide batter among 4 greased cans. Place cans on cookie sheet.
- Bake at 350 degrees for 55 minutes or until wooden pick inserted in center comes out clean.
- Remove loaves from cans and cool on rack.

*Serve with whipped cream cheese.*

# LEMON OR ORANGE BREAD

Makes 1 loaf

**BREAD**

| | |
|---|---|
| 6 | Tbsp. butter |
| 1 | cup sugar |
| 2 | eggs |
| 1½ | cups flour |
| 1 | tsp. baking powder |
| ½ | cup milk (may be part lemon or orange juice) |
| | Grated rind of 1 lemon or 1 orange |
| ½ | cup chopped walnuts, dusted with flour |

- Preheat oven to 325 degrees.
- Cream butter, sugar and eggs. Combine flour and baking powder; add to egg mixture.
- Add milk and rind; mix well. Add nuts; mix.
- Pour into greased 8-cup loaf pan.
- Bake at 325 degrees for 60 minutes.

**GLAZE**

| | |
|---|---|
| ⅓ | cup sugar |
| | Juice of 1 lemon or 1 orange |

- Mix well and pour over warm baked loaf while still in pan.
- Cool slightly before removing from pan.

# CARROT BREAD

Makes 2 loaves

| | |
|---|---|
| 2 | cups flour |
| 2 | tsp. baking soda |
| 2 | tsp. cinnamon |
| ½ | tsp. salt |
| 1½ | cups sugar |
| ½ | cup currants |
| ½ | cup shredded coconut |
| ½ | cup chopped pecans |
| 1 | cup vegetable oil |
| 2 | tsp. vanilla |
| 2 | cups grated carrots |
| 3 | eggs, beaten |

- Combine dry ingredients. Add currants, coconut and pecans; mix well.
- Add remaining ingredients and blend thoroughly. Pour into 2 greased 6-cup loaf pans and let stand 20 minutes.
- Preheat oven and bake at 350 degrees for 60 minutes.

# CRANAPANA BREAD

Makes 1 loaf

| | |
|---|---|
| 2½ | cups self-rising flour |
| 1 | cup sugar |
| 2 | Tbsp. salad oil |
| ¾ | cup milk |
| 2 | eggs |
| 1 | large ripe banana, mashed |
| 1 | cup chopped cranberries |
| 1 | apple, peeled and chopped |
| ½ | cup chopped walnuts |
| ¼ | cup raisins |

- Preheat oven to 350 degrees.
- Mix first 6 ingredients in large bowl.
- Fold in cranberries, apple, walnuts, and raisins.
- Spoon into greased 9 x 5-inch loaf pan.
- Bake at 350 degrees for 60 minutes.

**TOPPING**

Confectioners sugar
Cream

- Mix together and spread over cooled loaf.

*Decorative and delicious bread for Christmas presents.*

# SPICY ZUCCHINI BREAD

Makes 2 loaves

| | |
|---|---|
| 2 | cups grated zucchini |
| 3 | eggs |
| ¾ | cup salad oil |
| 1½ | cups sugar |
| 2 | tsp. grated lemon or orange rind |
| 2½ | cups flour |
| 2 | tsp. baking soda |
| 1 | tsp. baking powder |
| 1 | tsp. salt |
| ½ | tsp. nutmeg |
| ¼ | tsp. ginger |
| ½ | cup chopped pecans |

- Preheat oven to 350 degrees.
- Drain zucchini and set aside.
- Blend eggs, oil, sugar and lemon rind in processor, using steel blade, or mix by hand.
- In large bowl, sift dry ingredients together and add 1 cup at a time to egg and oil mixture. Blend only until flour disappears.
- Fold in zucchini and nuts.
- Pour into two greased loaf pans.
- Bake at 350 degrees for 60 minutes.

# CORNBREAD

Serves 6

2  eggs, beaten
1  cup sour cream
½  cup salad oil
1  8¾-ounce can cream-style corn
1  cup water ground corn meal
1  tsp. salt
3  tsp. baking powder

- Preheat oven to 375 degrees.
- Combine all ingredients and mix until smooth.
- Pour into 8 x 8-inch greased pan.
- Bake at 375 degrees for 45 minutes.

*More moist than most cornbread;*
*great with Local Catch, Tantalizing Tomatoes and Artichokes.*

# HAITIAN FRENCH BREAD

Serves 6-8

¼  pound plus 2 Tbsp. butter
2  tsp. Dijon mustard
1  medium onion, finely chopped
2  Tbsp. poppy seeds
2  Tbsp. lemon juice
8  ounces Monterey Jack cheese, sliced
1  loaf French bread

- Preheat oven to 350 degrees.
- Combine first 5 ingredients in saucepan. Simmer until onions are soft.
- Slice bread diagonally about 1 inch thick. Do *not* cut through the bottom crust.
- Spoon butter mixture in between slices. Stuff each cut with cheese. Wrap in foil, leaving part of the top exposed.
- Bake at 350 degrees for 20 minutes.

# PARMESAN FRENCH BREAD

Serves 8-10

1  Tbsp. chopped chives
⅛  tsp. garlic salt
¼  cup grated Parmesan cheese
¾  cup butter, softened
1  16-ounce loaf French bread, sliced

- Preheat oven to 375 degrees.
- Combine seasonings and cheese with butter, mixing well.
- Spread butter between bread slices. Wrap in foil.
- Bake at 375 degrees for 20 minutes. For crisper bread, leave top of foil open.

# CHEESE PUFF RING

Makes 8

1 **cup milk**
4 **Tbsp. butter**
½ **tsp. salt**
 **Dash pepper**
1 **cup flour**
4 **eggs**
1 **cup shredded Swiss cheese**

- Preheat oven to 375 degrees.
- In a large saucepan, heat first 4 ingredients. Bring to a full boil and add flour all at once, stirring over medium heat about 2 minutes or until mixture leaves sides of pan and forms a ball.
- Remove from heat and beat in each of the eggs by hand until mixture is smooth and well blended. Beat in half the cheese.
- Using an ice cream scoop or large spoon, make 8 equal-sized mounds of dough in a circle on a greased baking sheet, using ¾ of the dough. Each ball should just touch the next one.
- With the remaining dough, place a small mound of dough on top of each large mound.
- Sprinkle the remaining cheese over all.
- Bake at 375 degrees for about 55 minutes or until puffs are lightly browned and crisp. Serve hot.
- Puffs may be wrapped in foil, frozen and reheated in the foil.

*This popover-type bread is good for lunch when served with the Dig Deep salad.*

# BISCUITS SUPREME

Makes 24-36

2 **cups flour**
4 **tsp. baking powder**
¼ **tsp. cream of tartar**
1 **tsp. salt**
1-2 **Tbsp. sugar**
½ **cup plus 1 Tbsp. shortening**
⅔ **cup milk**

- Preheat oven to 425 degrees.
- Sift dry ingredients together. Cut in shortening until lumps form.
- Pour milk in all at once; stir with fork until dough forms a ball.
- Roll out on lightly floured board and cut. Do not handle dough too much or biscuits will be tough.
- Bake at 425 degrees for 8-10 minutes.

# PARTY ROLLS

Makes 36-48

| | |
|---|---|
| 1 | cup boiling water |
| 2 | heaping Tbsp. shortening |
| 2 | packages dry yeast |
| ½ | cup lukewarm water |
| 1 | cup sugar |
| 4 | cups self-rising flour |
| 1 | cup cold water |
| 4 | cups flour |
| | Butter, melted |

- Pour water over shortening. Set aside to cool.
- In large bowl, dissolve yeast in warm water; add sugar. Add 4 cups of flour. Beat thoroughly. Add cold water; mix thoroughly.
- Add 4 more cups flour. Knead until dough forms a smooth ball. Cover and let rise in warm place until doubled, approximately 1 hour.
- Make into rolls. Dip tops in melted butter.
- Place close together in 13 x 9-inch baking pans. Let rise again, approximately 45 minutes.
- Bake in preheated 400-425 degree oven for 10-15 minutes.

*Do not allow dough to rise too much or rolls will be dry.*

# GREAT GRANDMOTHER'S SALLY LUNN BREAD

Makes 2 loaves

| | |
|---|---|
| 4 | eggs, well beaten |
| 1 | cup sugar |
| 1 | package dry yeast, dissolved in 1 cup warm water |
| 2 | cups scalded milk |
| 2 | tsp. salt |
| 1 | cup *butter,* melted |
| 8 | cups flour |

- Dissolve yeast in water.
- Combine ingredients in large bowl in order listed and mix.
- Allow to rise in warm place in glass bowl, covered with damp towel, until doubled (about 3 hours).
- Punch down. Put into 2 greased and floured tube pans. Let rise, covered with damp towel, until nearly doubled (2-3 hours).
- Bake at 350 degrees for 30 minutes or until brown on top.

# ANGEL BISCUITS

Makes 2-3 dozen

| | |
|---|---|
| 5 | cups flour |
| 3-5 | Tbsp. sugar |
| 1 | Tbsp. baking powder |
| 1 | tsp. salt |
| 1 | tsp. baking soda |
| ¾ | cup butter |
| 1 | package yeast |
| 2-3 | Tbsp. warm water |
| 2 | cups buttermilk |
| | Small amount melted butter |

- Preheat oven to 400 degrees.
- Sift dry ingredients together; cut in butter until crumbly.
- Dissolve yeast in water. Stir yeast and buttermilk into flour mixture.
- Roll out onto a floured surface and cut out biscuits. Brush with melted butter.
- Bake at 400 degrees for 10-15 minutes or until brown.

*To freeze: bake only 10 minutes, cool and freeze. When ready to use, bake 15 minutes without thawing.*

# ENGLISH MUFFIN LOAF

Makes 2 loaves

| | |
|---|---|
| 5 | cups flour |
| 2 | packages dry yeast |
| 1 | Tbsp. sugar |
| 2 | tsp. salt |
| ¼ | tsp. baking soda |
| 2 | cups milk |
| ½ | cup water |
| | Corn meal |

- Combine first 5 ingredients in large bowl.
- Heat milk and water until very warm (120-130 degrees).
- Add liquids to dry mixture and beat well by hand. Batter will be sticky.
- Spoon into 2 greased 8-cup loaf pans dusted with corn meal.
- Sprinkle tops with corn meal. Cover and let rise in a warm place until doubled.
- Bake at 400 degrees for 25 minutes. Remove from pans immediately and cool. Slice and toast.

*Freezes well.*

# FRENCH BREAD

Makes 3 loaves

| | |
|---|---|
| 4 | packages dry yeast |
| 2¼ | cups warm water |
| 1 | Tbsp. salt |
| 1 | Tbsp. sugar |
| 6-7 | cups flour |
| | Corn meal |
| 1 | egg white, lightly beaten with 1 Tbsp. water |

- Dissolve yeast with water in large bowl.
- Add dry ingredients to yeast and mix well.
- Knead dough on a floured surface until smooth and elastic (10-12 minutes).
- Let dough rise in a greased bowl, covered with a damp towel, until doubled (1-1½ hours). Punch down and let rise again (1 hour).
- Divide dough into 3 equal portions. Roll out each into a rectangle and roll up dough to shape loaves.
- Place loaves on a corn meal-covered cookie sheet; slash tops and brush with egg white mixed with water. Let dough rise again uncovered (1 hour). Brush again with egg mixture before baking.
- Bake at 400 degrees for 15 minutes. Brush again and bake 10-15 minutes longer.

### HERB BUTTER OPTION

| | |
|---|---|
| ½-¾ | pound butter |
| 1-2 | tsp. garlic salt |
| 2 | Tbsp. dried minced onion |
| 1 | tsp. oregano |
| 2 | Tbsp. dried parsley |
| ½ | cup grated Parmesan cheese |

- Preheat oven to 350 degrees.
- Melt butter in sauce pan. Add seasonings; stir until blended.
- Slice bread but do not cut completely through.
- Spoon butter mixture on slices, pulling apart slightly.
- Sprinkle with cheese and heat in 350 degree oven.

# POPOVERS DELUXE

Makes 8

| | |
|---|---|
| 3 | eggs |
| 1 | cup milk |
| 3 | Tbsp. vegetable oil |
| 1 | cup sifted flour |
| ½ | tsp. salt |

- Preheat oven to 400 degrees.
- In medium bowl, beat eggs, milk and oil with rotary beater until well mixed.
- Sift flour with salt and pour over egg mixture. Beat just until smooth.
- Fill lightly greased custard cups ½ full and place on a large cookie sheet.
- Bake at 400 degrees for 45-50 minutes or until golden brown. Serve hot.

# HERB-CHEESE BREAD

Makes 1 loaf

| | |
|---|---|
| 1 | package dry yeast |
| 1 | tsp. sugar |
| ¼ | cup warm water |
| ¼ | cup finely ground Parmesan cheese |
| 1 | cup flour |
| 1¼ | cups bread flour |
| 1 | Tbsp. butter |
| ½ | tsp. mixed herbs |
| 2 | Tbsp. chives |
| ¼ | cup heavy cream |
| 2 | Tbsp. cold milk |
| 2 | Tbsp. cold water |
| 1 | extra large egg |
| ½-1 | tsp. salt |

- In a 2-cup measure dissolve sugar and yeast in water, stirring briefly to mix.
- In workbowl of food processor using metal blade, mix cheese, flours, butter, herbs and chives for about 30 seconds. Scrape down bowl if necessary.
- Stir cream, milk, water, egg and salt into yeast mixture. With food processor running, add mixture to flour in a steady stream, as quickly as flour absorbs it. Dough will clean workbowl when ready.
- Process an additional 50 seconds to knead. If dough is too sticky, add flour 1 Tablespoon at a time; if too dry, add milk 1 teaspoon at a time.
- Lightly flour hands and remove dough to a lightly floured 1-gallon bag. Twist closed and put in a warm place to double in size (approximately 1½-2 hours).
- When dough has doubled, punch down and allow to rest 5 minutes.
- Lightly oil a 9 x 5-inch loaf pan and shape dough to fit. Press into pan and cover with oiled plastic wrap. Allow to double in size, approximately 45-60 minutes.
- Just before baking, top of loaf may be brushed with a wash of 1 beaten egg mixed with 1½ Tablespoons water.
- Bake at 375 degrees for 35 minutes or until lightly browned. Remove from pan and cool on wire rack.

# TOMATO-BASIL BREAD

Makes 1 large loaf

| | |
|---|---|
| 1 | tsp. yeast |
| 1 | tsp. sugar |
| 1 | Tbsp. warm water |
| 3¾ | cups bread flour |
| 2 | Tbsp. butter |
| 2 | Tbsp. heavy cream |
| 1 | extra large egg |
| 1 | cup tomato sauce |
| 2 | tsp. fresh basil, chopped |
| 2 | tsp. fresh parsley, chopped |
| ½-1 | tsp. salt |

**CHILI BREAD VARIATION**
**Substitute a chili or Mexican-flavored sauce for tomato sauce. Substitute 1 tsp. chili powder and 1 tsp. cumin for basil.**

- In a 2-cup measure, dissolve the sugar and yeast in the water.
- Using metal blade of food processor, process the flour and butter in workbowl.
- Add cream, egg, sauce, basil, parsley and salt to yeast. Stir. Pour through processor feed tube steadily, as fast as flour will accept liquid.
- Process dough until it cleans inside of workbowl. Add flour by Tablespoons if dough is too moist and tomato sauce or cold water by teaspoons if dough is too dry.
- At this point, continue to process for 45-50 seconds to knead.
- Flour hands lightly; remove dough from processor. Place in lightly floured 1-gallon plastic bag. Twist top closed and set aside in a warm place until dough doubles in size, about 1½-2 hours.
- Punch dough down; allow to rest 5 minutes.
- Divide dough into thirds; stretch into oblong strips. Put one end of strips together and make a braid, stretching dough to make approximately a 15-inch loaf. Tuck remaining ends under loaf.
- Place loaf on lightly greased baking sheet. Cover with oiled plastic wrap and allow to rise until doubled, approximately 45 minutes.
- If desired, glaze with a beaten egg and water mixture.
- Bake at 375 degrees for 30 minutes or until loaf is lightly browned and sounds hollow when tapped on bottom crust. Transfer to a wire rack to cool.
- Do not overbake.

# CINNAMON-RAISIN BREAD

Makes 2 loaves

| | |
|---|---|
| 2 | cups milk |
| ¼ | cup butter, melted |
| 2 | cups flour |
| ½ | cup plus 1 Tbsp. sugar |
| ½ | tsp. salt |
| 1 | package dry yeast |
| 3-3¾ | cups flour |
| 1½ | cups raisins |
| 2 | Tbsp. plus 2 tsp. sugar |
| 2 | tsp. ground cinnamon |
| ¼ | cup butter, melted |

- Combine milk and butter; heat to 105-115 degrees.
- Combine flour, sugar, salt and yeast. Gradually add milk mixture to flour, mixing on low speed. Beat for 2 minutes.
- Add ¾ cup flour; beat 2 minutes. Stir in enough of remaining flour to make a soft dough. Stir in raisins.
- Knead on a floured board about 7 minutes until smooth and elastic.
- Place in a covered greased bowl; let rise in a warm place until doubled (about 80 minutes). Punch down and let rest for 15 minutes, covered.
- Combine sugar and cinnamon.
- Divide dough in half and roll out into 2 rectangles 18 x 8 inches on a floured board.
- Brush each half with 2 Tbsp. butter. Sprinkle both halves with sugar mixture.
- Roll each half in jelly roll fashion. Pinch seams and ends together.
- Place seam side down in 2 greased 8-cup loaf pans.
- Cover and let rise until doubled (55 minutes).
- Bake at 350 degrees for 25 to 30 minutes or until loaves sound hollow.
- Remove from pans and cool.

# RAISIN-APPLE WHEAT BREAD

Makes 2 loaves

| | |
|---|---|
| ⅔ | cup milk |
| ¼ | cup cracked wheat bulgar |
| 2 | packages dry yeast |
| ½ | cup warm water |
| 1 | egg |
| 2 | Tbsp. vegetable oil |
| 2 | Tbsp. honey |
| 2 | tsp. salt |
| 1 | cup chopped tart apple |
| 1½ | cups whole wheat flour |
| 2½ | cups all-purpose flour |
| 1½ | cups raisins |

- Heat milk to lukewarm in saucepan. Stir in bulgar; set aside.
- In large bowl, dissolve yeast in water. Add egg, oil, honey, salt, apples and milk mixture. Beat until just blended. Add the whole wheat flour and 1 cup all-purpose flour. Beat at low speed to blend, then beat at high speed for 2 minutes. With wooden spoon, add remaining flour and raisins.
- Turn dough out onto floured board and knead 8 to 10 minutes, working in enough of remaining flour to make a smooth, non-sticky dough.
- Place in a greased bowl. Cover with a damp towel and let rise until doubled, about 1-1½ hours.
- Punch dough down and divide in half and form 2 loaves. Place in 2 greased 8 x 4-inch loaf pans. Cover and let rise in warm place until dough rises just above the tops of the pans, about 45 minutes to 1 hour.
- Bake at 350 degrees for 30-40 minutes until tops are browned and loaves sound hollow when tapped.
- Cool in pans for 5 minutes, then turn out onto racks.
- Cooled loaves may be wrapped and frozen.

# APRICOT SPREAD

Yields 1 cup

| | |
|---|---|
| 3 | ounces cream cheese, softened |
| 1 | cup canned apricots, drained and chopped |
| ¼ | cup chopped walnuts or pecans |
| 1 | Tbsp. honey |

- Blend cream cheese with electric mixer or food processor until smooth and fluffy; stir in remaining ingredients.
- Best with white or whole wheat bread.

# TOAST OF THE COAST

Makes 12
Do ahead

| | |
|---|---|
| 12 | slices, 1½-inch thick, French bread |
| 4 | eggs |
| 1 | cup milk |
| 2 | Tbsp. Grand Marnier |
| 1 | Tbsp. sugar |
| ⅛ | tsp. salt |
| | Butter |

- Combine all ingredients except bread and beat well.
- Dip bread slices in egg mixture. Place in pyrex dish and pour remaining egg mixture on the bread. Cover and refrigerate overnight.
- Sauté bread in melted butter in skillet for about 5 minutes on each side.

*Good for a special breakfast or brunch.*

# WAFFLED FRENCH TOAST

Makes 8

| | |
|---|---|
| ½ | cup milk |
| 4 | eggs |
| 2 | Tbsp. butter, melted |
| 1 | Tbsp. sugar |
| ½ | tsp. salt |
| 8 | slices bread |

- Preheat waffle iron.
- Mix all ingredients except bread in shallow bowl.
- Dip bread slices, one at a time; let drain.
- Bake in an oiled waffle iron 2-3 minutes, or until brown.

*Wonderful with warm maple syrup and sausage links.*

# STRAWBERRY BUTTER

Yields 1¾ cups

| | |
|---|---|
| ½ | pound unsalted butter, softened |
| 10 | ounces frozen strawberries, thawed and drained |
| ½ | cup confectioners sugar |

- Combine all ingredients in electric mixer or food processor. Blend until *smooth* and *creamy*.
- Store in refrigerator.

*Serve on muffins, toast, pancakes or waffles.*

# TROPICAL "HEALTH-SPIKED" PANCAKES

Makes 12-14

| | |
|---|---|
| 2 | cups buttermilk baking mix |
| 1 | cup milk |
| 2 | eggs |
| 1 | ripe banana |
| ½ | cup crushed pineapple with juice |
| ¼ | cup honey |
| ¼ | cup bran |
| ¼ | cup wheat germ |
| 1 | Tbsp. brewer's yeast flakes |
| 1 | tsp. ground ginger |

- Blend all ingredients until well mixed.
- Pour by spoonfuls onto well greased griddle and cook each side until golden.

*Batter may be made the night before, refrigerated, and mixed immediately before using.*

# BRANCAKES

Makes 20-24

| | |
|---|---|
| 3 | eggs, slightly beaten |
| ½ | cup honey |
| 6 | Tbsp. corn oil margarine, melted |
| 2⅔ | cups milk |
| 2 | cups All-Bran cereal |
| 1 | cup whole wheat flour |
| 1 | cup unbleached flour |
| ½ | cup wheat germ |
| 2 | Tbsp. baking powder |
| ½ | tsp. baking soda |
| 1 | tsp. salt |

- In a large bowl, combine first 4 ingredients, mixing well. Stir in cereal.
- In a separate bowl, mix all remaining ingredients. Add to bran mixture, folding until just blended.
- Pour ¼ cup batter per pancake onto a preheated and buttered heavy skillet. Cook on each side until golden, turning once.
- Batter may be refrigerated and cooked a day or two later.
- Pancakes may be cooked and frozen and popped into toaster for a quick treat.

*Serve with butter and preserves or honey.*

# ENTRÉES

# ENTRÉES

## BEEF

Beef Stir-Fry  143
Beefsteak and Onions  144
Corned Beef Brisket  146
Fillet of Beef in Mushroom
  Sauce  142
Grilled Beef Tenderloin
  Diablo  139
Italian Meatloaf  142
Mexicali Casserole  145
Perfect Tenderloin  139
Pot Roasted Meatloaf  144
Spaghetti Sauce and
  Meatballs  146
Teriyaki over Rice  143
Virginia Wellington  140

## VEAL

Dilled Veal  149
Sautéed Veal Scallopini with
  Lemon Sauce  147
Spectacular Scallopini  148
Veal in Pecan Sauce  150
Veal Scallopini with
  Tomatoes  149

## PORK AND HAM

Bohannon Barbeque  157
Choucroute Alsacienne  154
Country Pride Pork
  Chops  152
Foolproof Smithfield Ham  156
Marinated Pork Roast  151
Pork Chop Surprise  152
Pork Tenderloin with Orange
  Sauce  151
Roast Pork  150
Sausage Supreme  155
Sausage-Zucchini Bake  155
Sherried Ham  157
Smithfield Ham  156
Southern Shish-Kabob  153
Sweet and Sour Pork  153
Tarragon Pork Chops  152

## LAMB

Bachelor's Curry  159
Butterflied Leg of Lamb  158
Roast Spring Lamb  158

## CHICKEN

Breezy Point Chicken
  Curry  159
Chicken Breasts Marne  163
Chicken Florentine  165
Chicken Provençal  161
Chicken Spaghetti  170
Chicken Surprise  161
Chicken in Tortilla Crepes  174
Chinese Chicken Dinner  173
Classic Chicken Tetrazzini  169
Company Chicken  166
Crab-Stuffed Chicken  166
Curried Cornish Hens  176
Easy Cornish Hens  175
Elegant Chicken and
  Crab  172
Gourmet Cornish Hens with
  Smithfield Ham  175
Grilled Lemon-Mustard
  Chicken  162
Hawaiian Chicken  162
Imperial Chicken  164
Lemon Chicken  163
Mediterranean Chicken  168
Mushroom and Chicken
  Cutlets  164
Party Chicken  171
Poulet Nouveau  167
Rosemary Chicken with
  Tangerine Rice  160

## GAME

Quail or Dove  178
Roast Quail  177
Wild Duck  176
Wild Goose  177

## SAUCES

Barbeque Sauce  171
Béarnaise Sauce  147
Beef Marinade  142
Green Peppercorn Sauce  174
Island Marinade  165
Jezebel Sauce  170
Orange-Raisin Sauce  152
Marinade for Beef  145
Palmer Sauce  168
Raisin-Sour Cream
  Sauce  154
Red Wine Marinade  145
Sweet and Creamy Mustard
  Sauce  172
Tangy Barbeque Sauce  178

# GRILLED BEEF TENDERLOIN DIABLO

Serves 10
Do ahead

| | |
|---|---|
| 1½ | cups dry Sherry |
| 1½ | cups sesame oil |
| ½ | cup orange or pineapple juice |
| 3 | cloves garlic, mashed |
| 1 | small onion, minced |
| 2 | Tbsp. chopped shallots |
| 1 | Tbsp. chopped fresh chives |
| 1 | Tbsp. chopped fresh oregano |
| 1 | Tbsp. chopped fresh basil |
| 1½ | tsp. Tabasco sauce or to taste |
| 1 | tsp. salt |
| 1 | tsp. ground pepper |
| | Soy sauce to taste |
| | Worcestershire sauce to taste |
| 2 | bay leaves |
| | Kosher salt |
| 1 | whole beef tenderloin, trimmed of excess fat |

- Mix all marinade ingredients except Kosher salt in a large pyrex dish.
- Immerse tenderloin in marinade, turning once to coat. Cover with foil and marinate for 24-48 hours, turning every 6 hours.
- While waiting for charcoal to heat, remove meat from marinade and roll in Kosher salt to coat all sides; allow to rest for a few minutes, then roll again.
- Gently place tenderloin on grill, turning and cooking to desired temperature. Some of salt will fall off during grilling and some during slicing. The salt coating, diluted by the juices, is quite good and may be eaten with the beef.

# PERFECT TENDERLOIN

| | |
|---|---|
| 1 | whole beef tenderloin, trimmed and tied |

- Broil tenderloin for 8 minutes on one side on center rack of oven.
- Turn and broil 10 minutes on other side.
- Set oven temperature to 325 degrees and bake for 30 minutes for rare to medium rare.

# VIRGINIA WELLINGTON

Serves 8-12
Do ahead

**PUFF PASTRY**

| | |
|---|---|
| 4½-5 | cups flour |
| 1 | tsp. salt |
| 1 | cup water |
| 1 | pound butter |

- Place 4 cups flour in large bowl. Make well in center; add salt and 1 cup water.
- Mix together to make firm but slightly sticky dough, adding more water gradually if needed.
- Form dough into ball; knead 15-20 minutes or until smooth and elastic. Refrigerate in plastic bag 30 minutes.
- Roll out onto floured surface to form an 18 x 8-inch rectangle.
- Cut ¼ pound of butter into thin squares; cover top two-thirds of dough lengthwise. Fold bottom one-third halfway over buttered section, then fold buttered section over bottom.
- Roll dough again into 18 x 8-inch rectangle. If butter breaks through, flour broken pieces well.
- Fold ends to meet center, fold again, making 4 layers.
- Refrigerate 1 hour, covered.
- Repeat rolling, buttering, folding and refrigeration 3 more times.
- Let rest well covered in refrigerator for 2 hours before final rolling into rectangle for wrapping beef.

**BROWN SAUCE**

| | |
|---|---|
| 1½ | Tbsp. butter |
| 1½ | Tbsp. flour |
| 1 | 10½-ounce can condensed beef broth, plus enough water to make 2 cups |
| ⅓ | cup dry white wine |

- Melt butter in saucepan. Add flour. Cook, stirring until browned.
- Stir in broth. Bring to boil, cook 3-5 minutes, stirring occasionally. Add wine. Set aside.

## HAM AND MUSHROOM PÂTÉ

| | |
|---|---|
| 1 | pound fresh mushrooms, chopped |
| ⅓ | pound Smithfield ham, chopped |
| ¼ | pound butter |
| 1 | Tbsp. chopped shallots |
| 1 | tsp. black pepper |
| ½ | tsp. marjoram |
| ¼ | tsp. nutmeg |
| ½ | cup brown sauce |

- Mince mushrooms and ham in food processor. Sauté in butter for 3-5 minutes.
- Add remaining ingredients. Cook until almost dry yet still binds together, 1-1½ hours.

## BEEF

| | |
|---|---|
| 4 | pounds center cut tenderloin, trimmed of fat, at room temperature |
| 4 | Tbsp. oil |
| | Salt and pepper |
| 1 | egg, beaten |
| | Fresh parsley for garnish |

- Preheat oven to 400 degrees.
- Sear beef on all sides in hot oil for 5 minutes. Cool. Set aside skillet and juices for later use.
- Sprinkle with salt and pepper. Cover top with ⅛-¼-inch thick layer of pâté.
- Roll out refrigerated pastry and wrap around fillet. Seal ends and place seam down on cookie sheet.
- Use leftover scraps of pastry to decorate top of pastry. Cut into shapes of flowers or leaves.
- Brush entire pastry lightly with beaten egg. Allow to dry; brush again. If first application does not dry in 5-10 minutes, refrigerate for 5 minutes. Make 3 slits in top of pastry.
- Bake at 400 degrees for 45 minutes for rare. Cool 10 minutes before slicing. Serve on top of mushroom sauce, with parsley garnish.
- Slice into individual servings, place on top of a couple of tablespoons of mushroom sauce.

## MUSHROOM SAUCE

| | |
|---|---|
| 1 | Tbsp. chopped shallots |
| ¼ | pound fresh mushrooms, chopped |
| ⅓ | cup Madeira |
| 1 | cup brown sauce |
| | Salt and pepper |

- Add shallots, mushrooms and Madeira to skillet containing juices left over from searing meat. Simmer until mushrooms are tender. Add remaining brown sauce, simmer 1 minute. Season to taste.

*Leftover pâté is great on crackers.*

# FILLET OF BEEF IN MUSHROOM SAUCE

Serves 6

| | |
|---|---|
| 6½ | Tbsp. butter |
| 1½ | Tbsp. flour |
| 2 | cups beef broth |
| 6 | fillets of beef |
| 1 | pound mushrooms, sliced |
| 1 | tsp. salt |
| ⅛ | tsp. pepper |
| ½ | cup Madeira |
| 2 | tsp. chopped onions |

- Melt 1½ Tablespoons butter in saucepan. Stir in flour, cook until brown. Gradually add beef broth, stirring to boiling point. Reduce heat; simmer for 30 minutes.
- Skim fat and strain. Measure out 1 cup; reserve.
- In skillet, melt remaining butter. Brown fillets quickly, remove. Add mushrooms, sauté for 5 minutes. Return beef. Add remaining ingredients including brown sauce. Cook over low heat for 5-10 minutes.

# BEEF MARINADE

Yields ¾ cup

| | |
|---|---|
| ¼ | cup salad oil |
| ¼ | cup dry Vermouth |
| ¼ | cup soy sauce |
| 1 | tsp. dry mustard |
| 1 | tsp. prepared mustard |
| 1 | clove garlic, minced |
| ¼ | tsp. pepper |
| ½ | tsp. salt |
| 1 | Tbsp. Worcestershire sauce |

- Mix all ingredients for 2 minutes in food processor or blender.
- Pour marinade over steaks in glass dish.
- Refrigerate, turning steaks every hour for 4 hours or more.

# ITALIAN MEATLOAF

Serves 6-8

| | |
|---|---|
| 1½ | pounds ground beef |
| 1 | cup diced bread |
| ½ | cup tomato juice |
| 1 | tsp. salt |
| ½ | tsp. pepper |
| ¼ | tsp. oregano |
| 1 | clove garlic, minced |
| 2 | Tbsp. parsley |
| 3-4 | slices ham |
| 3-4 | slices Mozzarella cheese |

- Combine all ingredients except ham and cheese.
- On a 18 x 10-inch sheet of foil, spread mixture into a rectangle ¾-inch thick.
- Cover alternately with ham and cheese.
- Starting on long side, begin to roll in jelly roll fashion. Pinch ends together and press top slightly. Place on baking sheet.
- Bake at 325 degrees for 1 hour.

# TERIYAKI OVER RICE

Serves 4-6

| | |
|---|---|
| 2 | pounds round steak, thinly sliced |
| 2 | Tbsp. sugar |
| ½ | cup soy sauce |
| ½ | cup oil |
| ½ | cup orange juice |
| 1 | tsp. ground ginger |
| 1 | clove garlic, pressed |
| | Hot cooked rice |

- Combine all ingredients for marinade. Add beef; let stand for 1 hour.
- Preheat large skillet until water drops sizzle.
- Pour meat and marinade into pan and cook 1-2 minutes for medium rare.
- Serve over rice immediately.

*Sunset Salad is a good accompaniment.*

# BEEF STIR-FRY

Serves 4

| | |
|---|---|
| 1 | pound round steak |
| 1 | cup hot water |
| 2 | Tbsp. cornstarch |
| 1 | Tbsp. sugar |
| 1 | Tbsp. lemon juice |
| 1 | Tbsp. soy sauce |
| ½ | tsp. salt |
| 1 | beef bouillon cube |
| 3 | Tbsp. salad oil |
| 1 | cup thinly sliced fresh mushrooms |
| ½ | cup green onions sliced in 1-inch lengths |
| 1 | 8-ounce can water chestnuts, drained and sliced |
| 2 | cups fresh broccoli pieces |
| | Hot cooked rice |

- Partially freeze beef. Cut into ¼-inch thick slices.
- Combine next 7 ingredients. Stir well and set aside.
- Heat oil and stir-fry beef over high heat for 2 minutes.
- Add mushrooms, onions, water chestnuts and broccoli. Stir-fry 2 minutes.
- Add bouillon mixture; cook until sauce thickens. Serve immediately over rice.

*Fresh ginger root may be added if desired.*

# BEEFSTEAK AND ONIONS

Serves 4

| | |
|---|---|
| 1½ | tsp. salt |
| 1 | tsp. seasoned salt |
| ½ | tsp. black pepper |
| ½ | cup flour |
| 1½ | pounds round steak, well pounded and cut into serving-size pieces |
| 4 | Tbsp. shortening |
| 1 | cup sliced onions |
| 1 | green pepper, sliced |
| 1 | 16-ounce can tomatoes |
| 1 | 8-ounce can tomato sauce |

- Combine first 4 ingredients. Dredge beef.
- Melt shortening; brown beef. Add remaining ingredients. Cover, reduce heat and simmer for 1-1½ hours or until tender.

# POT ROASTED MEATLOAF

Serves 4

| | |
|---|---|
| 1 | pound ground beef |
| ⅔ | cup evaporated milk |
| ⅓ | cup dry bread crumbs |
| ¼ | cup ketchup, chili sauce or tomato sauce |
| 2 | tsp. Worcestershire sauce |
| 1 | tsp. oregano |
| 1 | tsp. salt |
| ¼ | tsp. pepper |
| 3 | medium potatoes, peeled and sliced |
| 3 | medium onions, sliced |
| 3 | carrots, sliced |
| 2 | tsp. chopped parsley |
| ½ | tsp. salt |
| ¼ | tsp. pepper |

- Preheat oven to 375 degrees.
- In large bowl, combine first 8 ingredients. Shape into loaf in center of 13 x 9-inch baking pan.
- Place vegetables, sliced ¼-inch thick, around meat; sprinkle with remaining seasonings. Cover with foil.
- Bake at 375 degrees for 1 hour or until vegetables are tender. Uncover and bake 10 minutes more to brown meat. Allow to set for about 15 minutes to make slicing easier.

# MEXICALI CASSEROLE

Serves 6-8

| | |
|---|---|
| 1 | pound ground round |
| 1 | onion, chopped |
| 1 | clove garlic, minced |
| 1 | 15-ounce can tomato sauce |
| ½ | cup water |
| 2 | Tbsp. chili powder |
| ¼ | tsp. oregano |
| 1 | 16-ounce can kidney beans, drained |
| 1 | 8-ounce bag corn chips |
| ½ | cup grated Cheddar cheese |

- Brown beef, onion and garlic. Stir in tomato sauce, water and seasonings.
- In a greased 3-quart casserole, alternate layers of meat, beans and corn chips.
- Bake covered at 350 degrees for 30 minutes. Uncover, top with cheese, bake 10 minutes more.
- Serve with garnishes of grated cheese, shredded lettuce, chopped onion, chopped tomato and chopped jalapeño peppers.

*A favorite with children.*

# RED WINE MARINADE

Yields 1½ cups

| | |
|---|---|
| 1 | cup red wine |
| ¼ | cup soy or teriyaki sauce |
| 1 | tsp. garlic juice |
| 1 | Tbsp. seasoned salt |
| ¼ | cup vegetable oil |
| 1 | tsp. oregano |
| 1 | tsp. salt |
| 1 | tsp. pepper |

- Mix all ingredients. Marinate steaks in sauce overnight or for at least 8 hours.

# MARINADE FOR BEEF

Makes 1 cup

| | |
|---|---|
| 1 | clove garlic, minced |
| ⅓ | cup soy sauce |
| 1-2 | onions, sliced |
| ½ | cup oil |
| 3 | Tbsp. vinegar |
| 2 | Tbsp. ketchup |

- Mix all ingredients.
- Pour over meat which has been pricked all over with fork.
- Marinate meat at least 6 hours, overnight preferably.

# SPAGHETTI SAUCE AND MEATBALLS
Yields 2 quarts

## SAUCE

| | |
|---|---|
| 2 | 28-ounce cans tomatoes |
| 2 | 16-ounce cans tomato purée |
| 2 | 16-ounce cans tomato sauce |
| 1 | medium onion, chopped |
| 1 | Tbsp. oregano |
| 1 | tsp. garlic salt |
| ⅓ | cup Parmesan cheese |

- Simmer tomatoes in their own juice in large Dutch oven until thick, about 40 minutes, stirring occasionally.
- Add remaining sauce ingredients, simmering while preparing meatballs.

## MEATBALLS

| | |
|---|---|
| 1 | cup fresh white bread crumbs |
| 1 | pound ground beef |
| 3 | Tbsp. diced green pepper |
| 3 | Tbsp. diced celery |
| 3 | Tbsp. diced onion |
| 1 | egg, beaten |
| ¼ | tsp. garlic salt |
| | Salt and pepper to taste |

- Mix all ingredients for meatballs. Shape into balls and fry lightly in small amount of oil.
- Place in sauce, simmer slowly for about 1 hour.
- Serve over spaghetti.

# CORNED BEEF BRISKET

| | |
|---|---|
| 1 | flat cut corned beef brisket |
| | Prepared mustard |
| | Red pepper flakes |
| | Parsley flakes |
| | Chopped onions |
| 1-2 | Tbsp. vinegar |

- Preheat oven to 400 degrees.
- Trim fat from brisket. Spread mustard on top of beef. Sprinkle pepper flakes, parsley and onions over mustard topping.
- Place meat on heavy-duty foil in pan. Add vinegar. Seal.
- Bake at 400 degrees for 10-15 minutes until beef sizzles. Reduce heat to 275 degrees for 2-3 hours until tender when tested with fork. After first 1½ hours, open the foil, test meat and drain off some of the liquid.

*Delicious with Sautéed Cabbage and Sherried Sweet Potatoes.*

# SAUTÉED VEAL SCALLOPINI WITH LEMON SAUCE

Serves 2-4

| 1 | pound boneless veal slices |
| 2 | Tbsp. vegetable oil |
| ¼ | cup butter |
| | Flour |
| | Salt and pepper to taste |
| 2 | Tbsp. lemon juice |
| 2 | Tbsp. finely chopped fresh parsley |
| ½ | lemon, thinly sliced |

- Heat oil and 2 Tablespoons butter over medium high heat.
- Dredge veal in flour, shake off excess. Cook veal until lightly brown on both sides, about one minute.
- Transfer to warm platter and season with salt and pepper.
- Remove skillet from heat, add lemon juice, scraping loose the cooking residue. Add remaining butter and parsley. Add veal, turning pieces in sauce to warm.
- Transfer to serving dish; pour sauce over veal. Garnish with lemon slices.

# BÉARNAISE SAUCE

Yields 1 cup

| 1 | Tbsp. finely chopped green onions |
| ½ | cup tarragon vinegar |
| 1 | Tbsp. dried tarragon |
| 3 | egg yolks |
| 3 | Tbsp. cold water |
| ¼ | pound butter, melted |
| | Salt and pepper |
| | Fresh parsley, chopped |

- Combine first 3 ingredients in small saucepan, reducing until only 1 teaspoon of juice remains.
- Add egg yolks and cold water, whisking vigorously over heat.
- Whisk in melted butter a drop at a time.
- Season with salt, pepper and parsley.
- Serve with meat or grilled fish.

# SPECTACULAR SCALLOPINI

Serves 3-4

1½   **pounds veal loin, scallopini or cutlets**
2   **eggs, beaten**
4   **Tbsp. flour, seasoned with salt and pepper**
4-6   **Tbsp. butter**

- Pound veal until very thin; cut into 3-4 inch squares or rectangles. Dip into egg, then dredge in flour.
- Sauté in butter, about 2-3 minutes per side. Keep cutlets warm in 250 degree oven as you finish each batch and complete sauce embellishment.
- Serve with one of the following sauces.

## FRANCESE

¼   **cup chicken stock**
¼   **cup dry white wine**
1   **Tbsp. butter**
1   **Tbsp. lemon juice**
1   **lemon, sliced thinly**
    **Pinch of parsley**

## MARSALA

¼   **cup chicken stock**
¼   **cup Marsala or Madeira**
1   **Tbsp. butter**
    **Pinch of Parsley**

## MORELS IN CREAM

1   **cup dry white wine**
2   **cups morels or sliced mushrooms**
2   **cups heavy cream**

*SAUCES*

- After cooking veal, deglaze pan juices with stock and/or wine. Simmer for 5 minutes.
- Add remaining ingredients. Adjust seasonings.
- Cook over low heat 10-20 minutes. Pour over veal and serve immediately.

# VEAL SCALLOPINI WITH TOMATOES

Serves 2-4

| | |
|---|---|
| 1 | pound veal cutlets |
| 1 | Tbsp. butter |
| 1 | Tbsp. olive oil |
| ½ | pound fresh mushrooms, sliced |
| 1 | cup peeled tomatoes or 8 ounces tomato sauce |
| ½ | cup Marsala or any white wine |
| 4 | Tbsp. Parmesan cheese |
| 2 | Tbsp. chopped parsley |
| 2 | Tbsp. chopped basil |
| 1 | tsp. garlic salt |

- Pound veal with wooden mallet and dredge in flour.
- Brown in skillet with butter and oil.
- Place veal and juices in a covered casserole.
- Combine remaining ingredients and pour over veal.
- Bake covered at 325 degrees for 45 minutes.

# DILLED VEAL

Serves 4
Do ahead

| | |
|---|---|
| ¼ | cup sour cream |
| ½ | cup heavy cream |
| 2 | tsp. dill weed |
| 1½ | pounds veal scallops |
| 3 | Tbsp. butter |
| | Juice of ¼ lemon |
| 1 | tsp. salt |

- Combine sour cream, heavy cream and dill weed. Cover; refrigerate at least 4 hours.
- Pound veal between wax paper until thin and tender.
- Sauté veal in butter until done. Pour lemon juice over veal and stir.
- Remove veal to heated dish and keep warm in oven.
- Stir cream mixture into pan juices, add salt. Heat through and pour over veal.

# VEAL IN PECAN SAUCE

Serves 4

1½    pounds veal, cubed
½    cup water
¼    cup chopped onion
1    tsp. chicken bouillon granules
1    clove garlic, minced
½    tsp. salt
¼    tsp. thyme
¼    tsp. oregano

- In saucepan, combine all ingredients. Simmer, covered, 45-60 minutes until meat is tender. Drain; reserve broth and add water to make 1½ cups liquid.

## SAUCE

1    Tbsp. butter
¼    cup chopped onion
½    cup chopped pecans
3    Tbsp. flour
½    cup sour cream

- In skillet, sauté onion and pecans in butter until tender. Remove from heat.
- Blend flour into sour cream; stir in broth. Add to onion mixture. Add veal.
- Return to heat to thicken. DO NOT BOIL.
- Serve with rice or pasta.

# ROAST PORK

Serves 8-10

1    4-pound boned, rolled and tied pork loin roast
2    cloves garlic
2    tsp. salt
1    tsp. sage
½    tsp. pepper
½    tsp. nutmeg
2    carrots, sliced
2    onions, sliced
1    cup water
¾    cup currant jelly
2-3    tsp. dry mustard
     Whole cloves

- Mash garlic with salt, sage, pepper, and nutmeg. Rub well into pork loin.
- Spread carrots and onions in shallow roasting pan. Set meat, fat side up, on top of vegetables. Splash water over meat.
- Roast at 325 degrees for 1½ hours. Remove meat from oven. Slash fat in crisscross pattern and stud with whole cloves.
- Combine jelly with mustard. Spread mixture on meat. Roast for 1 hour more.
- Jelly-mustard mixture may be doubled and used as a warm sauce to serve over sliced pork.

*For a complete dinner add Parmesan Artichokes Atlantic, Cran-Apple Delight and Festive Asparagus Salad.*

# PORK TENDERLOIN WITH ORANGE SAUCE Serves 6

| | |
|---|---|
| 2 | 2-pound pork tenderloins |
| 2 | Tbsp. butter |
| 2 | Tbsp. olive oil |
| 1 | cup chopped onion |
| 2 | tsp. salt |
| ¼ | tsp. pepper |
| ¾ | cup white wine |
| 4 | oranges |
| 3 | Tbsp. sugar |
| 1 | bay leaf |
| 1 | Tbsp. chopped fresh parsley |
| 2 | tsp. arrowroot |
| 1 | Tbsp. water |
| 4 | cups hot cooked rice, seasoned with mixed herbs, salt and pepper |
| 2 | Tbsp. chopped fresh parsley |

- Sauté tenderloins in butter and oil until golden. Remove from pan and set aside. Add onion, salt and pepper. Sauté until tender. Return meat to pan.
- Pour wine and juice of 2 oranges over meat. Add sugar, bay leaf and parsley. Cover; simmer for 45 minutes, until tender.
- Peel 2 oranges and section. Cut peel in thin uniform strips and boil in small amount of water until tender.
- Remove meat from pan. Mix arrowroot with water. Add to broth and stir until thickened and smooth.
- Cut meat in thick slices. Place on platter with rice. Pour sauce over meat.
- Garnish with orange peel, sections and parsley.
- For a visually interesting touch, orange peel strips may be tied in bow knots before cooking.

# MARINATED PORK ROAST

Serves 8-10
Do ahead

| | |
|---|---|
| ½ | cup soy sauce |
| ½ | cup dry Sherry |
| 2 | cloves garlic, minced |
| 1 | Tbsp. dry mustard |
| 1 | tsp. ginger |
| 1 | tsp. thyme, crushed |
| 1 | 4-5 pound boned, rolled and tied pork loin roast |

- Combine all ingredients except roast. Mix well.
- Place roast in large plastic bag; set in deep bowl. Pour in marinade and close bag tightly. Let stand 2-3 hours at room temperature or overnight in refrigerator. Turn meat occasionally.
- Remove meat from marinade and place on rack in shallow roasting pan.
- Roast uncovered at 325 degrees for 2½-3 hours, or until meat thermometer registers 175 degrees.
- Baste occasionally with marinade during last hour of roasting.

*Nice accompaniments are Spinach Soufflé and Baked Pineapple.*

# PORK CHOP SURPRISE

Serves 6

| 6 | thick-cut pork chops |
|---|---|

- Brown pork chops. Place in baking dish.

**ORANGE-RAISIN SAUCE**

| 1 | cup raisins |
|---|---|
| 1¾ | cups water |
| ⅓ | cup brown sugar |
| 1¼ | Tbsp. cornstarch |
| ¼ | tsp. cinnamon |
| ¼ | tsp. dry mustard |
| ¼ | tsp. ground cloves |
| ¼ | tsp. salt |
| 2 | Tbsp. butter |
| 1 | Tbsp. vinegar |
| ¼ | cup orange juice |

- Cook raisins in boiling water for 5 minutes.
- Mix dry ingredients. Add to raisins. Cook 10 minutes on medium-low heat. Stir in butter and vinegar. Add orange juice.
- Pour sauce over pork chops. Bake at 350 degrees for 40 minutes.

*Pork chops could be stuffed prior to adding sauce.*

# COUNTRY PRIDE PORK CHOPS

Serves 4
Do ahead

| ½ | cup soy sauce |
|---|---|
| ¼ | cup packed brown sugar |
| ¼ | cup dry Sherry |
| 1 | tsp. ground cinnamon |
| ½ | tsp. garlic salt |
| ½ | tsp. seasoned salt |
| | Dash ground ginger |
| 4 | 1-inch thick pork chops |

- Combine first 7 ingredients; stir well.
- Arrange chops in single layer in baking dish.
- Pour marinade over chops. Cover and refrigerate for 24 hours.
- Grill chops 6-8 inches from heat over gray-white coals for 1 hour or until done, basting with marinade and turning occasionally.

# TARRAGON PORK CHOPS

Yields 6

| 6 | thick-cut pork chops (¾-1 inch) |
|---|---|
| 1-2 | tsp. tarragon per chop |
| | Salt and pepper to taste |

- Sprinkle tarragon, salt and pepper on both sides of pork chops and rub in.
- Grill until done.

# SWEET AND SOUR PORK

Serves 4

Peanut oil
1½ pounds lean pork shoulder cut into 2 x ½-inch strips
½ cup water
1 20-ounce can pineapple chunks, syrup reserved
¼ cup brown sugar
2 Tbsp. cornstarch
¼ cup white vinegar
2-3 Tbsp. soy sauce
½ tsp. salt
1 small green pepper, cut in strips
¼ cup coarsely chopped onion
1½ cups coarsely chopped Chinese celery
Cooked rice or noodles

- Brown pork in small amount of oil. Add water, cover and simmer 1 hour, or until done.
- Combine sugar and cornstarch. Add pineapple syrup, vinegar, soy sauce and salt. Add to pork, stirring until gravy thickens.
- Add pineapple and vegetables. Simmer covered, 2-3 minutes.
- Serve over rice or noodles.

# SOUTHERN SHISH-KABOB

Makes 6 skewers
Do ahead

3 pounds pork butt or sirloin steak cut into 1½ x ½-inch cubes
1 clove garlic, crushed
4 Tbsp. soy sauce
Salt to taste
1 tsp. ground black pepper
½ cup lemon juice
1 cup 7-Up
¼ cup sugar
Onion pieces
Green pepper pieces
Green olives

- Place meat cubes in pyrex dish.
- Mix marinade ingredients. Pour over meat, marinating for at least 2 hours at room temperature or overnight in refrigerator.
- Skewer meat alternately with onions, peppers and olives.
- Grill over charcoal until cooked.
- Serve immediately.

# CHOUCROUTE ALSACIENNE

Serves 8

¼ cup shortening
3 large onions, diced
2 large cloves garlic
2 pounds salt pork
5 pounds fresh sauerkraut, well rinsed and drained
1 pound thick-sliced bacon
20 juniper berries (optional)
2 bay leaves
2 quarts water
1 pound Polish sausage, sliced into 8 pieces
8 smoked pork chops
8 knockwurst or frankfurters
8 medium potatoes

- Melt shortening in 8-quart Dutch oven or roasting pan. Sauté onions until golden; remove and set aside.
- Cut salt pork in half, slit each piece and insert a clove of garlic.
- Place ⅓ of sauerkraut in pan. Layer ½ of salt pork, ½ of bacon and ½ onions.
- Combine 10 juniper berries and 1 bay leaf in cheese cloth bag. Place on top of layers. Repeat layers and seasonings. Top with remaining ⅓ of sauerkraut. Add water.
- Bake covered at 400 degrees for 3 hours.
- Remove from oven. Arrange pork chops and sausage on top of sauerkraut. Cover and cook 30 minutes more.
- Meanwhile, steam potatoes and boil knockwurst or franks.
- To serve, arrange in dome shape on a large platter, discarding seasoning bags.
- Place meats attractively atop sauerkraut. Remove salt pork if desired.
- Arrange potatoes around edge of platter or serve separately.

*Accompany with assortments of mustards, breads and German beers.*

# RAISIN-SOUR CREAM SAUCE

Yields 2½ cups

½ cup raisins
2 cups sour cream
1 Tbsp. horseradish
2 tsp. lemon juice

- Pour enough boiling water over raisins to cover. Let stand for 10 minutes.
- Drain raisins well and add remaining ingredients. Chill overnight. Serve with ham.

# SAUSAGE-ZUCCHINI BAKE

Serves 8-10

| | |
|---|---|
| 1 | pound bulk sausage |
| 5 | Tbsp. flour |
| 6 | medium zucchini, sliced |
| ½ | cup chopped onion |
| 2 | Tbsp. butter |
| 16 | ounces cottage cheese |
| ½ | cup grated Parmesan and Romano cheese |
| 4 | eggs |
| 1 | tsp. salt |
| ½ | tsp. garlic salt |
| 1 | cup grated Cheddar cheese |

- Brown sausage, drain off grease. Stir in flour. Set aside.
- Sauté zucchini and onions in butter.
- Combine cottage cheese, Parmesan and Romano, eggs, salt and garlic salt.
- Layer sausage, zucchini and cottage cheese mixture in a 13 x 9-inch baking dish. Sprinkle Cheddar cheese over top.
- Bake at 350 degrees for 40-45 minutes or until bubbly.

# SAUSAGE SUPREME

Serves 8
Do ahead

| | |
|---|---|
| 1½ | pounds lean pork sausage |
| 2 | Tbsp. butter, melted |
| 4-5 | spring onions, including tops, chopped |
| 4-5 | stalks of celery, chopped |
| 1 | large green pepper, chopped |
| | Salt and pepper to taste |
| 2 | packages chicken noodle soup mix |
| 1 | cup brown rice |
| 4½ | cups boiling water |
| 1 | 8-ounce can water chestnuts, chopped and drained |

- In large skillet, cover crumbled sausage with water. Cook until done. Drain water from sausage and set aside.
- Sauté onions, celery and green pepper in butter. Salt and pepper to taste.
- Cook chicken noodle soup in water for about 7 minutes. Add rice and cook 3 minutes longer. Add water chestnuts.
- Mix all ingredients. Place in casserole. May cover and refrigerate at this point.
- Bake covered at 350 degrees for 1½ hours.

*A combination of hot and mild sausage may be used.*

# SMITHFIELD HAM

1     **Smithfield or country ham**
      **Whole cloves**
2     **Tbsp. brown sugar**
2     **Tbsp. cracker crumbs**
      **Pepper**

Do ahead

- In large pot, completely immerse ham in water. Soak overnight or at least 12 hours. (May need to saw off the hock.)
- Drain. Scrub ham thoroughly. Place back in pot, skin side up.
- Cover with fresh water and bring to a boil. Reduce heat; cover and simmer slowly for 4-5 hours or until done. Meat should be separating from bone.
- Cool in liquid. Remove from pot. Skin the ham and remove some of the fat.
- With a sharp knife, make criss-cross marks on ham. Place a clove in each diamond.
- Sprinkle with mixture of cracker crumbs, brown sugar and pepper.
- Bake at 425 degrees until lightly brown.
- Cool and slice paper thin.

# FOOLPROOF SMITHFIELD HAM

1     **14-15 pound Smithfield or**
      **country ham**
2     **cups water**

Do ahead

- Soak ham, completely submerged in water, overnight. Drain water; scrub with a stiff brush.
- Place water in large roaster. Put ham in skin side up and cover.
- Cook ham in preheated 500 degree oven for 1 minute per pound.
- Turn oven off for 2 hours. DO NOT OPEN OVEN.
- Reheat oven to 500 degrees, cook ham 1 minute per pound.
- Turn off heat and leave ham in oven for at least 6 hours without opening oven.
- Remove ham from cooking liquid; trim off skin and excess fat while still warm.

# SHERRIED HAM

Serves 4

| | |
|---|---|
| 3 | Tbsp. butter |
| ¼ | cup flour |
| 1 | cup chicken stock |
| 2 | cups light cream |
| 2 | Tbsp. dry Sherry |
| 1½ | cups cubed ham |
| ½ | pound mushrooms, chopped |
| 2 | Tbsp. chopped onion |
| 2 | Tbsp. chopped green pepper |
| 1 | Tbsp. chopped pimiento |
| ¾ | cup grated Swiss cheese |
| | Salt and pepper to taste |

- In medium saucepan, melt butter and slowly add flour and chicken stock. Slowly stir in cream and Sherry.
- Add remaining ingredients, cook over medium heat until as thick as desired.
- Serve over rice or English muffins.

# BOHANNON BARBEQUE

Yields 3 quarts
Do ahead

| | |
|---|---|
| 1 | 6-pound fresh picnic ham |
| ½ | cup ketchup |
| ½ | cup barbeque sauce |
| ½ | cup water |
| ½ | cup cider vinegar |
| ¼ | cup packed brown sugar |
| 2 | Tbsp. Worcestershire sauce |
| 1 | tsp. salt |
| 1 | tsp. dry mustard |
| ½ | tsp. black pepper |
| ½ | tsp. Tabasco sauce |

- Cook ham, wrapped in foil and placed on cookie sheet, at 350 degrees for 3-4 hours, until it falls apart. Cool. Pull meat off bone.
- Boil remaining ingredients for 2 minutes, stirring constantly.
- Reduce heat and simmer uncovered 5-10 minutes.
- Pour sauce over meat and toss. Serve warm.

# BUTTERFLIED LEG OF LAMB

Serves 8
Do ahead

1   **6-7 pound leg of lamb, butterfly cut**

**MARINADE**

1   **cup dry red wine**
½   **cup olive oil**
2   **Tbsp. snipped parsley**
2   **Tbsp. chopped chives**
1   **large onion, coarsely chopped**
2   **cloves garlic, minced**
1   **tsp. salt**
½   **tsp. Worcestershire sauce**
¼   **tsp. pepper**
⅛   **tsp. marjoram**
⅛   **tsp. rosemary**
⅛   **tsp. thyme**

• Combine all ingredients. Pour over lamb. Refrigerate overnight.
• Grill lamb slowly on open grill. Baste with marinade often.
• Cooking time will vary, allow approximately 20 minutes per side.

*Great with Pasta Primavera.*

# ROAST SPRING LAMB

Serves 8-10

5-7   **pound leg of lamb**
1½   **tsp. salt**
¼   **tsp. pepper**
3   **cloves garlic**
¼   **cup melted butter**
¼   **cup lemon juice**
1   **tsp. rosemary or oregano**

• Wipe lamb with damp paper towel. Rub surface with salt and pepper. Cut 12-16 slits 1 inch deep in lamb.
• Peel and cut garlic into lengthwise slivers; insert in slits. Place lamb in shallow roasting pan.
• Brush with butter and pour lemon juice over meat. Sprinkle with rosemary or oregano.
• Bake at 350 degrees for 30-35 minutes per pound or until meat thermometer registers 170 degrees.

*Serve with Old Fashioned Mint Sauce.*

# BACHELOR'S CURRY

Serves 4-6

4   cups cooked lamb, beef, shrimp or chicken
6   slices bacon
1½  cups chopped onion
1   cup chopped green pepper
1   tsp. red pepper flakes
½   cup chopped unpared apple
6   Tbsp. flour
3   Tbsp. curry powder
4   cups clam, chicken or beef broth

- In large frying pan, sauté bacon, remove and drain on paper towel. Add onions, peppers and apples; sauté until soft.
- Mix flour and curry together; sprinkle on sautéed mixture, making a roux.
- Add broth to make thin sauce. Add meat, simmer covered at least 1 hour, stirring often.
- Serve over rice with condiments of bacon, chopped eggs, raisins and nuts.

# BREEZY POINT CHICKEN CURRY

Serves 8

4   slices bacon, cooked and crumbled
1   Tbsp. bacon drippings
¼   cup sliced celery
¼   cup chopped onion
1   clove garlic, minced
2   Tbsp. flour
2   chicken bouillon cubes
1   cup water
1   cup milk
½   cup applesauce
3   Tbsp. tomato paste
3-4 Tbsp. curry powder
3   cups cooked chicken, cubed
    Hot cooked rice
    Condiments

- Set bacon aside for use as condiment.
- Sauté celery, onion and garlic in bacon drippings until translucent.
- Add flour and blend. Dissolve bouillon cubes in water. Add milk, applesauce, tomato paste and curry; cook and stir until bubbly over medium heat. Stir in chicken and heat through.
- Serve over rice with an assortment of condiments: bacon, raisins, toasted coconut, chopped peanuts, chopped hard-boiled eggs, diced green pepper, diced celery and chutney.

*Fresh fruit salad with Poppy Seed Dressing is a good accompaniment.*

# ROSEMARY CHICKEN WITH TANGERINE RICE

Serves 8
Do ahead

### ROSEMARY SEASONING

| | |
|---|---|
| 2½ | Tbsp. rosemary, crushed |
| ⅔ | cup dry Vermouth |
| 3 | Tbsp. water |

- In saucepan, stir all ingredients together and let stand 1 hour in warm place.
- Start cooking rice to be used later.

### TANGERINE BUTTER

| | |
|---|---|
| 4 | Tbsp. butter, melted |
| 1 | 6-ounce can frozen tangerine concentrate (12 Tbsp.) |
| 2 | Tbsp. dry Vermouth |
| 2 | tsp. salt |
| ½ | tsp. pepper |

- Combine all ingredients.

### CHICKEN

| | |
|---|---|
| 3 | frying chickens, cut into parts or equivalent |
| ½ | cup orange juice |
| ¾ | cup flour |
| 1½ | tsp. salt |
| ½ | tsp. ginger |
| ¼ | tsp. pepper |
| 6 | Tbsp. butter |
| 6 | Tbsp. oil |

- Wash and pat chicken dry. Dip in orange juice and dust with flour, salt, ginger and pepper mixture.
- Brown chicken in large skillet in butter and oil.
- Add rosemary seasoning to chicken, cover loosely and simmer 15-20 minutes or until liquid evaporates. Chicken should be tender but not quite done.

### RICE

| | |
|---|---|
| 1½ | cups raw rice, cooked |
| | Half the tangerine butter |
| 6 | green onions, sliced, white only |
| 1 | 16-ounce package frozen peas, thawed and separated |
| 1 | 4-ounce can pimientos, sliced |

- Toss rice with remaining ingredients.
- Spread rice mixture on bottom of two 13 x 9-inch baking dishes. Arrange chicken in single layer over rice. Spread remaining half of tangerine butter on chicken.
- Bake covered at 375 degrees for 20 minutes. Remove cover and bake 10 minutes longer.

GARNISH

| 2 | avocados, sliced in wedges |
|---|---|
| 1 | 29-ounce can whole apricots, drained |

- To serve, place chicken in center of platter, surround with rice. Decorate with avocados and apricots.

# CHICKEN PROVENÇAL

Serves 8-10

| 1-1½ | chickens, cut into pieces, or equivalent |
|---|---|
| | Salt and pepper |
| 3 | Tbsp. cooking oil |
| 2 | cloves garlic, minced |
| 3 | slices bacon, diced |
| 1 | large onion, quartered |
| 2 | carrots, peeled and cut into pieces |
| 1 | 16-ounce can tomatoes, chopped |
| 1 | cup red wine |
| 2 | tsp. powdered bouquet garni |

- Preheat oven to 325 degrees.
- Salt and pepper chicken to taste. Brown in oil. Transfer to Dutch oven.
- Add all other ingredients. Cover and cook at 325 degrees for 2½ hours.
- Serve with rice or potatoes, using juice as gravy.

# CHICKEN SURPRISE

Serves 4-6

| 1-1½ | chickens, cut up |
|---|---|
| | Salt and pepper to taste |
| 2 | Tbsp. butter |
| 1-2 | Tbsp. flour |
| 1 | cup Sauterne |
| 1 | cup orange juice |
| 3 | onions, quartered |
| 6 | carrots, peeled and cut into pieces |
| 3 | stalks celery, cut up |
| 6-8 | small potatoes, cut up (optional) |

- Preheat oven to 325 degrees.
- Salt and pepper chicken. Brown in butter. Transfer to a large covered pot.
- Sprinkle chicken with flour. Add remaining ingredients. If using potatoes, add during last 30 minutes of cooking time.
- Bake at 325 degrees for 1½ hours.

# GRILLED LEMON-MUSTARD CHICKEN

Serves 6-8
Do ahead

| | |
|---|---|
| 8 | chicken breasts, skinned and boned |

- In large *non-metallic* shallow dish arrange chicken pieces and cover with marinade. Refrigerate 2-4 hours.
- Prepare grill for medium heat. Grill chicken 3 inches from flame for 7-10 minutes on each side.

**MARINADE**

| | |
|---|---|
| ½ | cup lemon juice |
| 1 | Tbsp. finely chopped lemon zest |
| ¼ | cup Dijon mustard |
| ¼ | cup finely chopped fresh herbs, any combination: thyme, rosemary, basil, oregano, parsley |
| ¾ | tsp. salt |
| ¼ | tsp. coarsely ground pepper |

- Combine marinade ingredients and mix well.
- If fresh herbs are not available, use 4 Tablespoons of dried herbs.

# HAWAIIAN CHICKEN

Serves 12
Do ahead

| | |
|---|---|
| 12 | chicken breasts, boned |
| ½ | cup soy sauce |
| ⅝ | cup Sherry |
| 1¾ | cups pineapple juice |
| ¼ | cup red wine vinegar |
| ⅜ | cup sugar |
| ½ | tsp. garlic powder |

- Place chicken in baking dish.
- Mix remaining ingredients and pour over chicken.
- Marinate in refrigerator for 2 days.
- Cook on grill, over medium heat, for 10-12 minutes per side or until juices run clear when pierced.

*Serve with Rice Pilaf.*

# CHICKEN BREASTS MARNE

Serves 4

| 4 | large chicken breasts, skinned and boned |
| ½ | tsp. salt |
| ¼ | tsp. ground white pepper |
| ½ | tsp. cayenne pepper |
| 1 | cup flour |
| 1 | Tbsp. mixed herbs |
| 2 | eggs, beaten with ¼ tsp. salt and 1 tsp. oil |
| ½ | cup grated Parmesan cheese |
| ½ | cup bread crumbs |
| 8 | Tbsp. clarified butter |

- Season breasts with salt and peppers.
- Mix flour and herbs; roll breasts in mixture.
- Dip breasts in egg then in combined cheese and crumb mixture.
- Let stand for 15 minutes.
- Sauté chicken in hot clarified butter for 6-7 minutes on each side.

# LEMON CHICKEN

Serves 6-8
Do ahead

| 8 | chicken breasts, boned |
| 2 | cups dry Sherry |
| | Juice of 2 lemons |
| 4 | eggs |
| ½ | cup heavy cream |
| 2 | tsp. salt |
| 1 | tsp. white pepper |
| | Few drops onion juice |
| | Bread crumbs |
| ¼-½ | pound butter |
| | Lemon wedges |

- Marinate chicken in Sherry and lemon juice for 2 hours.
- Pat dry and flatten to ½-inch thickness.
- Beat eggs with cream; add salt, pepper and onion juice.
- Dip chicken in egg mixture; roll in bread crumbs. Sauté in butter until golden brown.
- Serve with lemon wedges.

# IMPERIAL CHICKEN

Serves 8

| | |
|---|---|
| 8 | chicken breasts, skinned and boned |
| ¼ | cup flour |
| ¼ | pound butter |
| 1 | pound small mushrooms, quartered |
| 1 | Tbsp. minced onion |
| 1 | cup heavy cream |
| ¼ | cup dry Sherry |
| 1 | tsp. salt |
| ⅛ | tsp. pepper |
| 1 | Tbsp. flour |
| 2 | Tbsp. cold water |

- Coat chicken with flour. In a large skillet, brown chicken in butter, a few pieces at a time, over medium heat until lightly brown. Set aside.
- Add mushrooms and onions; sauté for 5 minutes, stirring frequently. Stir in cream, Sherry, salt and pepper. Blend well. Return chicken to skillet.
- Reduce heat to low and simmer for 20-30 minutes, covered, until chicken is tender.
- Remove chicken to platter and keep warm.
- Blend flour and water. Gradually add to pan liquids, stirring until thickened. Spoon over chicken.

# MUSHROOM AND CHICKEN CUTLETS

Serves 6

| | |
|---|---|
| 6 | chicken breasts, skinned and boned |
| 3 | eggs, well beaten |
| | Salt to taste |
| | Garlic powder |
| 1 | cup bread crumbs |
| ¼-½ | pound butter |
| ½ | pound fresh mushrooms, sliced |
| 3 | slices deli-thin Muenster or Swiss cheese |
| ½ | cup chicken broth |
| | Juice of 1 lemon |

- Add seasonings to eggs. Immerse chicken in egg mixture for one hour.
- Roll chicken in crumbs. Sauté in butter until golden. Place in large casserole dish. Reserve butter.
- Sauté mushrooms in reserved butter. Sprinkle mushrooms over chicken.
- Place ½ slice of cheese over each chicken piece. Pour broth over all and cover with foil.
- Bake at 350 degrees for 30 minutes.
- Remove foil for last 10 minutes of baking. Pour or squeeze lemon juice over chicken just before serving.

# CHICKEN FLORENTINE

Serves 8

| 8 | chicken breasts, skinned and boned |
| | Salt and pepper to taste |
| 1 | 10-ounce package chopped spinach, cooked and drained |
| 2 | Tbsp. butter, melted |
| 3 | ounces cream cheese |
| ½ | tsp. lemon juice |
| ½ | cup shredded Swiss cheese |
| 6 | Tbsp. butter |
| ⅓-½ | cup grated Parmesan cheese |

- Preheat oven to 400 degrees.
- Pound chicken until thin; season to taste. Set aside.
- Mix butter, cream cheese and lemon juice with spinach.
- In center of each breast, spread Swiss cheese and ¼ cup spinach mixture.
- Fold chicken to cover stuffing completely. Place in baking dish seam side down and spread 1½ teaspoons butter on each. Sprinkle with Parmesan cheese. Add small amount of water and remaining butter.
- Bake at 400 degrees for 25 minutes or until brown.

*Serve with wild rice and Popovers Deluxe.*

# ISLAND MARINADE

Yields 3 cups

| 1½ | cups soy sauce |
| ½ | cup water |
| ⅓ | cup brown sugar |
| ¼ | cup oil |
| ¼ | cup Bourbon |
| 1 | Tbsp. chopped ginger |
| 2 | cloves garlic, crushed |

- Mix all ingredients
- Pour over chicken or beef and marinate overnight.
- Use marinade as basting sauce while cooking meat.

# CRAB-STUFFED CHICKEN

Serves 6

| | |
|---|---|
| 6 | chicken breasts, boned |
| ½ | cup chopped onion |
| ½ | cup chopped celery |
| 3 | Tbsp. butter |
| 3 | Tbsp. dry white wine |
| 8 | ounces crabmeat |
| ½ | cup herb seasoned stuffing |
| 2 | Tbsp. flour |
| ½ | tsp. paprika |
| 2 | Tbsp. butter, melted |

- Pound chicken to flatten; sprinkle with salt and pepper.
- Cook onion and celery in butter until tender. Remove from heat; add wine, crabmeat and stuffing; toss well to blend.
- Divide mixture and place on chicken; roll up and secure.
- Combine flour and paprika; coat chicken.
- Place chicken in a 12 x 7-inch baking dish and drizzle with butter.
- Bake at 375 degrees for 1 hour. Transfer to platter.

**SAUCE**

| | |
|---|---|
| 1 | envelope hollandaise sauce mix |
| ¾ | cup milk |
| 2 | Tbsp. dry white wine |
| ½ | cup shredded Swiss cheese |

- Blend sauce mix with milk; cook until thick.
- Add remaining ingredients and stir until cheese melts.
- Pour some of the sauce over chicken; pass remaining sauce at the table.

*Never-Fail Hollandaise may be substituted.*

# COMPANY CHICKEN

Serves 16

| | |
|---|---|
| 16 | chicken breasts, skinned and boned |
| 2 | 14-ounce cans artichoke hearts, drained |
| ¾ | cup butter, melted |
| | Salt and pepper to taste |
| 2 | cups Never-Fail Hollandaise |
| 1 | Tbsp. finely chopped parsley |

- Preheat oven to 350 degrees.
- Place artichoke hearts in a generously greased baking dish. Place chicken on top and drizzle with butter; season.
- Bake at 350 degrees for 35 minutes, basting often. Drain excess juices if any.
- Just before serving, top with hollandaise sauce; sprinkle with parsley.

*Sauce and chicken may be prepared early in day and reheated.*

# POULET NOUVEAU

Serves 6-8

8    chicken breasts, skinned and boned
     Salt and pepper to taste
1    Tbsp. chives
¼    cup butter
1    4-ounce can mushroom caps
1    8½-ounce can artichoke hearts, cut in half
1    7½-ounce can hearts of palm, cut in thirds
1    8-ounce can water chestnuts, quartered
1    10¾-ounce can cream of asparagus soup
1    cup sour cream
½    cup dry white wine
     Paprika
     Parsley, chopped

- Preheat oven to 350 degrees.
- Sprinkle chicken with salt, pepper and chives.
- Brown chicken in butter. Set pan aside with drippings. Arrange chicken in shallow baking dish.
- Place mushrooms, artichokes, hearts of palm and water chestnuts on top of chicken.
- Stir soup, sour cream and wine into pan drippings. Simmer and pour mixture over chicken and vegetables.
- Bake covered at 350 degrees for 1 hour. Garnish with paprika and parsley.

*For a wonderful buffet dinner, serve with Vegetables Virginia and Black Cherry Ring.*

## MEDITERRANEAN CHICKEN

Serves 4

| | |
|---|---|
| 4 | large chicken breasts, skinned and boned |
| 2 | Tbsp. clarified butter |
| 1 | fresh red pepper, blanched and diced |
| 1 | medium onion, chopped |
| 1 | garlic clove, minced |
| 4 | ounces fresh mushrooms, sliced |
| 1 | Tbsp. flour |
| 1 | cup dry white wine |
| 1½ | tsp. chicken bouillon granules |
| 1 | Tbsp. tomato paste |
| | Bouquet garni (1 bay leaf, 2 sprigs of thyme and parsley tied in a square of cheesecloth) |
| 2 | ounces sliced, drained, pitted black olives |
| 1 | 10-ounce package frozen artichoke hearts, thawed |

- Sauté chicken in butter to seal in the juices, turning on all sides. Remove from pan.
- Cook pepper, onion, garlic and mushrooms in butter.
- Stir in flour; add wine, bouillon granules, tomato purée, and bouquet garni and bring to a boil.
- Replace chicken and simmer covered for 15 minutes. Additional butter or wine may be added to insure a sufficient quantity of sauce.
- Add olives and artichoke hearts and simmer 10 minutes until chicken is tender. Remove bouquet garni and serve.

## PALMER SAUCE

Yields 3 cups

| | |
|---|---|
| 1 | 16-ounce can tomatoes |
| 1 | cup sugar |
| 1 | cup cider vinegar |
| 1 | medium onion, chopped |
| ¼ | tsp. ground cloves |
| ¼ | tsp. cinnamon |
| ½-1 | tsp. salt |
| | Dash cayenne pepper |

- Mix all ingredients in a medium saucepan. Heat until almost boiling. Reduce heat to simmer.
- Cook slowly, uncovered, until mixture reduces, about 1-1½ hours. Stir occasionally.
- Serve sauce hot or cold with roast beef or hamburgers. As a garnish serve with scrambled eggs or omelets.

*Tightly covered, sauce will keep 6 months in refrigerator.*

# CLASSIC CHICKEN TETRAZZINI

Serves 5-6

| | |
|---|---|
| 1 | large chicken |
| 3 | 10-ounce cans chicken broth |
| ¼ | cup butter |
| 12 | ounces fresh mushrooms, sliced |
| 1 | green pepper, chopped |
| 1 | clove garlic, minced |
| 3 | Tbsp. flour |
| 4 | tsp. salt, divided |
| ¼ | tsp. pepper |
| 1 | cup heavy cream, warmed |
| ¼ | cup dry white wine |
| 2 | egg yolks, slightly beaten |
| 1 | bay leaf |
| 8 | ounces thin spaghetti |
| ⅔ | cup grated Parmesan cheese |
| | Black olives |

- In large pot, cook chicken in broth, adding water to cover, simmering until done. Remove chicken; strain and reserve broth. Skin, bone and cut chicken into pieces.
- In large fry pan, melt butter; add mushrooms, green pepper and garlic; sauté about 5 minutes. Stir in flour, 1 teaspoon of salt and the pepper. Slowly add 1½ cups of reserved broth and warmed cream, stirring until thickened, about 3 minutes; reduce heat to low, add wine.
- Add several Tablespoons of hot white wine sauce to egg yolks, then add egg mixture to skillet, stirring. Add chicken pieces, stirring until heated through, about 3 minutes.
- While making sauce, cook spaghetti in remaining broth, adding enough water to make 3 quarts. Add remaining salt and bay leaf. Drain.
- Place spaghetti in a greased 2-quart shallow baking dish. Spoon chicken mixture over top and sprinkle with cheese.
- Bake at 300 degrees for 30 minutes or until bubbly. Garnish with black olives.

*May be doubled or tripled easily and then frozen until needed.*

# CHICKEN SPAGHETTI

Serves 8-10

| | |
|---|---|
| 1 | large chicken, cut up |
| 4-6 | chicken breasts |
| 3 | Tbsp. oil |
| 1½ | cup chopped celery |
| 1 | cup chopped onion |
| 1 | green pepper, chopped |
| 1 | 16-ounce can tomatoes |
| 1 | 15-ounce can tomato sauce |
| 1 | cup reserved broth |
| 1 | 6-ounce can sliced mushrooms |
| 1 | Tbsp. chili powder |
| | Tabasco sauce to taste |
| 3 | Tbsp. Worcestershire sauce |
| | Salt and pepper to taste |
| 1 | cup chopped black olives |
| 8 | ounces thin spaghetti |
| 1 | cup reserved broth |
| 4 | cups grated sharp Cheddar cheese |

- Cook chicken in salted water for approximately 25 minutes.
- Cool; remove skin and bones; chop chicken. Reserve 2 cups broth, strain and degrease.
- In large skillet, brown celery, onion and peppers in oil. Add next 9 ingredients and chicken and simmer for ½ hour.
- Cook spaghetti according to package directions, using water and 1 cup broth.
- Combine spaghetti with chicken mixture and cheese in large casserole.
- Bake at 350 degrees for 30-40 minutes or until bubbly. If refrigerated before cooking, additional time must be allowed.

*Best made the day before. Serve with tossed salad and Great Grandmother's Sally Lunn Bread.*

# JEZEBEL SAUCE

Yields 6 ½-pints

| | |
|---|---|
| 1 | 18-ounce jar pineapple or apricot preserves |
| 1 | 18-ounce jar apple jelly |
| 1 | 1.12-ounce can dry mustard |
| 5 | ounces horseradish |
| 1 | Tbsp. cracked black pepper |

- Combine all ingredients. Blend well. Pour into jelly jars and store in refrigerator.
- Serve with meat, cheese, bread or crackers. Also good on cold turkey or chicken sandwiches.

# PARTY CHICKEN

Serves 18
Do ahead

| | |
|---|---|
| 1 | envelope onion soup mix |
| 2 | cups sour cream |
| 3 | 2½-pound roasting chickens |
| 2 | cups dry Sherry |
| 1 | cup water |
| 1 | tsp. salt |
| | Dash of pepper |
| ½ | tsp. dried basil |
| ½ | tsp. thyme |
| 2 | tsp. curry powder |
| 6 | Tbsp. minced parsley |
| 1 | 10¾-ounce can cream of mushroom soup |
| 2 | 6-ounce packages long grain and wild rice, cooked |

- Blend soup mix and sour cream, set aside for 2 hours.
- In a large roasting pan, place chickens, Sherry, water and seasonings. Cover tightly.
- Bake at 300 degrees for 1½ hours.
- Remove chickens from roaster. Allow to cool; reserve juices and degrease.
- Combine cooled juices with sour cream mixture and add mushroom soup.
- Cook rice according to package directions.
- Skin and bone chickens and cut up meat. Combine with cooked rice. Pour sauce over all. Place in two 13 x 9-inch shallow baking dishes.
- Bake uncovered at 350 degrees for 30 minutes or until bubbly.

*Good served with Winter Salad and Parmesan French Bread.*

# BARBEQUE SAUCE

Yields 3 cups

| | |
|---|---|
| 5 | ounces steak sauce |
| 5 | ounces Worcestershire sauce |
| 14 | ounces ketchup |
| ¼ | pound butter |
| 4 | Tbsp. vinegar |
| | Dash hot sauce |
| 1 | small onion, chopped |
| 2 | cloves garlic, crushed |
| | Juice of 1 lemon |
| | Small piece of leafy celery |

- Combine all ingredients in medium saucepan and simmer 1 hour.
- Stir occasionally.
- Use in cooking chicken, pork or beef.

# ELEGANT CHICKEN AND CRAB

Serves 8

| | |
|---|---|
| 5-6 | chicken breasts |
| 2½ | cups water |
| 3 | tsp. chicken bouillon |
| ¼ | cup sliced onions |
| 1 | stalk celery cut in thirds |
| | Salt and pepper to taste |
| ½ | cup sliced fresh mushrooms |
| ¼ | cup chopped onion |
| 3 | Tbsp. butter |
| 3 | Tbsp. flour |
| | Salt and pepper to taste |
| 1½ | cups reserved chicken broth |
| ½ | cup dry white wine |
| 2 | egg yolks, beaten |
| 1 | pound crabmeat |
| ½ | cup heavy cream, whipped |
| ¼ | cup grated Parmesan cheese |
| | Paprika to garnish |

- Cook chicken in water with bouillon, onions, celery and seasoning for 30-40 minutes. Remove chicken. Strain stock and reserve 1½ cups broth. Place skinned, boned and cut-up chicken in a shallow baking dish.
- Sauté mushrooms and onions in butter until tender. Blend in flour, salt and pepper. Gradually add reserved broth and wine. Cook, stirring until thickened.
- Add small amount of hot mixture to egg yolks and blend thoroughly. Return to hot mixture and cook 2 minutes. Remove from heat.
- Stir in crabmeat. Gently fold in cream. Pour sauce over chicken in casserole.
- Sprinkle with cheese and paprika.
- Bake at 350 degrees for 30 minutes.

*Serve with Oregano Peas and Mandarin Delight.*

# SWEET AND CREAMY MUSTARD SAUCE

Yields 1¾ cups

| | |
|---|---|
| ½ | cup sugar |
| 1½ | Tbsp. flour |
| 2 | Tbsp. dry mustard |
| 1 | egg yolk |
| 1 | cup light cream |
| ½ | cup cider vinegar |
| ½ | tsp. salt |

- Mix first 3 ingredients in top of double boiler. Stir in egg yolk and cream. Cook, stirring constantly over boiling water until thick.
- Stir in vinegar and salt. Continue cooking just until well mixed and heated through.
- Serve immediately on ham, beef or corned beef.

# CHINESE CHICKEN DINNER

Serves 6

| | |
|---|---|
| 3 | Tbsp. soy sauce |
| 3 | Tbsp. Sherry |
| 1 | tsp. ground ginger |
| 1 | clove garlic, crushed |
| 4 | chicken breasts, skinned, boned and cut in bite-size pieces |
| 4-8 | Tbsp. butter |
| 2 | cups sliced fresh mushrooms |
| 1 | cup thinly sliced celery |
| ½ | cup chopped scallions |
| 1 | 10-ounce package frozen snow peas, thawed |
| 1 | 8-ounce can water chestnuts, drained and sliced |
| 1 | Tbsp. cornstarch |
| 2 | Tbsp. water |
| 3 | cups hot cooked rice |

- Blend soy sauce, Sherry, ginger and garlic. Pour over chicken in bowl and marinate at least 30 minutes.
- Melt butter in skillet or wok over medium high heat. Add chicken, mushrooms, celery, scallions and snow peas. Sauté for 10-15 minutes, stirring constantly until chicken is tender and vegetables are crisp.
- Stir in water chestnuts.
- Combine cornstarch and water, add to chicken. Cook, stirring until thickened.
- Serve immediately over rice.

*Peanuts or pineapple could be added for an unusual and delicious combination.*

# CHICKEN IN TORTILLA CREPES

Serves 4-6

| | |
|---|---|
| 1 | 4-ounce can whole green chilies, cut in wide strips |
| 1 | pound Monterey Jack cheese, cut in strips |
| 4 | cups cooked, diced chicken |
| 12 | flour tortillas |

- Place a chili strip, some cheese, and some chicken on each tortilla; roll up and secure. Arrange in large casserole dish.

**SAUCE**

| | |
|---|---|
| ⅓ | cup flour |
| ⅓ | cup butter |
| 2 | cups chicken broth |
| 2 | cups milk |
| 2 | cups grated sharp Cheddar cheese |
| 1 | cup sour cream |
| ½ | tsp. Worcestershire sauce |
| ½ | tsp. seasoned salt |
| 2-3 | dashes cayenne pepper to taste |
| 1 | tsp. dry mustard |

- In saucepan, combine flour and butter, stirring until well blended.
- Slowly blend in broth. Add milk and cheese, stirring constantly.
- Add small amount of sauce to sour cream; return to pan. Add remaining ingredients. Cook over medium heat, stirring frequently until thick. Pour over tortillas.
- Bake at 350 degrees for 45 minutes or until golden brown.

# GREEN PEPPERCORN SAUCE

Yields 1 cup

| | |
|---|---|
| 1-2 | ounces green peppercorns, drained |
| 2 | tsp. beef bouillon granules |
| ½ | cup dry white wine |
| 2 | Tbsp. butter |
| 2 | tsp. dried thyme |
| 1 | cup heavy cream |
| 2 | Tbsp. Brandy |
| | Cornstarch |

- Combine all ingredients except butter in a small saucepan. Simmer until slightly reduced, whisking in butter a teaspoon at a time while cooking. Do not allow to boil.
- If sauce is too thin, thicken over low heat by adding a little cornstarch (approximately 1 teaspoon) dissolved in a small amount of water (approximately 2 Tablespoons). If sauce should separate, try beating in a little ice cold water.
- Serve immediately with beef or roast chicken.

# EASY CORNISH HENS

Serves 2

| | |
|---|---|
| 2 | 1-pound Cornish hens |
| ¼ | tsp. garlic powder |
| 2 | tsp. thyme |
| ½ | tsp. salt |
| ½ | tsp. pepper |
| ⅓ | cup butter |

- Combine all spices. Wipe out cavities of hens and rub each inside with half of the spice mixture.
- Tie wings behind the back of each hen and secure legs.
- In heavy skillet, brown the hens in butter on all sides. Remove and place breast-side up in a roasting pan.

## BASTING SAUCE

| | |
|---|---|
| ¼ | pound butter, melted |
| ¼ | cup lemon juice |
| ¼ | tsp. paprika |
| 1 | fat pinch thyme |

- Combine all ingredients and use to baste hens frequently while roasting.
- Roast at 425 degrees for 45 minutes.

*Serve cold for a tailgate party, backyard picnic or sailing supper.*

# GOURMET CORNISH HENS WITH SMITHFIELD HAM

Serves 6

| | |
|---|---|
| 4 | Tbsp. butter (for sautéeing) |
| 1 | cup sliced fresh mushrooms |
| ¼ | cup slivered almonds |
| ¼ | cup diced celery |
| 1 | 6-ounce box long grain and wild rice, cooked |
| 6 | thin slices Smithfield ham |
| 3 | small Cornish hens, halved |
| | Coarsely ground pepper |
| 4 | Tbsp. butter, melted (for basting) |
| ½ | cup dry white wine |

- Sauté mushrooms, almonds and celery in butter until celery is tender crisp. Mix with cooked rice.
- In shallow 3-quart casserole, arrange ham in single layer. Spoon a mound of rice mixture in center of each slice.
- Season hens with pepper and place one half on top of each mound, skin side up.
- Combine butter and wine.
- Bake at 350 degrees for 60 minutes, basting with wine mixture every 15 minutes.

# CURRIED CORNISH HENS

Serves 4

| | |
|---|---|
| 2 | Cornish hens |
| 4 | Tbsp. butter, melted |
| 1 | 6-ounce package curry rice |
| 1 | 17-ounce can whole apricots |
| ¼ | cup butter for sautéeing |
| ½ | cup sliced onion |
| ½ | cup sliced celery |
| 2 | Tbsp. flour |
| 1 | tsp. curry powder |
| 1 | cup water |
| ½ | cup apricot syrup |
| 2 | chicken bouillon cubes |

- Preheat oven to 350 degrees.
- Split hens and place in a 13 x 9-inch baking dish, skin side up. Brush with butter.
- Bake at 350 degrees for 1-1¼ hours.
- Cook rice as directed on package.
- Drain apricots and reserve ½ cup syrup.
- In saucepan, melt butter and sauté onion and celery until almost tender. Stir in flour and curry; remove from heat.
- Gradually stir in water and syrup. Add bouillon cubes; cook, stirring constantly until thickened and cubes melt. Cook for 2 minutes.
- To serve, place hens on top of rice on a serving platter; surround with apricots and spoon sauce over all.

*Makes a gorgeous party dish.*

# WILD DUCK

Serves 2

| | |
|---|---|
| 1 | wild duck, prepared for cooking |
| | Salt and pepper |
| 1 | onion |
| 1 | potato, peeled |
| | Flour |
| | Shortening |
| 1 | orange, including rind, sliced |
| 1 | 6-ounce can mushrooms, liquid reserved |
| | Dash Worcestershire sauce |
| ¼ | cup Sherry |
| 1 | cup light cream |

- Sprinkle duck with desired amount of salt and pepper inside and out. Place onion and potato inside cavity, or pieces of each if too large. Dust with flour.
- Lightly brown duck in shortening. When brown, place duck in heavy roaster. Add orange slices.
- Combine reserved mushroom liquid, Worcestershire sauce and Sherry. Pour around duck.
- Cover and bake at 300 degrees for 2-2½ hours until tender.
- Remove duck to platter. Discard orange slices. Add mushrooms to broth and adjust seasonings. Stir in cream; serve as gravy.

# WILD GOOSE

Serves 4
Do ahead

| | |
|---|---|
| 1 | goose |
| 2 | apples, chopped |
| 2 | onions, chopped |
| 2 | stalks celery, chopped |
| 2 | bacon slices |

- Soak goose for 2 hours in salted water to cover.
- Combine apples, onions and celery; spoon into cavity.
- Place goose in pan. Place slice of bacon on each side of breast.

**BASTING SAUCE**

| | |
|---|---|
| 2 | Tbsp. butter |
| 1 | cup beef bouillon |
| 1 | cup dry red wine |
| 1 | cup water |
| 1 | Tbsp. Worcestershire sauce |
| | Salt and pepper |

- Combine ingredients over low heat. When well mixed, pour over goose.
- Cover and bake at 350 degrees for 2 hours, basting frequently.

# ROAST QUAIL

Serves 6-8
Do ahead

| | |
|---|---|
| 6-8 | quail |
| 2 | cups milk |
| ⅓ | cup flour |
| 1 | tsp. salt |
| ⅛ | tsp. pepper |
| | Salad oil |
| 1½ | cups chicken broth |
| 2 | Tbsp. flour |
| | Scant amount of Sherry |

- Place quail in milk in shallow covered container in refrigerator overnight.
- The next day, combine flour, salt and pepper in a large bag and shake quail in mixture to coat evenly. Discard milk.
- Brown quail in skillet with ½ inch hot oil. Set aside pan, pouring off all but 2 Tablespoons oil.
- Put broth in large roaster. Place browned quail on rack in roaster and cover. Steam in 350 degree oven for about 1½ hours.
- For gravy, mix flour with reserved oil in browning pan; add steaming liquid. Stir and cook about 5 minutes until thick. Add Sherry to color. Spoon over quail when serving.

# QUAIL OR DOVE

Serves 2

| | |
|---|---|
| 4 | quail or dove, prepared for cooking |
| ¼ | pound butter |
| ½ | cup sliced mushrooms |
| ¼ | cup chopped onion |
| ¼ | cup chopped celery leaves |
| ½ | cup white wine |
| | Salt and pepper to taste |
| ¼ | tsp. dried tarragon |

- Sauté birds in butter until lightly browned.
- Remove birds; add all ingredients except tarragon. Heat.
- Add birds; cover and simmer 35 minutes.
- Uncover and sprinkle with tarragon. Simmer 15 minutes longer.

# TANGY BARBEQUE SAUCE

Yields 1¾ cups

| | |
|---|---|
| ¼ | cup vinegar |
| ½ | cup water |
| 2 | Tbsp. sugar |
| 1 | Tbsp. Dijon mustard |
| ½ | tsp. pepper |
| 1½ | tsp. salt |
| ¼ | tsp. cayenne pepper |
| 1 | slice lemon |
| 1 | slice onion |
| 4 | Tbsp. butter |
| ½ | cup ketchup |
| 2 | Tbsp. Worcestershire sauce |

- Mix first 10 ingredients in small saucepan. Simmer 10 minutes uncovered.
- Add ketchup and Worcestershire. Bring to boil.
- Baste on chicken, ribs or turkey.

# SEAFOOD ENTRÉES

# SEAFOOD ENTRÉES

## FISH
Baked Bluefish  183
Baked Fish with Shrimp
 Sauce  185
Charcoaled Fish  181
Easy Bluefish  182
Italian Baked Fish  183
Local Catch  181
Quick Pan-Fried Fish  182
Surf Roll-Ups  184

## SHRIMP
Beer Shrimp and Sauce  186
Greek Shrimp  192
Jambalaya  189
Marinated Thai Shrimp  185
Sautéed Shrimp  187
Shrimp and Artichokes  192
Shrimp in Béchamel
 Sauce  191
Shrimp Curry Wiki Wiki  189
Shrimp Florentine  193
Shrimp Galore  188
Shrimp Mosca  187
Spicy Shrimp Creole  190
Szechuan Shrimp  188
Tom Jones Shrimp  186

## CRAB
Blue Crab Casserole  196
Company Crab Cakes  195
Crabmeat Eastern Shore  194
Crabmeat Imperial  195
Crabs for a Feast  193
Deviled Crab  197
Hampton Crab  194
Hearty Crab  197
Tidewater Crab Cakes  196
Wild Crab Casserole  198

## SCALLOPS
Broiled Scallops  198
Savory Scallops  199
Scallops in Wine and
 Cheese  199

## SEAFOOD SPECIALS
Fisherman's Catch  200
Neptune's Delight  200
Shad Roe with
 Asparagus  202
Waterside Medley  201

## OYSTERS
Lynnhaven Oysters and Wild
 Rice  204
Scalloped Oysters  203
Zesty Scalloped Oysters  202

## SAUCES
Chinese Shrimp Sauce  187
Cocktail Sauce  204
Granny's Dipping Sauce  203
Shrimp Sauce  184

# LOCAL CATCH

Serves 4
Do ahead

**Fresh fish fillet**
**½    cup dry white wine**
**Juice of ½ lemon**
**Salt**
**Paprika**

- Pour wine and lemon juice over fillet. Refrigerate 2-3 hours, turning once.
- Preheat oven to broil.
- Pour off liquid. Season fish with salt and paprika and place on greased foil-lined pan.
- Broil until brown; turn and broil other side.

*Additional seasonings may be added: fresh herbs, sliced/minced onions, peppers.*

# CHARCOALED FISH

Serves 2-4

**Large fillet of mackerel or**
**bluefish**
**¼    pound butter, melted**
**1    8-ounce bottle**
**unsweetened lime juice**
**Enough Worcestershire**
**sauce to make sauce**
**dark.**
**Other seasonings as**
**desired: basil, wine,**
**garlic, seafood seasoning**

- Marinate fillet in sauce made from remaining ingredients for at least 2 hours, turning several times if fish is not covered by sauce.
- After fire in grill is well started, cover grill top with foil and punch holes in foil about every 3 inches to allow smoke to escape.
- When fire is at medium heat, place fillets on grill, skin side down, and allow to cook slowly.
- Baste frequently with sauce. Do *not* turn. Cook 20-30 minutes.
- When fish is done, remove with spatulas to keep from falling apart.

# QUICK PAN-FRIED FISH

Serves 2

2   fresh trout, cleaned,
    filleted, weighing about
    1½ pounds
    Salt to taste
    White pepper to taste
2   Tbsp. clarified butter
6   Tbsp. freshly grated
    Parmesan cheese
½   cup clam juice
1-2 Tbsp. flour
¼   cup light cream or milk

- Season fillets well on both sides with salt and pepper.
- Heat butter in skillet until sizzling. Brown fish on one side until barely done; turn over.
- Sprinkle cheese evenly on one side of fish; add clam juice. Cook until fish begins to flake when pierced with fork. Remove to heated platter.
- Stir flour into pan drippings until smooth. Add cream. Cook over low heat, stirring to desired thickness. Taste to correct seasonings.
- Pour sauce over fish on heated platter. Garnish with parsley and serve with lemon wedges.

*Overnight Cabbage Slaw and Tomato Pie are good accompaniments.*

# EASY BLUEFISH

Serves 2

Fresh bluefish fillet (or
other fish)
Lemon juice
Mayonnaise
Grated Parmesan cheese

- Preheat oven to 350 degrees.
- Place fillet on lightly greased cookie sheet, skin side down.
- Sprinkle lightly with lemon juice. Totally cover fillet with mayonnaise, as if icing a cake. Sprinkle with cheese.
- Bake at 350 degrees until mayonnaise is golden on top and fish flakes when fork is inserted in the thickest part.

*Potatoes Pierre and cabbage strips topped with Celery Seed Dressing
will complete your dinner.*

# BAKED BLUEFISH

| | |
|---|---|
| 1 | **large bluefish or flounder fillet** |
| | **Salt and pepper to taste** |
| 2 | **cloves garlic, minced** |
| 1 | **small onion, minced** |
| | **Fresh parsley, chopped** |
| 1 | **tsp. thyme** |
| 1 | **tsp. dill** |
| 2 | **Tbsp. butter** |
| 1½ | **Tbsp. lemon juice** |
| | **Paprika** |

- Preheat oven to 400 degrees.
- Place fillet on large piece of foil on baking sheet. Sprinkle with several or all seasonings to taste. Dot with butter. Pour lemon juice over fillet; sprinkle with paprika.
- Close foil around fish and bake at 400 degrees for 1 hour. Open foil for last 10 minutes of baking time.

# ITALIAN BAKED FISH

| | |
|---|---|
| | **Fresh tomatoes, peeled** |
| | **Seasoned Italian bread crumbs** |
| | **Salt and pepper to taste** |
| 8 | **small flounder fillets (or other fish)** |
| ½ | **cup white Port wine** |
| 4 | **Tbsp. butter** |
| 1 | **tsp. lemon juice** |
| | **Freshly grated Parmesan cheese** |
| | **Paprika** |
| | **Squeeze of lemon** |

- Preheat oven to 500 degrees.
- In a buttered 13 x 9-inch baking dish, thinly slice enough tomatoes to cover bottom. Sprinkle with bread crumbs, salt and pepper.
- Arrange fish in a single layer over mixture.
- Combine wine, butter and lemon juice in saucepan. Heat to a boil and cook 3 minutes. Pour over fish.
- Sprinkle with cheese and paprika and a squeeze of lemon over all.
- Bake at 500 degrees for 10-20 minutes.

*Spice up your meal with Snaps with Herbs and Au Gratin Potatoes.*

## SURF ROLL-UPS

Makes 6

| | |
|---|---|
| 3 | fresh flounder fillets, skinned |
| 1 | 10-ounce package frozen chopped spinach, thawed and drained |
| 3 | eggs, beaten |
| ¾ | cup crumbled Feta cheese |
| ¾ | cup cottage cheese |
| 1 | bunch green onions, finely chopped |
| 1 | Tbsp. fresh dill |
| ½ | tsp. salt |
| ¼ | tsp. pepper |
| 3 | Tbsp. butter, melted |
| 1 | Tbsp. lemon juice |

- Preheat oven to 350 degrees.
- Halve each flounder fillet lengthwise. Set aside.
- Mix spinach, eggs, cheeses, onions, dill, salt and pepper. Spread mixture evenly over one side of fillets. Roll into jelly roll shapes and secure with toothpicks.
- Place fish on buttered, foil-covered broiling pan.
- Combine butter and lemon juice; pour over fillets.
- Bake at 350 degrees for 20-30 minutes or until fish flakes when pierced with a fork.
- Carefully remove fillets with a spatula and serve immediately.

*Serve with Tropical Salad and Party Rolls.*

## SHRIMP SAUCE

Makes 1 cup

| | |
|---|---|
| 1 | cup mayonnaise |
| 1 | Tbsp. vinegar |
| 1 | Tbsp. sweet relish |
| 1 | Tbsp. chili sauce |
| 1 | small onion, sliced |
| 1 | radish, quartered |
| ½ | tsp. parsley flakes |
| | Dash Worcestershire sauce |
| | Dash cayenne pepper |

- Place all ingredients in food processor or blender. Process a few seconds. Store in refrigerator overnight.
- Serve as a dip with fried shrimp or oysters.

# BAKED FISH WITH SHRIMP SAUCE

Serves 6

**SAUCE**

| | |
|---|---|
| 1 | **pound medium shrimp** |
| 1½ | **cups water** |
| 1 | **tsp. seafood seasoning** |
| 2 | **Tbsp. butter** |
| 3 | **Tbsp. flour** |
| ½ | **cup heavy cream, more if needed** |
| | **Salt to taste** |
| | **White pepper to taste** |
| | **Tabasco sauce to taste** |
| 1 | **tsp. dill** |
| | **Dash lemon juice** |

- Preheat oven to 350 degrees.
- Boil shrimp in water and seasoning for 5 minutes. Reserve cooking liquid. When shrimp are cool, peel and devein. Set aside.
- Melt butter and stir in flour. Stir over medium heat until smooth. Continue to cook, stirring constantly, for 2 minutes.
- Add shrimp broth, continuing to stir as sauce thickens. Bring to a boil and cook 2 minutes.
- Pour in cream and heat thoroughly. Add seasonings and shrimp, heating until warm. Do not boil. Set aside, keeping warm until fish is baked.

**FISH**

| | |
|---|---|
| 6 | **pieces fresh flounder, monkfish, bluefish, etc.** |
| 2 | **Tbsp. butter** |
| | **Parsley** |
| | **Lemon slices** |

- Bake fish with butter at 350 degrees for 15-20 minutes or until done.
- Pour sauce over fish and serve garnished with parsley and lemon slices.

# MARINATED THAI SHRIMP

Serves 6
Do ahead

| | |
|---|---|
| 1½ | **pounds jumbo shrimp** |
| ½ | **cup soy sauce** |
| ½ | **cup light vegetable oil** |
| 2 | **Tbsp. lemon juice** |
| 1 | **tsp. ginger** |
| 3 | **cloves garlic, finely minced** |

- Peel, devein and wash shrimp. Pat dry. Place in a bowl.
- Mix rest of ingredients and pour over shrimp. Cover and refrigerate for at least 3 hours.
- Skewer shrimp and cook over hot coals for 4-5 minutes on each side.
- Serve immediately.

*Shrimp may be marinated for 24 hours if desired.*
*Recipe may be varied by using half scallops and half shrimp.*

# BEER SHRIMP AND SAUCE

Serves 4

**SHRIMP**

| | |
|---|---|
| 3 | bottles of beer |
| 3 | bottles of water |
| 3 | Tbsp. salt |
| 3 | Tbsp. celery seed |
| 1 | medium onion, chopped |
| 3 | whole peppercorns |
| 1 | bay leaf |
| 3 | pounds shrimp |

- Boil all ingredients except shrimp for 5 minutes. Add shrimp and cook for 5 minutes. Test shrimp for doneness; do *not* overcook.
- Rinse under cool water. Peel and dip in sauce.

**SAUCE**

| | |
|---|---|
| 2 | parts mayonnaise |
| 1 | part chili sauce |
| 1 | clove garlic, mashed |
| | Tabasco sauce to taste |

- Mix ingredients well. Pour into bowl for dipping.

# TOM JONES SHRIMP

Serves 2

| | |
|---|---|
| 1 | pound shrimp |
| 1 | Tbsp. freshly ground pepper |
| 1½ | tsp. salt |
| | Juice of one lemon |
| 1 | Tbsp. Worcestershire sauce |
| | Several shakes of hot pepper sauce |
| 1 | clove garlic, minced |
| 3 | Tbsp. extra virgin olive oil |
| 3 | Tbsp. butter |

- Preheat oven to 350 degrees.
- Wash shrimp, then spread in a single layer in a baking dish.
- Mix all remaining ingredients except butter and pour over shrimp. Dot with butter.
- Bake at 350 degrees for 20 minutes. Stir several times while cooking.
- Serve shrimp in baking dish; peel when cool enough to handle. Use French bread for dipping in sauce.

## SHRIMP MOSCA

Serves 4

| | |
|---|---|
| ¼ | cup olive oil |
| 2 | pounds shrimp |
| 4-6 | cloves garlic to taste |
| 2 | bay leaves |
| 1 | tsp. rosemary |
| 1 | tsp. oregano |
| 1 | tsp. ground black pepper |
| 1 | Tbsp. salt |
| 2 | Tbsp. Sauterne wine |

- Heat oil in wok or heavy frying pan. Add remaining ingredients except wine.
- Sauté, stirring constantly, for 5 minutes or until shrimp are pink but *not* done.
- Add Sauterne and heat briefly until shrimp are cooked.
- Peel shrimp at the table, using French bread for dipping into sauce.

## SAUTÉED SHRIMP

Serves 6-8

| | |
|---|---|
| 2 | pounds shrimp, peeled and deveined |
| ¼ | cup extra virgin olive oil |
| 1 | pound fresh mushrooms, sliced |
| 1 | small onion, chopped |
| ½ | cup chopped fresh parsley |
| ½ | cup dry white wine |
| ½ | tsp. salt |
| 2 | cloves garlic, minced |
| ¼ | tsp. fresh ground pepper |

- Heat oil in a large wok or skillet. Add mushrooms and onion; sauté until tender. Add parsley and wine; stir.
- Gradually add shrimp, sautéeing until just pink. Season with salt, garlic and pepper. Stir and cook for several minutes.
- Serve immediately over rice or noodles.

## CHINESE SHRIMP SAUCE

| | |
|---|---|
| 2 | scallions, chopped |
| 2 | tsp. chopped fresh ginger |
| 1 | clove garlic, crushed |
| 3 | Tbsp. soy sauce |
| 1 | Tbsp. hoisin sauce |
| 1 | tsp. Tabasco sauce |
| 1 | Tbsp. dry Sherry |

- Combine ingredients in small bowl. Refrigerate.
- Serve as a dip with steamed shrimp.

## SHRIMP GALORE

Serves 6-8

| | |
|---|---|
| 4 | **pounds medium shrimp** |
| ½ | **pound butter, melted** |
| 2 | **cloves garlic, crushed** |
| ⅓ | **cup chopped fresh parsley** |
| ½ | **cup dry Sherry** |
| ½ | **tsp. paprika** |
| ½ | **tsp. cayenne pepper** |
| 2 | **cups soft bread crumbs** |

- Cook shrimp in seasoned water; peel and clean.
- Mix butter, garlic, parsley, Sherry, paprika and pepper. Set aside.
- Toss shrimp and bread crumbs in large bowl.
- Arrange shrimp mixture in a large buttered baking dish. Pour butter mixture over shrimp.
- Bake at 325 degrees for 15-20 minutes or until bubbly.

*Good with Dilly Tomato Aspic and Great Grandmother's Sally Lunn Bread.*

## SZECHUAN SHRIMP

Serves 4

| | |
|---|---|
| 1½ | **pounds shrimp** |
| ½ | **cup minced scallions** |
| ½ | **cup minced bamboo shoots** |
| ¼ | **tsp. minced fresh ginger** |
| 3 | **large cloves garlic, minced** |
| 1 | **tsp. hot pepper sauce** |
| ½ | **cup sliced green pepper** |
| ½ | **cup sliced water chestnuts** |
| 2 | **Tbsp. sugar** |
| ⅓ | **cup ketchup** |
| ¼ | **cup dry Sherry** |
| 3 | **Tbsp. soy sauce** |
| 2 | **Tbsp. sesame seeds, toasted** |
| 1 | **Tbsp. cornstarch** |
| 3 | **Tbsp. water** |
| ¼ | **cup peanut oil or as needed** |

- Peel and devein shrimp.
- In a small mixing bowl, combine next 7 ingredients. Set aside.
- In a smaller bowl, combine sugar, ketchup, Sherry, soy sauce and sesame seeds. Set aside.
- In a cup, combine cornstarch and water. Stir to mix.
- Stir-fry shrimp in hot oil in wok or large skillet until barely done. Remove, drain and set aside.
- Using 2 Tablespoons hot strained shrimp oil, stir-fry scallion mixture. Add shrimp, then ketchup mixture, stirring quickly. Add cornstarch mixture and stir until thickened. As wok is very hot, heat may be turned off at this point so that shrimp do not overcook while sauce thickens.
- Serve over rice accompanied by steamed vegetables or salad.

## SHRIMP CURRY WIKI WIKI
Serves 4

| | |
|---|---|
| 1½ | pounds shrimp, peeled and deveined |
| 2 | Tbsp. butter |
| 2 | Tbsp. flour |
| ¼ | tsp. salt |
| | Dash pepper |
| 2 | tsp. curry powder |
| 1 | tsp. ginger |
| 1 | Tbsp. minced onion |
| 2 | cups milk |
| 1½ | cups grated coconut |
| 2 | tsp. lemon juice |
| | Cooked white rice |
| | Condiments |

- Melt butter, adding next 6 ingredients. Stir until a roux forms, then add milk gradually and cook until mixture thickens. Sauce may be thinned with additional milk.
- Add coconut and lemon juice. Cook on low heat for 15-20 minutes.
- Add shrimp and cook until shrimp are done.
- Serve over fluffy rice with a choice of condiments: chopped peanuts, bacon bits, pineapple chunks, grated coconut, minced hard-boiled egg yolks, raisins, chopped green peppers, chopped green onion and mango chutney.

## JAMBALAYA
Serves 6

| | |
|---|---|
| ¼ | pound bacon, cut into 1-inch strips |
| 2 | onions, minced |
| 2 | green peppers, cut into strips |
| 1 | cup uncooked rice |
| 1 | 16-ounce can tomatoes |
| ½ | pound cooked smoked ham, cut into bite-size pieces |
| 1 | 14½-ounce can chicken broth |
| 1 | tsp. minced garlic |
| 1 | tsp. salt |
| | Black pepper to taste |
| ½ | tsp. thyme |
| 1 | pound medium shrimp, peeled and deveined |

- Preheat oven to 350 degrees.
- In medium skillet, sauté bacon until brown but not crisp. Remove bacon and reserve. Sauté onions in drippings until translucent.
- Add green pepper, stir and cook about 4 minutes. Add rice, stirring until rice is coated and turns opaque.
- Add tomatoes, ham, reserved bacon, chicken broth, garlic, salt, pepper and thyme. Pour mixture in a large shallow casserole.
- Bake at 350 degrees for 40-50 minutes or until rice is tender. More broth may be needed as casserole bakes. Add raw shrimp, pushing down into rice. Cook for an additional 10 minutes. Serve immediately.

# SPICY SHRIMP CREOLE

Serves 6-8

| | |
|---|---|
| ½ | lemon, sliced |
| 4 | black peppercorns |
| 2 | pounds shrimp, peeled and deveined |
| 4 | slices bacon |
| 2 | Tbsp. butter |
| 1 | clove garlic, finely chopped |
| 1 | cup chopped onion |
| 1½ | cups chopped green pepper |
| ¼ | cup chopped parsley |
| 1½ | cups thinly sliced celery |
| 1 | 28-ounce can tomatoes |
| 1 | 6-ounce can tomato paste |
| 1 | Tbsp. lemon juice |
| 1 | Tbsp. sugar |
| 1 | tsp. salt |
| ¼-½ | tsp. pepper |
| ¼-½ | tsp. crushed red pepper |
| 1 | bay leaf |
| ½ | tsp. dried thyme leaves |
| ½ | tsp. filé powder |
| | Cooked white rice |

- In a large saucepan, bring 1 quart of water to a boil. Add lemon, peppercorns and shrimp. Reduce heat and simmer uncovered for 3 minutes. Drain shrimp, reserving 1 cup cooking liquid. Shrimp should be barely cooked.
- In the same pan, sauté bacon over low heat until crisp. Remove bacon, reserving fat; drain bacon on paper towels and crumble.
- To the bacon fat, add butter, garlic, onion, green pepper, parsley and celery. Cook, stirring, until vegetables are tender.
- Add shrimp liquid, bacon, tomatoes, tomato paste, lemon juice, sugar, salt, pepper, red pepper, bay leaf and thyme. Bring to a boil. Reduce heat and simmer covered for 30 minutes.
- Just before serving, stir in filé powder and shrimp. Bring to a boil, then reduce heat and simmer for 3 minutes.
- Serve over cooked white rice.

# SHRIMP IN BÉCHAMEL SAUCE
Serves 4-6

## SHRIMP MIXTURE

| | |
|---|---|
| 1½ | **pounds shrimp, peeled and deveined** |
| 1½ | **cups sliced fresh mushrooms** |
| 2 | **Tbsp. butter** |
| | **Seasoned salt to taste** |
| | **White pepper to taste** |
| | **Dash Worcestershire sauce** |
| | **Dash Tabasco sauce** |
| 1 | **Tbsp. chicken stock** |
| ¼ | **cup dry Sherry or Cognac** |

- Sauté mushrooms in butter; add seasonings. Add shrimp and cook until just done, adding chicken stock to keep moist. Add Sherry, stir briefly and set aside.

## BÉCHAMEL SAUCE

| | |
|---|---|
| 1½ | **cups milk** |
| 2-3 | **Tbsp. chopped onions or shallots** |
| 2 | **Tbsp. chopped celery** |
| 6-8 | **whole peppercorns** |
| 2 | **bay leaves** |
| 3 | **Tbsp. butter** |
| 3 | **Tbsp. flour** |
| 1 | **Tbsp. chopped fresh parsley or tarragon** |
| 1 | **egg yolk** |

- On low heat, cook first 5 ingredients until milk steams. Strain and set aside.
- In medium pan, melt butter and whisk in flour. Add milk, whisking continuously until thick. Add parsley.
- Beat egg yolk in a small bowl. While whisking, gradually add some of the sauce, then slowly pour egg mixture into remaining sauce. Stir well, heating 1 minute. Do not boil.
- Pour sauce over reserved shrimp mixture. Heat thoroughly, but do not allow to boil. If sauce becomes too thick, add a little cream to thin.
- Serve over spinach pasta, rice or in pastry shells.

# SHRIMP AND ARTICHOKES

Serves 4-6

| | |
|---|---|
| 2 | 14 ½-ounce cans artichoke hearts, drained |
| 1 | pound shrimp, cooked, peeled and deveined |
| ½ | pound fresh mushrooms, sliced |
| 6 | Tbsp. butter |
| 4 | Tbsp. flour |
| 1½ | cups milk |
| | Salt and pepper to taste |
| 1 | Tbsp. Worcestershire sauce |
| ¼ | cup dry Sherry |
| 1 | ounce Parmesan cheese, grated |
| | Paprika |
| | Fresh parsley |

- Preheat oven to 375 degrees.
- In bottom of a buttered casserole, arrange artichoke hearts. Spread shrimp over artichokes.
- Sauté mushrooms in 2 Tablespoons of butter for 6 minutes. Layer over shrimp.
- Melt remaining 4 Tablespoons butter in a saucepan. Whisk in flour, stirring until well blended and smooth. Pour in milk, whisking constantly until mixture has thickened. Season with salt and pepper, then add Worcestershire sauce and Sherry. Pour over casserole. Sprinkle with cheese and paprika.
- Bake at 375 degrees for 30-40 minutes.
- Serve hot, garnished with an extra sprinkling of paprika and chopped fresh parsley.
- Chicken may be substituted for shrimp.

*Serve with Fall Salad.*

# GREEK SHRIMP

Serves 4

| | |
|---|---|
| 3 | Tbsp. extra virgin olive oil |
| 2 | cups chopped onions |
| 1 | clove garlic, minced |
| ¼ | cup finely chopped parsley |
| 2 | cups chopped fresh tomatoes or 16-ounce can Italian plum tomatoes, drained and chopped |
| ¼ | cup tomato paste |
| 1 | pound shrimp, peeled and deveined |
| | Pinch crushed red pepper |
| 1 | cup Feta cheese, crumbled |
| 2 | cups cooked rice |

- Preheat oven to 425 degrees.
- In large skillet, heat olive oil; sauté onions and garlic until onion is soft. Add parsley, tomatoes and tomato paste. Simmer covered for 20 minutes.
- Add shrimp and sauté for 2 minutes. Do not overcook. Stir in red pepper.
- Place mixture in a buttered 1½-quart casserole. Sprinkle with cheese.
- Bake at 425 degrees for 10-15 minutes or just until cheese melts and is bubbly.
- Serve over rice.

# SHRIMP FLORENTINE

Serves 4

| | |
|---|---|
| 1 | cup water |
| 1 | small onion, diced |
| 1 | clove garlic, diced |
| | Leaves from 2 stalks of celery |
| 1 | bay leaf |
| 6 | peppercorns |
| 1½ | pounds shrimp |
| 2 | 10-ounce packages frozen spinach, cooked |
| 1 | cup light cream |
| 4 | Tbsp. butter |
| ¼ | cup flour |
| 2 | Tbsp. dry Sherry |
| 2 | ounces Parmesan cheese, grated |
| | Ground pepper to taste |

- Preheat oven to 375 degrees.
- Bring water to a boil in a saucepan. Add onion, garlic, celery leaves, bay leaf and peppercorns. Cover and boil 5 minutes.
- Add shrimp and simmer 4 minutes. Drain and reserve broth. Discard bay leaf.
- When shrimp have cooled, peel and devein.
- Drain spinach thoroughly and place in a buttered 2-quart casserole.
- Bring cream and reserved shrimp broth just to boiling point.
- At the same time, melt butter in a saucepan. Add flour, whisking until well blended. Add shrimp mixture to roux all at once, whisking thoroughly until sauce is thick and smooth.
- Add Sherry, half of cheese and shrimp. Season with pepper. Pour on top of spinach. Sprinkle with remaining cheese.
- Bake at 375 degrees until top is brown and bubbly, about 20 minutes.

*May be prepared ahead, refrigerated and baked at 325 degrees for 40 minutes or until browned.*

# CRABS FOR A FEAST

Serves 6

| | |
|---|---|
| 12-18 | crabs |
| 6 | quarts water |
| ⅓ | cup salt or seafood seasoning |

- Place *live* crabs in seasoned boiling water. Cover and return to boiling point.
- Reduce heat and simmer 12-15 minutes. Remove and rinse; cool slightly. Gather your guests around a newspaper-covered table. Let everyone begin picking their own crabs; be sure to supply plenty of paper napkins.
- To steam, place live crabs on a rack in a steamer over 2 cups water or beer. Steam 12-15 minutes.

# CRABMEAT EASTERN SHORE

Serves 6-8

| | |
|---|---|
| 1 | cup mayonnaise |
| 1½ | cups heavy cream |
| 4 | ounces sharp Cheddar cheese, grated |
| 2 | Tbsp. Durkee Famous Sauce |
| 2 | hard-boiled eggs, chopped |
| 2 | cups cooked rice |
| 1 | Tbsp. Worcestershire sauce |
| ½ | tsp. Tabasco sauce |
| 1 | Tbsp. lemon juice |
| 1 | Tbsp. grated onion |
| | Parsley, chopped |
| 1 | pound backfin crabmeat |

- Preheat oven to 350 degrees.
- Combine all ingredients except crab, then fold in crab.
- Place in a 13 × 9-inch casserole.
- Bake at 350 degrees for 45 minutes.

# HAMPTON CRAB

Serves 4

| | |
|---|---|
| 4 | slices white bread, crusts removed |
| | Milk |
| 1 | pound backfin crabmeat |
| ¼ | pound butter, melted |
| 1 | boiled egg, chopped |
| ½ | cup mayonnaise |
| 3 | Tbsp. finely chopped parsley |
| | Salt to taste |
| | White pepper to taste |
| 1 | tsp. Worcestershire sauce |
| | Buttered bread crumbs |

- Preheat oven to 350 degrees.
- Cover the bottom of a casserole with bread. Cover with milk. Allow to soften, then mash.
- Mix remaining ingredients, except bread crumbs. Add to milk-bread mixture; blend.
- Cover with buttered crumbs.
- Bake at 350 degrees for 20-30 minutes or until bubbly.

*May be spooned over Smithfield Ham slices for an elegant luncheon entrée.*

# CRABMEAT IMPERIAL

Serves 4

| | |
|---|---|
| ½ | cup chopped green pepper |
| 1 | Tbsp. butter |
| ½ | tsp. salt |
| ¼ | tsp. ground black pepper |
| ¼ | tsp. dry mustard |
| 1 | tsp. Worcestershire sauce |
| ¼ | cup mayonnaise |
| 1 | pound backfin crabmeat |
| ⅓ | cup chopped pimiento |
| ⅔ | cup crushed herb seasoned stuffing |
| 2 | Tbsp. butter, melted |
| ½ | tsp. paprika |

- Preheat oven to 350 degrees.
- Sauté green pepper in butter for 1 minute, then mix in salt, pepper, mustard, Worcestershire sauce and mayonnaise.
- Flake crabmeat and add to mixture. Turn into a buttered 1-quart casserole.
- Combine remaining ingredients and sprinkle over top.
- Bake at 350 degrees for 30 minutes.
- Serve immediately.

# COMPANY CRAB CAKES

Serves 4

| | |
|---|---|
| 1 | pound backfin crabmeat |
| 1 | egg |
| 1 | tsp. salt |
| 1 | Tbsp. Worcestershire sauce |
| 1½ | tsp. chopped fresh parsley |
| 1 | Tbsp. baking powder |
| 1 | Tbsp. mayonnaise |
| 1 | Tbsp. butter, melted |
| | Dash Tabasco sauce |
| 6 | crackers, crumbled |

- Mix all ingredients except crackers with crabmeat, being careful not to break up lumps of crab. Shape into cakes. Roll in cracker crumbs.
- Fry in butter until golden brown and cooked through.

# BLUE CRAB CASSEROLE

Serves 8-10

| | |
|---|---|
| 2 | pounds backfin crabmeat |
| 2 | eggs, beaten |
| 1 | hard-boiled egg, mashed into a paste |
| ¼ | cup mayonnaise |
| 3 | slices stale bread, finely crumbled |
| 3 | Tbsp. minced pimiento |
| 3 | Tbsp. minced green pepper, parboiled 5 minutes |
| 2 | Tbsp. minced parsley |
| ¼ | cup Worcestershire sauce |
| | Salt and pepper to taste |
| 2 | Tbsp. butter, melted |
| 2 | Tbsp. dry white wine |

- Preheat oven to 350 degrees.
- Save largest lumps of crab for topping. Mix rest of crab with remaining ingredients. Blend well.
- Pile mixture into 8 buttered baking shells, partially flattening tops and pressing lumps into mixture.

**SAUCE**

| | |
|---|---|
| ½ | cup mayonnaise |
| | Heavy cream |
| | Paprika |

- Thin mayonnaise with a little cream and pour over each shell, allowing it to run down sides.
- Sprinkle with paprika and bake at 350 degrees for 15 minutes or until browned.

# TIDEWATER CRAB CAKES

Serves 4

| | |
|---|---|
| 1 | pound backfin crabmeat |
| 2 | eggs, beaten |
| ¼ | cup finely chopped onion |
| ½ | cup cracker crumbs |
| 3 | Tbsp. mayonnaise |
| 1 | Tbsp. prepared mustard |

- Gently mix all ingredients.
- Shape into cakes and sauté in butter until brown.
- Serve immediately.

# HEARTY CRAB

Serves 4-6

| | |
|---|---|
| 1½ | pounds backfin crabmeat |
| 4 | shallots, finely chopped |
| 4 | tender celery stalks, finely chopped |
| 8 | ounces mushrooms, sliced |
| 4 | Tbsp. butter |
| 2 | Tbsp. flour |
| 1 | cup milk |
| ¼ | cup dry Sherry |
| 2 | Tbsp. fresh lemon juice |
| 2 | tsp. Worcestershire sauce |
| | Dash red pepper |
| 2 | Tbsp. chopped fresh parsley |
| 1 | tsp. chicken bouillon granules |
| 8 | ounces Swiss cheese, grated |
| | Parmesan cheese |
| | Dried bread crumbs |

- Preheat oven to 325 degrees.
- Place crab in a well buttered 2-quart baking dish.
- Cook shallots, celery and mushrooms in butter. Stir in flour and add milk and Sherry. Bring to a boil and add lemon juice, Worcestershire sauce, pepper, parsley and bouillon.
- Remove from heat and stir in Swiss cheese until melted. Pour over crab. Cover top with Parmesan cheese and bread crumbs.
- Bake at 325 degrees for 30 minutes until bubbly.

# DEVILED CRAB

Serves 4-6

| | |
|---|---|
| ⅓ | cup mayonnaise |
| ⅓ | cup Durkee Famous Sauce |
| 1 | tsp. seasoned salt |
| ¼ | tsp. hot sauce |
| 1 | pound backfin crabmeat |
| | Seasoned bread crumbs |

- Preheat oven to 350 degrees.
- Mix first 4 ingredients. Fold in crabmeat.
- Fill individual shells with mixture. Sprinkle with seasoned bread crumbs.
- Bake at 350 degrees for 30 minutes.

# WILD CRAB CASSEROLE

Serves 6

| | |
|---|---|
| 1 | cup raw wild rice, cooked or ½ cup wild rice and ½ cup brown rice |
| ½ | pound butter |
| 1½ | cups chopped celery |
| 1 | cup chopped onions |
| 1 | cup chopped mushrooms |
| 1 | tsp. thyme |
| | Salt and pepper to taste |
| 3 | shallots, chopped |
| 2 | cloves garlic, minced |
| ½ | cup flour |
| 4 | cups light cream |
| 2 | egg yolks, beaten |
| 1 | cup grated Parmesan cheese |
| 1½ | pounds backfin crabmeat |

- Preheat oven to 425 degrees.
- Melt half of butter; add celery, onions and mushrooms. Brown slightly, adding thyme and seasonings to taste. Pour over cooked rice and mix. Place in a large oven-proof dish and set aside.
- Melt remaining butter, add shallots and garlic. Add flour and stir well. Add cream slowly. Remove from heat, stir in egg yolks and half of cheese. Beat well until smooth.
- Place crabmeat on top of rice. Pour sauce over crab and sprinkle with remaining cheese.
- Bake at 425 degrees until cheese browns and sauce bubbles.

# BROILED SCALLOPS

Serves 2
Do ahead

| | |
|---|---|
| ¼ | cup lemon juice |
| ¼ | cup dry Vermouth |
| 1 | clove garlic, crushed |
| ½ | tsp. salt |
| ¼ | tsp. pepper |
| ¼ | cup vegetable oil |
| 2 | Tbsp. chopped fresh parsley |
| 1 | pound scallops |
| 8 | ounces fresh mushroom caps |

- Mix first 7 ingredients in a bowl. Add scallops and mushrooms, marinating at least 1 hour.
- Remove scallops and mushrooms. Place on foil-lined shallow baking pan. Broil 8-10 minutes, 4-5 inches from heat, turning once.
- Scallops may be cooked in foil pouch on grill.

*Wonderful served with Tomatoes Rockefeller.*

## SAVORY SCALLOPS

Serves 4-6

¼  cup extra virgin olive oil
2  medium shallots, finely chopped
3  large tomatoes, peeled, seeded and chopped
⅔  cup dry white wine
1  tsp. chopped fresh basil
1  tsp. chopped fresh rosemary
1  Tbsp. finely chopped fresh parsley
1  clove garlic, finely minced
¼  tsp. salt
   Pinch freshly ground pepper
2  pounds scallops
1  Tbsp. flour
2  Tbsp. chopped parsley for garnish

- Heat 2 Tbsp. of oil in skillet over medium heat. Add shallots and sauté 3 minutes or until soft. Add tomatoes, wine, herbs and garlic. Simmer 5 minutes or until slightly reduced. Add salt and pepper. Set aside.
- Pat scallops dry. Sprinkle with flour, shaking off excess. Heat remaining oil in large skillet.
- Add scallops and sauté over medium-high heat for about 2 minutes per side in single layer.
- Spoon scallops onto serving plate and pour on sauce.

*Either bay or sea scallops may be used; if using sea scallops, remove small white muscle on side of each scallop.*

## SCALLOPS IN WINE AND CHEESE

Serves 4

1½  pounds sea scallops, halved
½  cup dry white wine
½  tsp. salt
1  bay leaf, crushed
1  small onion, minced
3  Tbsp. butter
3  Tbsp. flour
1  cup reserved broth
½  cup heavy cream
1  cup grated Cheddar cheese

- Preheat oven to 350 degrees.
- In saucepan, combine first five ingredients. Bring to a boil. Reduce heat and simmer covered for 5 minutes.
- Remove and reserve scallops. Strain and reserve *the broth*.
- In saucepan, melt butter and add flour. Stir and add reserved broth and cream. Stir until sauce is thickened; add cheese and stir until melted.
- Add scallops and bake uncovered at 350 degrees for 20 minutes in a 2-quart casserole.

# FISHERMAN'S CATCH

Serves 6-8

| | |
|---|---|
| 1 | pound scallops |
| 1 | pound shrimp, cooked, peeled and deveined |
| 1 | pound backfin crabmeat |
| ¼ | pound butter |
| 8 | Tbsp. flour |
| | Salt and pepper to taste |
| 3 | cups milk |
| 2 | Tbsp. chopped fresh parsley |
| 3 | Tbsp. Worcestershire sauce |
| 6 | Tbsp. lemon juice |
| 1 | cup bread crumbs |

- Preheat oven to 350 degrees.
- Place scallops in colander and pour 1 teakettle of boiling water over them. Drain.
- Mix scallops, shrimp and crabmeat and set aside.
- Melt butter over low heat, adding flour, salt and pepper. Add milk slowly, whisking rapidly to prevent lumps. Stir in remaining ingredients except breadcrumbs.
- Pour sauce over seafood; mix well. Pour mixture into buttered 3-quart casserole. Top with bread crumbs if desired.
- Bake at 350 degrees for 30-40 minutes or until hot and bubbly.
- Serve over long grain rice.

# NEPTUNE'S DELIGHT

Serves 6

| | |
|---|---|
| 3 | Tbsp. butter |
| ¼ | cup flour |
| 2 | cups heavy cream |
| 2 | ounces Parmesan cheese, grated |
| 2 | Tbsp. Sherry |
| ½ | tsp. paprika |
| 2 | cups backfin crabmeat |
| 1 | cup cooked, peeled and deveined shrimp |
| 1½ | cups onion-garlic croutons |
| ¼ | cup parsley sprigs |
| 4 | Tbsp. butter, melted |

- Preheat oven to 350 degrees.
- Melt butter in a pan. Remove from heat and whisk in flour. Add 1½ cups of cream; whisk well. Return to heat and add cheese, continuing to stir until creamy.
- Remove from heat, adding remaining cream. Stir in Sherry, paprika and seafood. Spoon into 6 large shell-shaped baking dishes.
- In food processor, blend croutons and parsley. Sprinkle over seafood mixture. Top with melted butter. Refrigerate until needed.
- Bake at 350 degrees for 20 minutes or until top is browned and bubbly.
- Serve accompanied by a green salad.

# WATERSIDE MEDLEY

Serves 4-6

| | |
|---|---|
| 1 | 10-ounce package frozen puff pastry patty shells |
| 1 | pound scallops, liquid reserved |
| 1 | cup dry white wine |
| 1 | small onion, sliced |
| 1 | Tbsp. chopped parsley |
| 2 | Tbsp. lemon juice |
| ½ | tsp. salt |
| 4 | Tbsp. butter |
| 6 | Tbsp. flour |
| 1 | cup light cream |
| 1 | cup reserved scallop liquid |
| 2 | ounces Gruyère or Swiss cheese, grated |
| | Dash pepper |
| 8 | ounces backfin crabmeat |
| 8 | ounces small shrimp |
| 1½ | cups sliced mushrooms |
| ½ | cup bread crumbs |

- Preheat oven to 350 degrees.
- Prepare pastry according to package directions; while baking, prepare filling.
- Combine first 6 ingredients in a pan and bring to a boil. Reduce heat and simmer 5 minutes. If necessary, reduce the cooking liquid to measure 1 cup. Reserve.
- In a medium saucepan, melt butter; stir in flour. Whisk cream in slowly to prevent lumps. Add scallop liquid, stirring over medium heat until sauce thickens.
- Remove sauce from heat. Stir in cheese and pepper. Add scallop mixture, crabmeat, shrimp and mushrooms.
- Pour into 1½-quart casserole; blend well. Top with bread crumbs.
- Bake at 350 degrees for 25 minutes; serve in patty shells.

*A light and savory luncheon dish.*

# SHAD ROE WITH ASPARAGUS

Serves 10

| | |
|---|---|
| 5 | pairs shad roe, separated |
| 10 | tsp. butter |
| 10 | tsp. dry white wine |
| 10 | tsp. fresh lemon juice |
| 2½ | tsp. chopped fresh tarragon |
| | Salt and freshly ground pepper |
| ¼ | pound butter, melted |
| | Juice of 1 medium lemon |
| 30 | asparagus spears (about 1½ pounds), stalks snapped at natural breaking point |
| | Vegetable oil for frying |
| 10 | lemon wedges for garnish |

- Center each half on right side of 12 × 12-inch square of waxed paper. Dot with 1 teaspoon butter and drizzle with 1 teaspoon wine and 1 teaspoon lemon juice. Sprinkle with ¼ teaspoon tarragon. Season with salt and pepper.
- Fold paper over and roll up edges to seal. Repeat with remaining halves. (Can be prepared up to 2 hours ahead to this point.)
- Blend melted butter and lemon juice. Cook asparagus in boiling salted water until crisp-tender.
- Meanwhile, pour oil into large skillet to depth of ¼ inch. Heat oil over medium heat. Add roe packages in batches and cook until paper is browned, about 4 minutes on each side.
- Keep roe warm in packages in preheated oven set at lowest temperature.
- Drain asparagus and pat dry. Unwrap roe and transfer to individual heated plates. Arrange 3 asparagus stalks on side of each roe. Drizzle lemon butter over asparagus. Garnish with lemon wedges and serve.

# ZESTY SCALLOPED OYSTERS

Serves 4

| | |
|---|---|
| ½ | cup bread crumbs |
| 1 | cup cracker crumbs |
| ¼ | pound butter, melted |
| 1 | pint oysters |
| ½ | tsp. salt |
| ¼ | tsp. pepper |
| | Dash cayenne pepper |
| | Dash mace or nutmeg |

- Preheat oven to 375 degrees.
- Mix first 3 ingredients and separate into thirds. Place first layer of crumbs in buttered 2-quart baking dish. Cover with half of the oysters. Sprinkle with seasonings.
- Add next layer of crumbs, then oysters. Sprinkle with additional spices if desired.
- Top with remaining crumbs.
- Bake at 375 degrees for 30 minutes.

# SCALLOPED OYSTERS

Serves 4

| | |
|---|---|
| 2 | Tbsp. chopped onion |
| ¼ | pound butter |
| 1 | tsp. celery salt |
| | Dash pepper |
| 1 | Tbsp. lemon juice |
| 1 | Tbsp. Worcestershire sauce |
| 1 | Tbsp. parsley flakes |
| 2 | cups cracker crumbs (rolled saltines) |
| 1 | quart oysters, liquor reserved |
| ½ | cup light cream |
| ½ | cup milk |

- Preheat oven to 400 degrees.
- Sauté onions in butter; add seasonings, then crumbs, mixing well.
- Beginning and ending with crumb mixture, layer crumbs 3 times and oysters 2 times in a 2-quart buttered casserole.
- Mix oyster liquor, milk and cream and pour over top.
- Bake at 400 degrees for 30 minutes.

# GRANNY'S DIPPING SAUCE

Yields 3 cups

| | |
|---|---|
| 7 | ounces ketchup |
| 6 | ounces chili sauce |
| 2 | Tbsp. mayonnaise |
| 2 | small white onions, finely chopped |
| ½ | green pepper, finely chopped |
| | Juice of ½ lemon |
| 1½ | tsp. horseradish or to taste |
| | Dash Worcestershire sauce |
| | Dash Tabasco sauce |
| | Salt and pepper to taste |

- Mix all ingredients, seasoning to taste.
- Serve with oysters or other seafood.

# LYNNHAVEN OYSTERS AND WILD RICE

Serves 10-12

| | |
|---|---|
| 1 | **6-ounce box long grain and wild rice, cooked** |
| ¼ | **pound butter, melted** |
| 4 | **dozen oysters, well-drained** |
| | **Salt and pepper to taste** |
| | **Dash Tabasco sauce** |
| | **Sprinkle of celery seed** |
| 1 | **cup heavy cream** |
| 2 | **chicken bouillon cubes, dissolved in ¼ cup hot water** |
| 1 | **cup light cream** |
| 1 | **medium onion, finely chopped** |
| ¾ | **tsp. thyme** |
| 1 | **Tbsp. curry powder, or to taste** |
| | **Fresh chopped parsley** |

- Preheat oven to 300 degrees.
- Toss rice and butter until thoroughly mixed. Place half of rice in bottom of 13 × 9-inch baking dish. Layer oysters on top of rice and season with salt, pepper and Tabasco sauce. Top with remaining rice.
- In heavy pan, add celery seed to heavy cream and heat; pour in chicken bouillon. Stir, then add light cream.
- Remove pan from heat and add remaining ingredients. Pour over casserole.
- Bake at 300 degrees for 45 minutes.
- Garnish with chopped parsley.

*First part of recipe, up to heating the cream, may be prepared early in the day and refrigerated. Sauce must be warm when added to the casserole prior to baking.*

# COCKTAIL SAUCE

Yields 1¼ cups

| | |
|---|---|
| 1 | **cup mayonnaise** |
| ¼ | **cup chili sauce** |
| 1 | **tsp. lemon juice** |
| 1 | **tsp. curry powder** |
| ½ | **tsp. finely minced onion** |
| ½ | **tsp. Worcestershire sauce** |
| ½ | **tsp. Tabasco sauce** |
| | **Salt and pepper to taste** |

- Combine all ingredients, mixing well. Refrigerate until ready to use.
- Good dipping sauce for seafood or raw vegetables.

# SALADS

# SALADS

## ENTRÉE
Avocado Stuffed with
    Crabmeat  208
Chicken Salad Pie  215
Chinese Chicken  217
Cold Chicken and
    Pasta  216
Crab Delight  212
Crab-Stuffed Artichokes  217
Curried Chicken Salad  214
Garnished Chicken and
    Grape Salad  207
Ham and Pasta  213
Hot Potuna  218
Mandarin Salad  212
Sail Along Salad  213
Salad Olé  209
Sea Shell Shrimp  211
Spicy Lemon Shrimp  210
Sumptuous Seafood  209
Surfside Salad  207
Tropical Tostada  215
Tuna Louis  211
Zesty Seafood Salad  208

## FRUIT
Black Cherry Ring  220
Cottage Pineapple  218
Cranberry Freeze  219
Frozen Fruit Basket  220
Mandarin Delight  221
Pineapple Dream  219
Spiced Peach Salad  221
Sunburst Salad  219
Sunset Salad  221

## VEGETABLE
Admiral's Egg Salad  231
Cold Potato and Green Bean
    Salad  234
Creamy Asparagus Ring  230
Dilly Tomato Aspic  226
Dockside Potato Salad  224
Festive Asparagus Salad  228
Fresh Mushroom Salad  232
Fresh Vegetable
    Marinade  228
"Gardens-by-the-Sea"
    Salad  233
Gazpacho Aspic  222
Gazpacho Salad  223
German Potato Salad  224
Golden Carrot Salad  229
Marinated Sliced
    Tomatoes  223
Mousse aux
    Concombres  233
Overnight Cabbage Slaw  226
Pineapple-Cabbage
    Slaw  222
Shrimp and Tomato
    Aspic  227
Spinach Ring  232
Tomato Aspic  231
Vegetable Pasta Salad  230
Very, Very Vegetable  229

## GREEN
Caesar Salad  225
Dig Deep  236
Fall Salad  236
Spinach Salad Supreme  238
Tropical Salad  225
Winter Salad  237

## DRESSINGS
Celery Seed Dressing  220
Country Dressing  234
Creamy French Dressing  239
Curry Dressing for Fruit  235
Dieter's Cucumber
    Dressing  235
French Dressing  240
German French
    Dressing  238
Glazed French Dressing  237
Honey-Nut Dressing  240
Mud Salad Dressing  235
Poppy Seed Dressing  214
Seaside Salad Dressing  216
Topopo Salad Dressing  240

# GARNISHED CHICKEN AND GRAPE SALAD    Serves 6

| | |
|---|---|
| 3 | cups diced, cooked chicken breast |
| 1 | cup diced green pepper |
| ½ | cup chopped celery |
| 2 | cups seedless green grapes, halved |
| ⅓ | cup mayonnaise |
| ⅓ | cup sour cream |
| 2 | Tbsp. lemon juice |
| 1 | tsp. salt |
| ¼ | tsp. pepper |

**GARNISH**

| | |
|---|---|
| | Lettuce leaves |
| 3 | ounces slivered almonds, toasted |
| 2 | hard-boiled eggs, sliced |
| 1 | large tomato, cut into wedges |

- Combine all ingredients in large bowl. Mix well. Cover and refrigerate at least 1 hour.
- Serve on lettuce leaves. Top with almonds. Arrange eggs and tomatoes around salad.

# SURFSIDE SALAD    Serves 6
Do ahead

| | |
|---|---|
| 1 | pound backfin crabmeat |
| ¼ | cup tarragon vinegar |
| 3 | Tbsp. drained and chopped pimiento |
| 2 | Tbsp. snipped chives |
| 2 | Tbsp. sweet pickle relish |
| ½ | cup mayonnaise |
| | Salt and pepper to taste |
| 6 | cleaned crab shells or lettuce |
| | Capers |
| | Pimiento to garnish |

- Pick over crabmeat and discard any shell; marinate in vinegar for 15 minutes.
- Drain crabmeat; add pimiento, chives, relish, mayonnaise, and salt and pepper.
- Divide mixture evenly into cleaned crab shells or crisp lettuce cups, shaping into domes.
- Sprinkle some well drained capers over the top of dome and garnish with pimiento. Serve very cold.

*Great as an appetizer.*

# AVOCADO STUFFED WITH CRABMEAT

Serves 2

½ pound backfin crabmeat
Mayonnaise to hold crab together
1 Tbsp. capers
1 avocado, peeled, halved and seeded
1 Tbsp. grated Parmesan cheese
1 tsp. bread crumbs

- Preheat oven to 350 degrees.
- Mix crabmeat, capers and mayonnaise. Fill avocado halves.
- Sprinkle with cheese and bread crumbs.
- Bake at 350 degrees for 20 minutes.

# ZESTY SEAFOOD SALAD

Serves 6-8
Do ahead

1 cup mayonnaise
½ cup chili sauce
2 Tbsp. French dressing
2 Tbsp. capers
1 Tbsp. minced onion
1 Tbsp. lemon juice
2 tsp. horseradish
1 tsp. seasoned salt
¾ tsp. salt
½ tsp. Worcestershire sauce
Pinch of pepper
1 pound crabmeat, flaked
1 pound large shrimp, cooked, peeled and deveined
Tomato wedges

- Combine ingredients except crabmeat, shrimp and tomatoes. Mix until well blended.
- Pour over crabmeat and shrimp. Cover and chill 2 to 3 hours. Serve on lettuce leaves with tomatoes for garnish.

# SUMPTUOUS SEAFOOD

Serves 6-8

| | |
|---|---|
| ¼ | cup olive oil |
| 12 | scallions, green tops included, thinly sliced |
| 1 | tsp. saffron (optional) |
| ½-1 | tsp. salt |
| 2 | cups uncooked rice |
| 4 | cups chicken stock |
| 1 | pound medium shrimp, peeled and deveined |
| ½ | pound salami or pepperoni, sliced thin and cut into small pieces |
| 1 | green pepper, cut into thin strips |
| 1 | red pepper, cut into thin strips |
| ½ | cup chopped parsley |
| | Salt and pepper |

- Heat oil in heavy pot on medium heat. Add scallions and sauté for 5 minutes or until wilted. Add saffron and cook 2 minutes.
- Add rice and stir, coating grains with oil. Add salt and chicken stock and stir. Bring to a simmer, cover and cook 20 minutes or until liquid is absorbed. Fluff with fork and let cool slightly.
- Bring 2 quarts of water to boil; add shrimp. Immediately remove from heat, cover and let stand for 2 minutes. Drain.
- Place rice in large bowl. Add shrimp, sausage, peppers, parsley, salt and pepper and toss well.
- If prepared ahead, bring to room temperature before serving.

# SALAD OLÉ

Serves 8-10

| | |
|---|---|
| 1 | head lettuce |
| 1 | medium onion, chopped |
| 2 | tomatoes, chopped |
| 1 | small can green chilies, drained and chopped |
| 1 | cup grated sharp Cheddar cheese |
| 1 | pound ground beef |
| 1 | package taco seasoning |
| ½ | cup mild taco sauce |
| ½ | cup red wine vinegar and oil dressing |
| 6 | ounces nacho chips, broken |

- Tear lettuce and place in bottom of large salad bowl. Layer with onion, tomatoes, green chilies and cheese.
- Sauté beef and drain. Add taco seasoning, following package directions using only ⅔ the amount of water.
- Mix taco sauce with dressing and blend well. Add beef, mix well.
- Place beef mixture in salad bowl. Sprinkle chips over beef and toss. Serve warm or chilled.

# SPICY LEMON SHRIMP

Serves 4-6
Do ahead

| | |
|---|---|
| 1 | pound shrimp, peeled and deveined, with tails left intact |
| 1 | cup water |
| 1 | cup dry white wine |
| 1 | bay leaf |
| 1 | small red bell pepper, seeded and thinly sliced |
| 1 | small red onion, thinly sliced |
| ½ | cup drained and halved black olives |
| 1 | lemon, thinly sliced |

- Combine water, wine and bay leaf in 2-quart saucepan and bring to a boil. Add shrimp; reduce heat and cook 3-5 minutes or until pink on the outside and just cooked in the center. Remove with a slotted spoon to a bowl.
- Simmer red pepper in shrimp liquid for 1 minute over medium heat. Remove and drain. Add to bowl of shrimp.
- Add onions, olives and lemon.

## MARINADE

| | |
|---|---|
| ½ | cup lemon juice |
| ½ | cup olive oil |
| 1 | Tbsp. red wine vinegar |
| 1 | medium clove garlic, minced |
| 1 | Tbsp. dry mustard |
| ¼ | tsp. cayenne pepper |
| ½ | tsp. salt |
| ⅛ | tsp. pepper, coarsely cracked |
| 1 | Tbsp. finely chopped parsley |

- In separate bowl, combine ingredients and pour over shrimp mixture. Refrigerate for 4 hours or more.
- Drain shrimp, retaining a little of the marinade.
- Serve over lettuce, pouring a small amount of marinade over shrimp.

# SEA SHELL SHRIMP

Serves 6-8

| | |
|---|---|
| 1 | 8-ounce package green sea shell pasta |
| 1½ | pounds shrimp |
| 1 | bay leaf |
| 1 | Tbsp. onion flakes |
| ¼ | tsp. cayenne pepper |
| ½ | pound snow peas |
| 3 | navel oranges |
| 3-5 | green onions |
| 2 | Tbsp. grated Parmesan cheese |
| | Fresh chopped parsley |
| | Italian dressing to taste |
| | Salt and pepper to taste |
| | Sesame seeds |

- Cook pasta according to package directions; drain and rinse in cold water.
- Boil shrimp with bay leaf, onion flakes and cayenne pepper until just pink, about 3 minutes. Peel and devein.
- Blanch snow peas in small amount of water until barely tender.
- Cut oranges, onions, snow peas and shrimp into bite-size pieces.
- Place all in large bowl with pasta. Sprinkle with cheese and parsley. Add dressing, salt and pepper to taste. Chill.
- Garnish with sesame seeds.
- For best flavor, allow to come to room temperature before serving.

# TUNA LOUIS

Serves 4

| | |
|---|---|
| ⅔ | cup mayonnaise |
| ⅓ | cup ketchup |
| 2 | Tbsp. lemon juice |
| 1 | Tbsp. dry mustard |
| 1 | Tbsp. grated onion |
| ¼ | cup chopped stuffed green olives |
| 1 | Tbsp. capers |
| 1-2 | heads Boston lettuce |
| 1 | 12½-ounce can tuna, chilled |
| | Parsley sprigs |

- Combine first 7 ingredients to make sauce. Chill.
- Break lettuce onto salad plates.
- Drain tuna and spread over lettuce. Spoon sauce over tuna and garnish with parsley sprigs.

*Serve with Popovers Deluxe for an easy summer supper.*

# MANDARIN SALAD

Serves 4-6

4    ounces egg noodles,
     cooked and drained
2    cucumbers, peeled,
     seeded and slivered
2    stalks celery, slivered
2    carrots, scraped and
     slivered
1-2  green peppers, slivered
4    eggs, beaten
2-3  chicken breasts, cooked
     and shredded
1    cup ham, slivered

- Pat dry all slivered vegetables.
- Cook eggs as you would a crépe. Allow to cool and sliver.
- Arrange all ingredients on a platter in layers in the order listed, forming a pyramid.

**SAUCE**

2    stalks green onion,
     peeled and minced
2    cloves garlic, minced
4    Tbsp. soy sauce
2    tsp. crushed red pepper
½    tsp. seasoned salt
⅔    cup sugar
½    cup white vinegar
4    Tbsp. sesame oil
     Dash of salt

- Combine all ingredients in a glass jar and shake well.
- Pour about half of the sauce over salad immediately before serving and provide remainder in a bowl at the table for anyone who wants additional sauce.

# CRAB DELIGHT

Serves 6

1    pound backfin crabmeat
½    cup mayonnaise
1    cup chopped celery
2    Tbsp. chopped onion
2    Tbsp. chopped sweet
     pickle
1    Tbsp. vinegar
½    tsp. salt
     Dash of pepper

- Mix all ingredients. Cover and refrigerate.
- Serve on lettuce.

# SAIL ALONG SALAD

Serves 6-8
Do ahead

3-4 cups cooked rice
1 8-ounce can pineapple chunks, liquid reserved
1 cup mayonnaise
1 tsp. prepared mustard
½ tsp. salt
½ cup chopped green pepper
¼ cup sliced green onion
1 pound ham, diced
1 cup shredded Swiss cheese
Slivered almonds

- Place rice in large bowl.
- Pour pineapple liquid into small bowl. Beat in mayonnaise, mustard and salt.
- To rice, add pineapple, peppers, onions and ham. Add dressing and mix. Add cheese. Toss lightly. Chill 1 hour. Top with almonds.

*Easy to take to the beach or on a boat trip.*

# HAM AND PASTA

Serves 8
Do ahead

8 ounces pasta shells, cooked and drained
4 ounces boiled ham, cut into strips
½ cup chopped black olives
1 large ripe tomato, diced
1 small green pepper, chopped
½ tsp. basil
½ cup mayonnalse
2 Tbsp. vinegar
Seasoned salt to taste
Freshly ground pepper to taste

- Mix all ingredients and chill.

# CURRIED CHICKEN SALAD

Serves 6
Do ahead

| | |
|---|---|
| 1 | cup diced, peeled cucumber |
| | Vinegar to cover cucumber |
| | Salt |
| 3 | cups diced, cooked chicken breast |
| 1½ | cups diced, cooked red potatoes |
| ½ | cup diced celery |
| 1 | tsp. chopped chives |
| 1 | tsp. chopped parsley |
| ½ | tsp. lemon herb seasoning salt |

• Marinate cucumber in vinegar and a little salt overnight.
• Drain cucumber well and combine with remaining ingredients in a large bowl.

**CURRY MAYONNAISE**

| | |
|---|---|
| 1 | cup mayonnaise |
| 2 | Tbsp. chutney |
| 1 | garlic clove, mashed |
| 1 | Tbsp. lime juice |
| 1 | tsp. honey |
| ½ | tsp. curry powder |
| ¼ | tsp. ginger |

• Combine ingredients and mix with salad. Chill.

# POPPY SEED DRESSING

Yields 1½ cups

| | |
|---|---|
| ½-¾ | cups sugar |
| 1 | tsp. dry mustard |
| 1 | tsp. salt |
| | Onion juice, or grated onion, to taste |
| 5 | Tbsp. vinegar |
| 1 | cup vegetable oil |
| 1½ | Tbsp. lemon juice |
| 3 | Tbsp. poppy seeds |

• Mix sugar, mustard, salt, onion, and 2 Tablespoons vinegar.
• Add oil slowly in thin stream, constantly beating with electric mixer. Add lemon juice and remaining vinegar and beat until thick. Stir in poppy seeds.
• Store in refrigerator; serve at room temperature.

# TROPICAL TOSTADA

Serves 4

| | |
|---|---|
| 1 | 20-ounce can crushed pineapple, drained |
| 4 | chicken breasts, cooked and cubed |
| ½ | cup mayonnaise |
| ½ | cup sour cream |
| ¼ | cup chopped green onion |
| 3 | Tbsp. diced green chilies |
| 1 | tsp. ground cumin |
| 4 | flour tortillas, fried |
| | Lettuce leaves, shredded |

**GARNISHES**
Diced tomatoes
Diced avocado
Sliced chili peppers

- Combine pineapple and chicken.
- Mix remaining ingredients except tortillas and lettuce and toss with chicken mixture.
- Top each tortilla with lettuce. Spoon chicken mixture on lettuce. Top with garnishes.

# CHICKEN SALAD PIE

Serves 8

| | |
|---|---|
| 2 | cups diced, cooked chicken |
| ¾ | cup shredded Cheddar cheese |
| ½ | cup diced celery |
| ½ | cup drained crushed pineapple |
| ⅓ | cup slivered almonds, toasted |
| ½ | tsp. paprika |
| ½ | tsp. salt |
| ¾ | cup mayonnaise (divided) |
| 1 | 9-inch baked pie shell |
| ½ | cup heavy cream, whipped |
| ½ | cup grated carrot |

- Combine first 7 ingredients with ½ cup mayonnaise. Toss well. Spoon into pie shell.
- Fold ¼ cup mayonnaise into whipped cream. Spread over chicken mixture.
- Sprinkle grated carrots around edge. Chill.

# COLD CHICKEN AND PASTA

Serves 6-8
Do ahead

| | |
|---|---|
| 4-6 | chicken breasts |
| 2 | chicken bouillon cubes |
| 2-2½ | cups water |
| ¼ | cup chopped onion |
| 6 | ounces vermicelli |
| 1 | 14-ounce can plain artichoke hearts, halved |
| 1 | pint cherry tomatoes, halved |

- Dissolve bouillon cubes in water. Simmer chicken and onion in bouillon until done, about 45 minutes. Strain and reserve broth. Remove chicken; allow to cool and chop coarsely.
- Break vermicelli into 2-inch pieces. Add enough water to broth to cook pasta according to package instructions.

## DRESSING

| | |
|---|---|
| 1½ | Tbsp. grated onion |
| ⅓ | cup oil |
| 3 | Tbsp. red wine vinegar |
| 3 | Tbsp. lemon juice |
| 1½ | Tbsp. sugar |
| 1½ | tsp. seasoned salt |
| 1½ | tsp. dried basil, crushed |

- Combine all ingredients and mix well.
- When vermicelli is done, drain thoroughly and mix with chicken and dressing. Add artichoke hearts and toss.
- Refrigerate at least 2 hours.
- To serve, add tomatoes and toss.

# SEASIDE SALAD DRESSING

Yields 1 quart

| | |
|---|---|
| ½-¾ | cup sugar |
| 1 | Tbsp. prepared mustard |
| 1 | Tbsp. salt |
| 1 | Tbsp. sweet basil |
| 1 | Tbsp. marjoram |
| 4 | cloves garlic, finely chopped |
| 1½ | cups salad oil |
| 1½ | cups white vinegar |

- Mix all ingredients well.
- Refrigerate until needed.

# CHINESE CHICKEN

Serves 4-6
Do ahead

| | |
|---|---|
| 3 | chicken breasts |
| 3 | slices fresh ginger |
| 4 | Tbsp. sugar |
| 2 | tsp. salt |
| 1 | tsp. seasoned salt |
| ½ | tsp. black pepper |
| 4 | Tbsp. white vinegar |
| ½ | cup salad oil |
| ½ | package Chinese rice sticks |
| 1 | medium package slivered almonds |
| 1 | 2½-ounce box sesame seeds |
| 1 | head lettuce |
| 3-6 | green onion stalks |

- The day before serving, cook chicken in water with ginger until done. Remove from heat and allow to cool in liquid, covered. When cool, remove chicken from bones and shred. Refrigerate overnight.
- Place sugar, salt, seasoned salt, pepper and vinegar in pan and cook over low heat for 10 minutes, stirring until all solids are dissolved. Do not boil. Allow to cool, add salad oil and store in refrigerator.
- Deep fry Chinese rice sticks in 2 inches of oil. Drain, cool and store in tight container.
- Toast almonds and sesame seeds in a dry skillet; store.
- To serve, shred lettuce. Slice onions lengthwise, add almonds, sesame seeds, chicken and dressing. Toss. Just before serving, add Chinese rice sticks and toss.

# CRAB-STUFFED ARTICHOKES

Serves 5

| | |
|---|---|
| 5 | fresh artichokes |
| 1 | pound backfin crabmeat |
| 4 | ounces Swiss cheese, shredded |
| ¼ | cup chopped green pepper |
| ¼ | cup finely chopped onion |
| 1 | tsp. salt |
| ½ | cup mayonnaise |
| 2 | tsp. lemon juice |

- Preheat oven to 375 degrees.
- Trim artichoke stems and cut off tips of leaves with scissors or a knife. Place artichokes, stemside down, in a Dutch oven with 1 inch water. Simmer 25-30 minutes. Drain and cool. Remove thistle center from the top. Set artichokes aside.
- Mix next 5 ingredients. Blend in mayonnaise and lemon juice. Toss.
- Fill artichokes with crab. Place in a shallow dish and add 1 inch of hot water. Cover.
- Bake at 375 degrees for 35 minutes or until cheese melts and bubbles.

# HOT POTUNA

Serves 4-6

6    slices bacon, cooked and crumbled
¼    cup sugar
6    Tbsp. vinegar
2    Tbsp. water
1    tsp. celery seed
1    egg, beaten
4    medium potatoes, cooked and coarsely chopped
¾    cup diced celery
1    medium onion, chopped
1    7-ounce can tuna, drained
     Salt and pepper to taste
     Seasoned salt to taste

• Preheat oven to 350 degrees.
• Pour off all but ¼ cup bacon drippings. Add sugar, vinegar, water and celery seed to skillet. Bring to a boil and simmer 5 minutes.
• Stir small amount of vinegar mixture into egg. Pour the egg mixture into the skillet; mix well and remove from heat.
• Pour mixture over potatoes, celery, onion and tuna; mix well. Season to taste.
• Place salad in a 1½-quart casserole and sprinkle with crumbled bacon.
• Bake at 350 degrees for 30 minutes. Serve warm or chilled.

# COTTAGE PINEAPPLE

Serves 12
Do ahead

1    6-ounce package lime gelatin
1    6-ounce package lemon gelatin
2    cups hot water
1    20-ounce can crushed pineapple, drained
16   ounces cottage cheese
1    cup mayonnise
1    cup heavy cream, whipped
½    cup chopped nuts

• Dissolve gelatin in hot water; chill until partially set.
• Add remaining ingredients in order listed; mix well. Refrigerate until firm.

*Delicious topped with a dressing of mayonnaise flavored with horseradish.*

# PINEAPPLE DREAM

Serves 6
Do ahead

| | |
|---|---|
| 1 | Tbsp. flour |
| ½ | cup sugar |
| 3 | eggs, beaten |
| 1 | 20-ounce can pineapple chunks in light syrup, liquid reserved |
| ¼ | pound butter |
| 1-2 | bananas, sliced |
| | Lettuce leaves |

- Combine flour and sugar with eggs. Set aside.
- In saucepan, combine pineapple liquid and butter. Bring to a boil. Add small amount of hot liquid to egg mixture, stirring vigorously.
- Add egg mixture to saucepan, stirring constantly until thickened. Add pineapple. Chill.
- When ready to serve, stir in bananas and spoon onto lettuce leaves.

# CRANBERRY FREEZE

Serves 8
Do ahead

| | |
|---|---|
| 1 | can whole cranberry sauce |
| 1 | 8-ounce can crushed pineapple |
| 1 | cup chopped pecans |
| 8 | ounces sour cream |
| 2 | Tbsp. mayonnaise |
| 2 | Tbsp. sugar |

- Combine ingredients.
- Pour into cupcake papers placed in muffin tins. Freeze.
- Remove papers and serve on bed of lettuce.

# SUNBURST SALAD

Serves 6-8
Do ahead

| | |
|---|---|
| ¾ | cup sugar |
| ½ | cup pineapple liquid |
| 1 | Tbsp. unflavored gelatin |
| ¼ | cup cold water |
| 1 | cup drained crushed pineapple |
| 1 | cup grated Cheddar cheese |
| 1 | cup heavy cream, whipped |

- Dissolve sugar in pineapple liquid over low heat. Soften gelatin in water. Add to sugar mixture. Chill until partially set.
- Add pineapple and cheese, fold in whipped cream. Pour into ring mold. Chill until firm.

# FROZEN FRUIT BASKET

Serves 10
Do ahead

| | |
|---|---|
| 6 | ounces cream cheese, softened |
| ½ | cup mayonnaise |
| 2 | tsp. lemon juice |
| 1 | tsp. lemon extract |
| 1 | 8-ounce can crushed pineapple, drained |
| ½ | cup diced maraschino cherries |
| ½ | cup chopped pitted dates |
| ½ | cup chopped pecans |
| 2 | cups sliced bananas |
| 1 | cup whipping cream |
| ¼ | cup sugar |

- Beat cream cheese until smooth; add mayonnaise, lemon juice and lemon extract. Mix well.
- Stir in pineapple, cherries, dates and pecans. Add bananas and toss gently to coat.
- Beat cream until foamy; gradually add sugar and beat until soft peaks form. Fold into fruit mixture.
- Spoon into a 9 x 5-inch loaf pan; cover and freeze.
- To serve, unmold salad on lettuce. Let stand at room temperature 20-30 minutes before serving.

# BLACK CHERRY RING

Serves 10-12
Do ahead

| | |
|---|---|
| 2 | 3-ounce packages black cherry gelatin |
| 1 | 17-ounce can pitted Bing cherries, drained, liquid reserved |
| 6 | ounces cream cheese, softened |
| ½ | cup chopped pecans |

- Add water to cherry liquid to equal 3½ cups. Dissolve gelatin in 2 cups of boiling cherry liquid. Add 1½ cups cool liquid. Chill until partially set.
- Shape cheese into balls, using a level teaspoon for each. Roll in pecans.
- Place cherries and cheese balls in 9-inch ring mold. Add partially set gelatin. Chill.
- Unmold on large serving plate.

# CELERY SEED DRESSING

Yields 2 cups
Do ahead

| | |
|---|---|
| 10 | Tbsp. sugar, or less to taste |
| 1 | tsp. prepared mustard |
| 1 | cup vegetable oil |
| 1 | Tbsp. celery seed |
| 1 | tsp. salt |
| ⅓ | cup vinegar |
| 1 | medium onion, grated |

- Mix all ingredients and refrigerate overnight.
- Serve on crisp cabbage strips or fruit salad.

# MANDARIN DELIGHT

Serves 8
Do ahead

1¾ cups boiling water
2 3-ounce packages lemon gelatin
1 6-ounce can frozen orange juice concentrate, thawed
1 15½-ounce can crushed pineapple, with juice
1 11-ounce can mandarin oranges, drained and cut

- Dissolve gelatin in water. Add remaining ingredients.
- Pour into 13 x 9-inch pan. Chill until set.

# SUNSET SALAD

Serves 9
Do ahead

2 3-ounce packages apricot gelatin
2 cups boiling water
1 8-ounce carton vanilla yogurt
1 11-ounce can mandarin oranges, ½ cup liquid reserved

- Dissolve gelatin in boiling water.
- Measure 1 cup gelatin, blend in yogurt. Pour into 8 x 8-inch pan. Chill until set but not firm.
- Add reserved liquid to remaining gelatin and chill until slightly thickened.
- Arrange orange sections on top of set gelatin-yogurt layer. Top with clear gelatin. Chill until firm, about 3 hours. Cut into squares to serve.

# SPICED PEACH SALAD

Serves 6
Do ahead

1 17-ounce jar spiced peaches, chopped, liquid reserved
1 15¼-ounce can pineapple tidbits, drained
1 3-ounce package lemon gelatin
½ cup pecans
2 Tbsp. Grand Marnier

- Add water to peach liquid to make 1½ cups and bring to a boil. Dissolve gelatin in hot liquid. Stir in remaining ingredients.
- Pour into square pan or 4-cup mold. Chill.

*Serve with Chicken Florentine.*

# GAZPACHO ASPIC

Serves 12
Do ahead

| | |
|---|---|
| 2 | **envelopes unflavored gelatin** |
| 1¼ | **cups tomato juice** |
| ⅓ | **cup red wine vinegar** |
| 1 | **tsp. salt** |
| | **Dash Tabasco sauce** |
| 1 | **Tbsp. chives** |
| 2 | **small tomatoes, chopped** |
| 1 | **medium cucumber, chopped** |
| ½ | **green pepper, chopped** |
| ¼ | **cup chopped onion** |

- In medium saucepan, sprinkle gelatin over ¾ cup tomato juice. Stir over low heat until dissolved. Remove from heat.
- Stir in remaining ingredients except vegetables. Set in bowl of ice and stir 15 minutes or until consistency of unbeaten egg whites. Fold in vegetables.
- Pour into 1½-quart mold. Chill. Serve plain or with dressing.

## AVOCADO DRESSING

| | |
|---|---|
| 2 | **large ripe avocados** |
| 1 | **cup sour cream** |
| 1 | **cup light cream** |
| 2 | **Tbsp. minced onion** |
| 2 | **Tbsp. lemon juice** |
| 3 | **tsp. salt** |
| ¼ | **tsp. sugar** |
| 2 | **cloves garlic, mashed** |

- Blend ingredients in mixer or food processor. Cover with plastic wrap smoothed over surface of dressing until ready to serve.

# PINEAPPLE-CABBAGE SLAW

Serves 6-8
Do ahead

| | |
|---|---|
| 1 | **large head cabbage, finely chopped** |
| ¾ | **cup vinegar** |
| ¾ | **cup sugar** |
| 3 | **egg yolks, beaten** |
| 1 | **lump butter, size of small egg** |
| 1 | **cup mayonnaise** |
| 1 | **cup heavy cream** |
| 1 | **cup drained crushed pineapple** |
| 2 | **carrots, shredded** |

- Combine vinegar, sugar, yolks and butter. Cook, stirring often, until consistency of custard. Cool.
- Add remaining ingredients. Toss with cabbage and chill.

# GAZPACHO SALAD

Serves 8
Do ahead

| | |
|---|---|
| 4-5 | tomatoes, chopped |
| 2 | cucumbers, diced |
| 2 | green peppers, chopped |
| 2 | bunches radishes, sliced |
| 1 | large sweet red onion, sliced |
| 12-14 | black olives |
| 2 | cloves garlic, minced |
| ¼ | cup olive oil |
| ⅓ | cup white wine vinegar |
| 1 | tsp. salt |
| ¼ | tsp. Tabasco sauce |
| 1 | Tbsp. minced parsley |
| 2 | Tbsp. minced chives |
| ⅛ | tsp. pepper |
| | Lettuce |

- Alternate layers of tomatoes, cucumbers, peppers, radishes, onions and olives.
- Combine remaining ingredients except lettuce. Pour over vegetables. Cover and refrigerate for several hours.
- Serve in glass bowl with a separate bowl of lettuce for individuals to make their own salads.

# MARINATED SLICED TOMATOES

Serves 4

| | |
|---|---|
| 2-3 | large ripe tomatoes |
| ½ | cup olive or salad oil |
| 2 | Tbsp. cider vinegar |
| 1 | Tbsp. basil |
| 1 | Tbsp. minced parsley |
| 1 | Tbsp. finely chopped onion |
| 1 | clove garlic, pressed |
| 1 | tsp. salt |
| 1 | Tbsp. capers |
| | Parsley to garnish |

- Wash tomatoes, pat dry and slice into thick slices. Arrange on platter or shallow dish slightly overlapping.
- In a bowl, mix remaining ingredients. Drizzle over tomatoes.
- Refrigerate at least 1 hour. Garnish with parsley.

*For variation, add sliced Bermuda onion and fresh mushrooms to tomatoes.*

# DOCKSIDE POTATO SALAD

Serves 6-8
Do ahead

| 5-6 | medium red potatoes |
| ¼ | cup finely chopped onion |
| ¼ | cup finely chopped celery, including some leaves |
| 1 | dill pickle, chopped |
| 2 | Tbsp. dried parsley |
| 6 | strips bacon, cooked crisp and crumbled |
| ½-1 | tsp. salt |
| ¼ | tsp. pepper |
| 1½ | Tbsp. vinegar |
| 4 | Tbsp. vegetable oil |
| 1-1¼ | cups mayonnaise |

• Cook potatoes in salted water until tender, 30-40 minutes. *Cool completely* in refrigerator. Peel and cut into thin bite-size pieces. Place in large bowl.
• Add next 5 ingredients. Sprinkle salt, pepper, vinegar and oil over all.
• Gently turn all ingredients over with wooden spoon until well mixed.
• Add mayonnaise and turn again until well moistened.
• Refrigerate several hours before serving.

# GERMAN POTATO SALAD

Serves 10-12

| 5 | pounds new or red potatoes |
| 1 | pound siced bacon, cut into thirds |
| 1 | large onion, diced |
| ⅓ | cup flour |
| | Parsley, freshly snipped |
| ½ | cup water |
| ½ | cup vinegar |
| 1 | Tbsp. sugar |
| ½ | tsp. salt |
| | Pepper to taste |

• Cook potatoes in salted water for 45 minutes. Peel and slice into oven-proof dish.
• Fry bacon; reserve grease. Sauté onion in 1-2 Tablespoons bacon grease. Add onions, bacon and parsley to potatoes. Mix.
• Add flour to remaining bacon grease and mix well. Stir in remaining ingredients. When thickened, pour over potato mixture; mix well. More parsley may be sprinkled on top for color.
• Bake at 350 degrees for 45 minutes.

# CAESAR SALAD

Serves 6

¼   cup olive oil
    Juice of 1 lemon
2   cloves garlic, sliced
¼   tsp. salt
    Pepper, coarsely ground
1   medium head romaine
    lettuce, torn
1   cup croutons
¼   cup grated Parmesan
    cheese
4   anchovy fillets, chopped
1   egg, beaten

- In large glass bowl, combine oil, lemon juice, garlic, salt and pepper. Cover and let stand 50 minutes or more. Discard garlic when ready to prepare.
- Just before serving, toss lettuce in dressing. Add cheese, anchovies and egg; toss well. Add croutons and toss. Serve immediately.

# TROPICAL SALAD

Serves 6-8

½   head romaine lettuce,
    torn into bite-size pieces
3   medium bananas, sliced
3   oranges, peeled and
    sliced
1   green pepper, sliced into
    rings
1   small red onion, thinly
    sliced and separated into
    rings

- Combine all ingredients and pour dressing over salad just before serving; toss.
- Note: for perfect orange sections, cut a slice from top and bottom of orange. Trim off peel in strips from top to bottom, cutting deep enough to remove white membrane. Cut along the dividing membrane from outside to middle of core and remove section.

**LEMON DRESSING**

½   cup salad oil
2   Tbsp. wine vinegar
2   Tbsp lemon juice
2   tsp. sugar
1   tsp. dry mustard
½   tsp. salt

- Combine dressing ingredients and chill thoroughly.

*A good winter salad.*

# DILLY TOMATO ASPIC

Serves 6-8
Do ahead

| | |
|---|---|
| 3 | envelopes unflavored gelatin |
| ¾ | cup cold water |
| 5 | cups tomato juice |
| 3 | Tbsp. grated onion |
| ¼ | cup chopped green pepper |
| 1 | cup finely chopped celery |
| 4 | tsp. dill seed |
| ¼ | tsp. basil |
| ½ | tsp. Worcestershire sauce |
| 1 | tsp. salt |
| ½ | tsp. sugar |
| | Juice of ½ lemon |

- Soften gelatin in water. Heat tomato juice until just boiling. Remove from heat and stir in gelatin until dissolved. Let cool, then add remaining ingredients.
- Pour into well oiled 2-quart mold. Chill until set. Serve with dressing.

## DRESSING

| | |
|---|---|
| 1 | cup whipped cream cheese |
| ⅓ | cup chopped green olives |
| | Dash of garlic powder |
| | Light cream |

- Mix cream cheese, olives and garlic. Add enough light cream to make creamy consistency.

# OVERNIGHT CABBAGE SLAW

Serves 6
Do ahead

| | |
|---|---|
| ½ | medium cabbage, sliced |
| 1 | small red onion, sliced |
| ½ | medium green pepper, sliced |
| 2 | carrots, shredded |

- Place vegetables in large bowl.

## DRESSING

| | |
|---|---|
| ⅔ | cup vinegar |
| ⅓ | cup vegetable oil |
| ¼ | cup sugar |
| 1 | tsp. salt |
| ¼ | tsp. pepper |

- Combine dressing ingredients; mix well. Pour over vegetables and stir.
- Cover and refrigerate 8 hours.
- To serve, stir thoroughly and drain.

# SHRIMP AND TOMATO ASPIC

Serves 6
Do ahead

## ASPIC

| | |
|---|---|
| 1½ | tsp. unflavored gelatin |
| 1 | 3-ounce package lemon gelatin |
| 1 | cup hot V-8 juice |
| ¾ | cup cold V-8 juice |
| ¼ | cup horseradish |
| ¾ | cup chopped green pepper |
| ¾ | cup chopped celery |
| 1 | cup cooked, chopped shrimp |
| 1 | Tbsp. Worcestershire sauce |

- Dissolve unflavored and lemon gelatins in hot vegetable juice. Add remaining ingredients. Mix well.
- Pour into ring mold and chill until firm.
- Serve with dressing.

## DRESSING

| | |
|---|---|
| 3 | ounces cream cheese |
| | Crumbled Blue cheese to taste |
| 1-2 | Tbsp. milk |

- Whip ingredients until thick and creamy. Chill.

# FRESH VEGETABLE MARINADE

Serves 8-10
Do ahead

| | |
|---|---|
| 4 | stalks fresh broccoli, broken into florets |
| 8 | large mushrooms, sliced |
| 1 | green pepper, chopped |
| 3 | stalks celery, sliced |
| 1 | head cauliflower, broken into florets |

• Combine all vegetables in a large bowl.

**MARINADE**

| | |
|---|---|
| ¾-1 | cup sugar |
| 2 | tsp. dry mustard |
| 1 | tsp. salt |
| ½ | cup vinegar |
| 1½ | cups vegetable oil |
| 1 | small onion, grated |
| 2 | Tbsp. poppy seed |

• Combine ingredients; pour over vegetables and cover. Chill for at least 3 hours before serving.

*Wonderful winter salad.*

# FESTIVE ASPARAGUS SALAD

Serves 8
Do ahead

| | |
|---|---|
| 2 | packages unflavored gelatin, dissolved in ½ cup cold water |
| 1 | cup sugar |
| 1 | cup water |
| ½ | cup vinegar |
| 1 | can asparagus tips, drained |
| 1 | small onion, chopped |
| ½ | cup chopped celery |
| 1 | small jar pimientos, drained |
| | Juice of ½ lemon |

• Combine sugar, water and vinegar and boil for 1-2 minutes. Remove from heat and stir in softened gelatin.
• Add remaining ingredients. Pour into casserole or mold. Chill until set.

# VERY, VERY VEGETABLE

Serves 20
Do ahead

| | |
|---|---|
| 2 | **16-ounce cans French style green beans** |
| 2 | **17-ounce cans early green peas** |
| 1 | **14-ounce can artichoke hearts, diced** |
| 1 | **4-ounce jar pimientos, chopped** |
| 1 | **medium green pepper, chopped** |
| 1 | **medium onion, chopped** |
| 1 | **8-ounce can water chestnuts, sliced** |

• Combine drained vegetables in a large bowl.

### MARINADE

| | |
|---|---|
| ¾ | **cup sugar** |
| 1 | **cup red wine vinegar** |
| ½ | **cup water** |
| ½ | **cup salad oil** |
| 1 | **clove garlic, minced** |

• Blend all ingredients and pour over vegetables.
• Marinate overnight.

# GOLDEN CARROT SALAD

Serves 8
Do ahead

| | |
|---|---|
| 6 | **cups julienne carrots, blanched** |
| 5 | **green onions, thinly sliced, including tops** |

• Toss carrots and onion lightly in bowl.

### MARINADE

| | |
|---|---|
| ¾ | **cup sugar** |
| 1 | **tsp. salt** |
| ½ | **tsp. pepper** |
| ½ | **cup salad oil** |
| ⅔ | **cup vinegar** |

• Combine all ingredients and pour over vegetables. Let stand overnight in refrigerator.
• To serve, drain.

# VEGETABLE PASTA SALAD

Serves 8
Do ahead

| | |
|---|---|
| 12 | ounces thin spaghetti, cooked and drained Vegetable oil |
| 1 | medium zucchini, thinly sliced |
| ¼ | pound green beans, cut in ½-inch pieces |
| 2 | green onions, chopped |
| ⅔ | cup sliced black olives |
| ⅔ | cup sliced mushrooms |
| 1 | cup sliced cherry tomatoes |
| 1 | tsp. salt |
| ½ | cup grated Parmesan cheese |

- Cool spaghetti and toss with a small amount of oil.
- Cook zucchini and beans until just tender. Rinse immediately in cold water. Drain.
- Add green beans, zucchini, onions, olives, mushrooms, tomatoes, salt and cheese to spaghetti.

## DRESSING

| | |
|---|---|
| ¼ | cup white vinegar |
| ⅔ | cup olive oil |
| 2 | Tbsp. water |
| 1 | envelope dry Italian salad dressing mix |

- Combine ingredients. Beat well. Pour over spaghetti. Store in tightly sealed container in refrigerator overnight.

*Pretty served in a glass bowl.*

# CREAMY ASPARAGUS RING

Serves 8
Do ahead

| | |
|---|---|
| 1 | 8-ounce can cut asparagus, liquid reserved |
| 1 | 3-ounce package lemon gelatin |
| 1 | envelope unflavored gelatin |
| 8 | ounces cream cheese, softened |
| 1 | cup mayonnaise |
| ¼ | cup almonds |

- Add enough cold water to asparagus liquid to make 2 cups. Soften gelatins in water, heat to dissolve.
- Put remaining ingredients in blender, adding liquid gradually while blending. Add almonds during last few seconds.
- Pour into ring mold and chill.

# TOMATO ASPIC

Serves 8-10
Do ahead

| | |
|---|---|
| 2 | Tbsp. unflavored gelatin |
| ½ | cup cold water |
| 3 | cups tomato juice |
| 2 | bay leaves |
| 2 | whole garlic cloves |
| | Dash of black pepper |
| 1 | cup sugar |
| 1 | tsp. salt |
| ½ | cup cider vinegar |
| 2 | tsp. chopped onion |
| 1 | cup shredded cabbage |
| 2 | stalks celery, chopped |
| 1 | small green pepper, chopped |

- In a large bowl, dissolve gelatin in water for several minutes.
- Boil tomato juice, bay leaves, garlic and pepper for 5 minutes. Strain into bowl with gelatin.
- Add sugar, salt, vinegar and onion. Chill until beginning to gel. Add remaining ingredients.
- Pour into 6-8 cup mold. Chill until firm—at least 4 hours. Unmold and serve with dressing.

## DRESSING

| | |
|---|---|
| ½ | cup mayonnaise |
| ½ | cup sour cream |

- Combine and chill.

# ADMIRAL'S EGG SALAD

Serves 6-8
Do ahead

| | |
|---|---|
| 1 | envelope unflavored gelatin |
| ¼ | cup cold water |
| 1 | cup chicken broth, boiling |
| 1 | cup mayonnaise |
| ¼ | cup diced green pepper |
| 1 | Tbsp. lemon juice |
| 1 | Tbsp. grated onion |
| 1 | Tbsp. chopped parsley |
| | Salt to taste |
| | White pepper to taste |
| 12 | hard-boiled eggs, riced |

- In a large bowl, dissolve gelatin in water; add broth.
- Mix in remaining ingredients, adding eggs last.
- Pour into greased 6-cup ring mold immediately; refrigerate overnight. Unmold to serve.

*Good served with Surfside Salad.*
*Center of mold may be filled with cherry tomatoes.*

# FRESH MUSHROOM SALAD

Serves 4
Do ahead

½   pound mushrooms, sliced
    ⅛ inch thick
1   cup water
1   Tbsp. lemon juice
¼   cup heavy cream
1   Tbsp. grated onion
    Pinch of sugar
½   tsp. salt
⅛   tsp. white pepper
    Lettuce leaves

- Bring water and lemon juice to a boil. Add mushrooms and cover. Reduce heat and simmer gently for 2-3 minutes.
- Remove from heat, drain mushrooms and pat dry with paper towels.
- Combine cream, onion, sugar, salt and pepper. Add mushrooms and toss lightly until well coated.
- Serve on lettuce leaves.

*Good with Perfect Tenderloin.*

# SPINACH RING

Serves 6-8
Do ahead

2     10-ounce packages frozen chopped spinach
1½-2  packages unflavored gelatin
1     10½-ounce can beef consommé
4     hard-boiled eggs, grated
¾     cup mayonnaise
1¾    tsp. salt
4     Tbsp. Worcestershire sauce
2     Tbsp. lemon juice
5     dashes Tabasco sauce

- Cook spinach according to package directions without salt. Drain well.
- Soften gelatin in ½ cup cold consommé. Heat remaining consommé and pour into gelatin, stirring until dissolved. Set aside to cool.
- Mix eggs, mayonnaise, and seasonings with spinach. Fold in gelatin.
- Pour into ring mold and chill overnight or until set.
- Serve with dressing.
- Broccoli may be substituted for spinach.

**DRESSING**

2     cups sour cream
      Horseradish to taste
      Lemon juice to taste

- Combine ingredients.

# "GARDENS-BY-THE-SEA" SALAD

Serves 6-8
Do ahead

| | |
|---|---|
| 8 | ounces spinach noodles, cooked and drained |
| 1 | bunch fresh broccoli, chopped |
| 1 | green pepper, chopped |
| 1 | carrot, chopped |
| 1 | onion, minced |
| 1 | 4-ounce can water chestnuts, drained and chopped |
| ¼ | pound mushrooms, chopped |
| 2 | firm rlpe tomatoes, chopped |
| 1 | tsp. garlic salt |
| 1 | tsp. pepper |
| ½-1 | cup Italian dressing |

- Toss noodles with remaining ingredients.
- Refrigerate until well chilled.

# MOUSSE AUX CONCOMBRES

Serves 12
Do ahead

| | |
|---|---|
| 1 | 3-ounce package lime gelatin |
| 1 | 3-ounce package lemon gelatin |
| 2 | cups boiling water |
| 2 | cucumbers, peeled, seeded and coarsely chopped |
| 1 | cup plain yogurt |
| 1 | cup sour cream |
| 1 | Tbsp. tarragon vinegar |
| 1 | Tbsp. lemon juice |
| 1 | Tbsp. grated onion |
| ½ | tsp. dill |
| | Salt and white pepper to taste |

- Dissolve gelatin in water.
- Combine ingredients. Adjust seasonings to taste.
- Pour half of mixture into blender. Blend 30-60 seconds. Repeat.
- Pour into oiled 5-6 cup mold. Chill overnight.
- To serve, unmold and decorate with cucumber slices and mint. Yogurt may be served in center of mold.

# COLD POTATO AND GREEN BEAN SALAD

Serves 12
Do ahead

| | |
|---|---|
| 24-30 | small red potatoes |
| 3 | pounds young green beans |
| 1½ | cups extra virgin olive oil |
| ⅓ | cup wine vinegar |
| 3 | cloves garlic, finely minced |
| 1 | Tbsp. mixed herbs |
| | Dash Tabasco sauce |
| | Dash Worcestershire sauce |
| 1½ | tsp. salt |
| | Ground pepper to taste |
| 2 | Tbsp. whole grain mustard |
| 2 | heads Boston or leaf lettuce |
| | Pimientos |
| | Fresh parsley, chopped |

- Boil potatoes in salted water until tender. Drain and set aside.
- Blanch green beans in salted boiling water until just tender. Do not cover as beans will stay greener. Drain and set aside.
- In a food processor or blender, mix remaining ingredients except mustard. Remove from processor. Add mustard, stirring well.
- Put vegetables in a large bowl or soup pot. Pour dressing over hot vegetables. Allow to reach room temperature, toss, cover and chill overnight. Toss several times more.
- Remove from refrigerator 1 hour before serving and toss well.
- Line a large salad bowl with leaf lettuce. Add beans and potatoes. Sprinkle pimientos over salad and pour any remaining dressing over top. Sprinkle with chopped parsley and serve.

*For a nice garnish, add Niçoise olives
which have been pitted and coarsely chopped.*

# COUNTRY DRESSING

Yields 2 cups
Do ahead

| | |
|---|---|
| 1 | cup mayonnaise |
| 1 | cup buttermilk |
| 1 | Tbsp. dried parsley |
| 1 | Tbsp. chopped fresh scallions |
| 1 | clove garlic, finely minced |
| ⅛ | tsp. English or Dijon mustard |
| ½ | tsp. salt |
| ⅛ | tsp. pepper |

- Mix all ingredients.
- Allow to stand in refrigerator, tightly covered, for one day to allow all flavors to blend.

# DIETER'S CUCUMBER DRESSING

Yields 3½ cups

| | |
|---|---|
| 1½ | large cucumbers, seeded |
| 1½ | cups diet mayonnaise |
| ½ | cup plain lowfat yogurt |
| 1 | Tbsp. dill weed |
| 1½ | Tbsp. minced onion |
| 1 | tsp. vinegar |
| ½ | tsp. salt |
| ¼ | tsp. black pepper |
| 3 | packages diet sweetener or to taste |

- Mix all ingredients in blender or processor.
- Refrigerate.
- Keeps for 1 week tightly sealed.
- Dressing may be used as a dip for raw vegetables or sauce for cold poached fish, as well as for salads.

*Only 9 calories per Tablespoon!*

# MUD SALAD DRESSING

Yields 4 cups

| | |
|---|---|
| 3 | cups vegetable oil |
| 1 | cup apple cider vinegar, or less to taste |
| 2 | Tbsp. oregano |
| 2 | Tbsp. crushed basil |
| 3 | cloves garlic, minced |
| 1 | Tbsp. paprika |
| ½ | cup soy sauce |

- Mix all ingredients and refrigerate.
- Use as needed.

*Good as a non-mayonnaise dressing for tuna salad.*

# CURRY DRESSING FOR FRUIT

Yields ½ cup

| | |
|---|---|
| 2 | Tbsp. vinegar |
| 1 | Tbsp. lemon juice |
| ½ | tsp. curry |
| 2 | ounces plain yogurt |
| 1 | Tbsp. mayonnaise |
| 1 | Tbsp. sugar |

- Mix all ingredients using blender or mixer. Chill.
- Pour over fruit one hour before serving.

# FALL SALAD

Serves 6-8

| | |
|---|---|
| 8 | cups torn salad greens, chilled |
| 1 | cup diced red apples |
| 1 | cup diagonally sliced celery |
| ¼ | cup crumbled Blue cheese |
| 1 | cup chopped nuts |

- Combine greens, apples and celery. Shake dressing, pour over salad. Add cheese and toss lightly. Garnish with nuts.

**DRESSING**

| | |
|---|---|
| ⅔ | cup vegetable oil |
| ½ | cup vinegar |
| 1 | tsp. sugar |
| ½ | tsp. salt |
| ⅛ | tsp. pepper |

- Combine dressing ingredients in a jar and shake well; chill.

# DIG DEEP

Serves 8
Do ahead

| | |
|---|---|
| 1 | large head lettuce, coarsely chopped |
| 4 | stalks celery, chopped |
| 1-2 | green peppers, chopped |
| 1-2 | medium red onions, thinly sliced |
| 1 | 10-ounce box frozen peas, thawed |
| 1 | 8-ounce can water chestnuts, sliced |
| 2 | cups mayonnaise |
| ¾ | cup grated Parmesan or Romano cheese |
| 1 | Tbsp. sugar |
| 1 | pound bacon, cooked and crumbled |
| 3 | hard-boiled eggs, sliced |
| 1-2 | tomatoes, sliced |

- In large glass bowl, arrange first 6 ingredients in layers as listed.
- Cover top well with mayonnaise to seal. Sprinkle with cheese and sugar. Top with bacon.
- Refrigerate at least 24 hours.
- Remove from refrigerator 20-30 minutes before serving; add eggs and tomato garnish.

# WINTER SALAD

Serves 8

| | |
|---|---|
| 1 | pound fresh spinach, washed and trimmed |
| ½ | small red onion, sliced |
| 2 | 11-ounce cans mandarin orange slices, drained |
| ½ | cup chopped sugared dates |
| ¾ | cup chopped pecans |

- Toss ingredients.

## DRESSING

| | |
|---|---|
| ¼ | cup oil |
| ¾ | cup wine vinegar |
| 2 | tsp. brown sugar |
| 1 | tsp. garlic salt |
| ½ | tsp. poppy seeds |
| | Salt and pepper to taste |

- Mix ingredients in a jar. Shake well and toss with salad just before serving.

# GLAZED FRENCH DRESSING

Yields 2 cups

| | |
|---|---|
| ¼ | cup vinegar |
| 1 | tsp. Worcestershire sauce |
| ½ | cup sugar |
| 1 | tsp. dry mustard |
| 1 | tsp. salt |
| 1 | tsp. paprika |
| 1 | Tbsp. minced onion |
| 1 | clove garlic, finely minced |
| 1 | tsp. salt or to taste |
| 1 | cup salad oil |
| ½ | cup crumbled Blue cheese |

- Mix first 9 ingredients with a food processor or electric mixer.
- In a thin stream, gradually add oil, beating until thick.
- Add cheese. Serve with fruit or green salad.

# GERMAN FRENCH DRESSING

Yields 3 cups
Do ahead

1   **Tbsp. salt**
1   **Tbsp. tarragon or wine vinegar**
4   **cloves garlic, finely minced**
1   **small onion, chopped**
4   **Tbsp. plain vinegar**
4   **Tbsp. water**
1   **tsp. Worcestershire sauce**
½   **tsp. paprika**
1   **tsp. celery salt**
    **Pinch black pepper**
    **Pinch red pepper**
1   **tsp. mustard**
2   **cups extra virgin olive oil,** *or* **1 cup olive oil and 1 cup vegetable oil**
    **Salt to taste**

- Combine first 4 ingredients in a quart jar and shake vigorously.
- Add the rest of the ingredients and again shake well. Refrigerate overnight before using.
- Remove from refrigerator one hour before serving.

# SPINACH SALAD SUPREME

Serves 8-10

1   **pound fresh small leaf spinach**
1   **medium Bermuda onion, thinly sliced**
¼   **pound fresh mushrooms, sliced**
8   **slices bacon, cooked and crumbled**
    **Dash of pepper**
4   **hard-boiled eggs, chopped**
    **Water chestnuts, sliced**
½   **cup grated Swiss cheese (optional)**

- Wash and dry spinach. Tear into bite-size pieces, discarding stems. Store in refrigerator.
- When ready to serve, remove spinach from refrigerator and add any or all of the additional ingredients.
- Toss with one of the following dressings.

### SOUR CREAM DRESSING

| | |
|---|---|
| 1 | cup salad oil |
| 5 | Tbsp. red wine vinegar |
| 4 | Tbsp. sour cream |
| 2 | Tbsp. sugar |
| 2 | tsp. chopped parsley |
| 1½ | tsp. salt |
| ½ | tsp. dry mustard |
| 2 | cloves garlic, crushed |
| | Pepper to taste |

- Combine dressing ingredients in a jar and shake well. Refrigerate until ready to serve salad.
- Immediately before serving, pour over salad and toss.

### COTTAGE CHEESE DRESSING

| | |
|---|---|
| 1 | cup chopped pecans |
| 3-4 | Tbsp. cottage cheese |
| ¼ | cup sugar |
| ½ | tsp. dry mustard |
| ¼ | tsp. salt |
| 2 | tsp. horseradish |
| 3 | tsp. wine vinegar |

- Mix all ingredients in a jar and shake well.
- Refrigerate until just before serving. Shake chilled dressing and pour over salad.

### OIL AND VINEGAR DRESSING

| | |
|---|---|
| 1 | cup oil |
| ⅓ | cup cider vinegar |
| ⅓ | cup sugar |
| 1 | tsp. dry minced onion |
| ½ | tsp. paprika |
| ½ | tsp. dry mustard |

- Place all ingredients in blender and blend 6-8 minutes. Pour half of the dressing over salad and toss.
- Dressing is best when made a day ahead and stored in refrigerator.
- Dressing is enough for 2 salads; remainder can be stored up to 1 month in refrigerator.

# CREAMY FRENCH DRESSING

Yields ½ cup

| | |
|---|---|
| 5 | Tbsp. extra virgin olive oil |
| 3 | Tbsp. vinegar |
| 1 | Tbsp. mayonnaise |
| 1 | tsp. Dijon mustard |
| | Dash pepper |
| | Dash soy sauce |

- Mix ingredients in a blender or food processor. Chill.

# TOPOPO SALAD DRESSING

*Yields 1½ cups*

| | |
|---|---|
| ⅔ | cup oil (walnut oil is preferred) |
| ⅔ | cup vinegar |
| 1 | tsp. salt |
| 1 | Tbsp. molasses or dark corn syrup |
| ½ | tsp. dry mustard |
| ½ | tsp. paprika |
| ½-1 | tsp. pepper |
| ⅛ | tsp. Tabasco sauce |

- Combine all ingredients in a quart jar and shake well.
- Serve on green salads.

# HONEY-NUT DRESSING

*Yields 2 cups*

| | |
|---|---|
| ¼ | cup sugar |
| 1 | tsp. dry mustard |
| 1 | tsp. paprika |
| 1 | tsp. celery salt |
| ¼ | tsp. salt |
| ⅓ | cup honey |
| ⅓ | cup vinegar |
| 1 | Tbsp. lemon juice |
| 1 | Tbsp. pineapple juice |
| 1 | cup vegetable oil |
| ½ | cup chopped pecans |

- Mix first 5 ingredients. Add honey, vinegar, lemon and pineapple juices. Mix.
- Using electric mixer, beat constantly while adding oil slowly in a thin stream.
- Add pecans. Stir just before serving.

# FRENCH DRESSING

*Yields 1 cup*

| | |
|---|---|
| ½ | cup vegetable oil |
| ¼ | cup red wine vinegar |
| ½ | cup ketchup |
| 1 | small onion, chopped |
| 2 | Tbsp. sugar |
| ½ | tsp. salt |
| 1 | tsp. paprika |
| | Juice of 1 lemon |

- Combine all ingredients in a blender or food processor. Mix well.

# ACCOMPANIMENTS

# ACCOMPANIMENTS

# CRAN-APPLE DELIGHT

Serves 6

| | |
|---|---|
| 3-4 | **tart apples** |
| 2 | **cups raw cranberries** |
| ¾-1 | **cup sugar** |
| 3-4 | **Tbsp. water** |

**TOPPING**

| | |
|---|---|
| ¾ | **cup uncooked oatmeal** |
| ¼ | **cup flour** |
| ½ | **cup brown sugar** |
| ½ | **cup chopped pecans** |
| ¼ | **pound butter, melted** |

- Preheat oven to 350 degrees.
- Peel, core and slice apples. Rinse and pick over cranberries. Mix fruit with sugar and water and place in a 2-quart casserole. Set aside.

- Mix dry ingredients. Add melted butter.
- Spread topping over fruit.
- Bake at 350 degrees for 45 minutes.

*Good side dish for Thanksgiving or Christmas dinner.*

# SCALLOPED APPLES

Serves 6

| | |
|---|---|
| 6 | **medium tart apples** |
| ¼ | **tsp. cinnamon** |
| ¼ | **tsp. salt** |
| ¼ | **tsp. nutmeg** |
| 1 | **Tbsp. lemon juice** |
| ¼ | **cup water** |
| ¾ | **cup brown sugar** |
| ¼ | **cup flour** |
| ⅓ | **cup butter** |

- Preheat oven to 400 degrees.
- Pare, core and slice apples. Place in buttered shallow casserole dish.
- Mix next five ingredients and pour over apples.
- Work sugar, flour and butter together until of crumb-like consistency. Sprinkle over apples.
- Bake uncovered at 400 degrees for 30 minutes. Serve warm as side dish or with ice cream for dessert.

*Smells as good as it tastes!*

# STUFFED PUMPKIN

Serves 6

| | |
|---|---|
| 1 | small pumpkin (8-9″ diameter) |
| 1 | cup chopped apples |
| 1 | cup cranberries |
| 1 | cup raisins |
| ½ | cup chopped nuts |
| ⅓ | cup sugar |
| 1 | tsp. lemon juice |
| ¼ | tsp. nutmeg |
| ¼ | tsp. cinnamon |
| 8 | ounces sour cream |

- Cut off top of pumpkin and set aside. Carefully remove seeds and wash.
- Mix all ingredients except sour cream. Set pumpkin on cookie sheet and fill with mixture.
- Bake uncovered at 350 degrees for 35-40 minutes. Cover with pumpkin top and continue baking for 20 minutes.
- Serve hot or cold with dollop of sour cream.

*Good Thanksgiving dinner accompaniment.*

# HOT FRUIT COMPOTE

Serves 12
Do ahead

| | |
|---|---|
| 1 | 12-ounce package pitted prunes |
| 1 | 12-ounce package dried apricots |
| 1 | 12-ounce package dried mixed fruits |
| 1½ | cups dry Sherry |
| 1 | cup water |
| 1 | cup cherry pie filling |
| 1 | 16-ounce can pineapple chunks with juice |

- Cut all dried fruit into bite-size pieces and marinate in Sherry overnight.
- Add water to Sherry-fruit mixture and simmer 20-30 minutes.
- Add pie filling and pineapple with juice. Pour into 2½-quart casserole dish and bake at 350 degrees for 30 minutes.
- Serve warm or cold.

# FESTIVE FRUIT

| | |
|---|---|
| 1 | 20-ounce can sliced pineapple |
| 1 | 16-ounce can peach halves |
| 1 | 16-ounce can pear halves |
| 1 | 16-ounce can apricot halves |
| 1 | 15-ounce jar spiced apple rings |
| ⅔ | cup blanched, slivered almonds |

- Drain fruit. Place fruit and almonds in layers in a shallow baking dish. Set aside.
- Select one of 2 sauces.

## SHERRY SAUCE

| | |
|---|---|
| ¼ | pound butter |
| 1 | cup Sherry |
| ½ | cup sugar |
| 2 | Tbsp. flour |

- Melt butter in top of a double boiler. Add Sherry, sugar and flour. Combine and cook until consistency of cream.
- Pour sauce over fruit and refrigerate overnight.
- Remove from refrigerator and bake at 350 degrees for 30 minutes.

## CURRY SAUCE

| | |
|---|---|
| ¾ | cup light brown sugar |
| 3 | tsp. curry powder |
| ⅓ | cup butter, melted |

- Combine brown sugar, curry and butter and pour over fruit. Refrigerate overnight.
- Remove from refrigerator and bake at 350 degrees for 30 minutes.

# APRICOT CASSEROLE

Serves 6

| | |
|---|---|
| 2 | 16-ounce cans apricot halves in extra light syrup, drained |
| 15 | Ritz crackers, crushed |
| ¾ | cup brown sugar |
| ½ | tsp. cinnamon |
| 6 | Tbsp. butter, melted |

- Preheat oven to 350 degrees.
- Layer half the apricots in 1-quart casserole.
- Mix crackers, sugar and cinnamon. Spread half of mixture over apricots.
- Place rest of apricots in casserole. Spread remaining cracker mixture over top.
- Pour melted butter over casserole.
- Bake at 350 degrees for 30 minutes.

# COLD SPICED FRUIT

Serves 12-16
Do ahead

| | |
|---|---|
| 1 | **20-ounce can pineapple chunks, drained, reserving ½ cup liquid** |
| 1 | **16-ounce can peach halves, drained, reserving ½ cup liquid** |
| 1 | **16-ounce can apricot halves, drained, reserving ½ cup liquid** |
| 1 | **16-ounce can pear halves, drained** |
| 3 | **sticks cinnamon** |
| 10 | **whole cloves** |
| 2 | **unpeeled oranges, sliced in eighths and seeded** |
| 1 | **cup sugar** |
| ⅔ | **cup vinegar** |
| 1 | **3-ounce package cherry gelatin** |

- Place fruit in bowl. Set aside.
- In pan combine cinnamon, cloves, oranges, sugar, vinegar, reserved juices and gelatin. Bring to a boil and simmer 30 minutes. Remove cinnamon and cloves. Pour hot liquid over fruit. Refrigerate overnight. Stir several times.
- Serve cold in a glass bowl for a summer buffet.

# BAKED PINEAPPLE

Serves 6

| | |
|---|---|
| 2 | **Tbsp. flour** |
| ½ | **cup sugar** |
| 2 | **eggs, beaten** |
| 1 | **20-ounce can crushed pineapple, undrained** |
| ¼ | **pound butter** |
| 5 | **slices of white bread, cubed** |

- Preheat oven to 375 degrees.
- Mix flour and sugar. Add beaten eggs, pineapple and juice.
- Melt butter in frying pan and add cubed bread. When coated with butter and slightly browned, add to pineapple mixture.
- Place in greased 1-quart casserole dish. Bake uncovered at 375 degrees for 30 minutes.

*Lovely holiday side dish.*

# FRESH BROCCOLI

Serves 6

2    pounds fresh broccoli,
     cleaned, trimmed and cut

- Cook broccoli until barely tender. Drain thoroughly. Place on serving dish.
- Select one of the sauces listed.

## CAPER SAUCE
⅓    cup butter, melted
4-6  tsp. capers, undrained

- Pour butter over broccoli. Spoon capers and their juice over all.

## LEMON SAUCE
½    cup slivered almonds
1    Tbsp. butter
⅓    cup milk
1    Tbsp. lemon juice
¼    tsp. salt
6    ounces cream cheese,
     softened

- Sauté almonds in butter until golden, stirring frequently. Set aside.
- Combine remaining ingredients, cook over medium heat, stirring until smooth and creamy.
- Pour over broccoli. Garnish with almonds.

## POPPY SEED BROWNED BUTTER
½    tsp. sugar
3    Tbsp. butter
2    tsp. poppy seed
⅛    tsp. freshly ground pepper

- Combine sugar and butter with poppy seed, cooking until browned. Add pepper and pour over broccoli.

# EASY BROCCOLI SOUFFLÉ

Serves 8

3    pounds fresh broccoli,
     washed and trimmed
4    eggs, slightly beaten
1    cup light cream
2    tsp. melted butter
1    tsp. salt
½    tsp. nutmeg
¼    tsp. pepper

- Cook broccoli, drain well.
- Place all ingredients in blender and whirl until mixed. Pour into deep buttered 2-quart casserole.
- Bake at 325 degrees for 45 minutes.

# BROCCOLI AND CHEESE BAKE

Serves 8

| | |
|---|---|
| 2 | 10-ounce packages frozen chopped broccoli |
| 2 | eggs, beaten |
| 2 | Tbsp. flour |
| 8 | ounces Cheddar cheese, grated |
| ¾ | cup cottage cheese |
| 2 | Tbsp. butter |
| | Salt and pepper to taste |

- Preheat oven to 350 degrees.
- Cook broccoli slightly. Drain.
- Add flour, cheeses and broccoli to eggs.
- Melt butter in 1½-quart casserole. Add mixture.
- Bake at 350 degrees for 25-30 minutes.

# BROCCOLI-CAULIFLOWER AU GRATIN

Serves 6-8

| | |
|---|---|
| 1 | 10-ounce package frozen broccoli |
| 1 | 10-ounce package frozen cauliflower |
| 2 | Tbsp. butter |
| 1½ | Tbsp. flour |
| ¼ | tsp. each of salt, seasoned salt, pepper |
| 1½ | cups milk |
| ¼ | cup chopped onion |
| 2 | ounces pimientos, chopped and drained |
| ¾ | cup grated Cheddar cheese |
| 10 | saltines, crushed |
| | Paprika |

- Cook vegetables according to package directions, drain well. Place in 2-quart casserole.
- In saucepan, melt butter. Blend in flour and seasonings. Remove from heat and gradually stir in milk.
- Cook over low heat, stirring constantly until thickened.
- Sprinkle onion, pimiento and cheese over vegetables in casserole.
- Pour sauce over all. Top with cracker crumbs and dash of paprika.
- Bake at 350 degrees for 45 minutes.

# OREGANO PEAS

Serves 4

4   Tbsp. butter, melted
1   10-ounce package frozen peas
1   Tbsp. minced onion
½   tsp. salt
½   tsp. oregano
¼   tsp. seasoned salt
¼   pound fresh mushrooms, sliced

- Add peas to butter and cook until tender.
- Add remaining ingredients. Sauté until hot.

# GREEN BEANS SUPREME

Serves 6-8

2   10-ounce packages frozen French-cut green beans
2   Tbsp. butter, melted
½   cup chopped onion
2   Tbsp. flour
    Salt and pepper
1   cup sour cream
½   cup shredded Cheddar cheese

- Cook beans according to package directions. Drain.
- Sauté onions in butter until tender. Add flour, salt and pepper; mix well.
- Blend in sour cream. Heat thoroughly. Do not boil. Add beans.
- Pour into 1½-quart casserole. Top with cheese.
- Bake at 350 degrees for 15 minutes.

# SNAPS WITH HERBS

Serves 4

1   pound fresh snap beans, cut in 1-inch pieces
3   Tbsp. butter
½   cup chopped onion
¼   cup chopped celery
1   clove garlic, minced
2   tsp. fresh rosemary or ½ tsp. dried
2   tsp. fresh basil or ½ tsp. dried

- Cook or steam snaps until almost tender; drain. Stir in remaining ingredients.
- Cook covered about 5 minutes or until beans are tender.

# CELERY BRAISED IN CONSOMMÉ

Serves 6

| | |
|---|---|
| 2-3 | small heads celery |
| 1 | medium onion, chopped |
| 2 | Tbsp. butter |
| | Dash of pepper |
| 1 | 10-ounce can beef consommé |
| | Grated Parmesan cheese |
| 1 | Tbsp. chopped parsley |

- Scrub celery, remove top leaves, cut each head lengthwise through heart, making 4 or 5 slender sections. If long, cut in half crosswise.
- Arrange celery on top of onions in casserole. Dot with butter and sprinkle with pepper. Add consommé.
- Bake covered at 375 degrees for 60 minutes. Top with Parmesan cheese before serving. Sprinkle with parsley.

# SAUTÉED CABBAGE

Serves 4

| | |
|---|---|
| ¼ | cup olive oil |
| 4 | cups coarsely chopped cabbage |
| 1 | large onion, coarsely chopped |
| | Garlic salt |

- Heat oil in large cast-iron skillet or wok.
- Gradually add cabbage and onion. Toss constantly to coat with oil.
- Sprinkle with garlic salt and cook over medium high heat tossing constantly for 5 minutes. Cabbage should be crisp. Serve immediately.

*Wonderful side dish with Tarragon Pork Chops and Sweet Potato Puff.*

# SUNSHINE CARROTS

Serves 4-6

| | |
|---|---|
| 4½ | cups sliced carrots |
| ½ | cup mayonnaise |
| 2 | Tbsp. chopped onion |
| 2 | Tbsp. prepared horseradish |
| ¼ | tsp. salt |
| | Dash pepper |
| ¼ | cup crushed saltine crackers |
| 2 | tsp. butter, melted |

- Cook carrots covered in boiling salted water until tender. Drain.
- Combine mayonnaise, onion, horseradish, salt and pepper. Toss with carrots. Place in 1-quart casserole.
- Mix crumbs and butter and sprinkle over carrots. Bake uncovered at 350 degrees for 30 minutes.

# CARROT-CAULIFLOWER CHEESE PIE

Serves 8-10

| | |
|---|---|
| 2 | cups herb seasoned croutons, finely crushed |
| ¼ | cup butter, melted |
| 1 | cup chopped onion |
| 1 | garlic clove, minced |
| 2 | Tbsp. butter, melted |
| ½ | tsp. dried savory |
| ½ | tsp. dried oregano |
| ½ | tsp. salt |
| | Dash pepper |
| 4 | cups cauliflorets |
| 2 | cups carrots, sliced |
| 1½ | cups shredded Cheddar cheese |
| 3 | eggs, slightly beaten |
| ½ | cup milk |

- Preheat oven to 375 degrees.
- Combine croutons and butter. Press into deep dish pie plate. Set aside.
- In a saucepan, combine onion, garlic and 2 Tablespoons butter. Cook until onion is tender but not brown.
- Add seasonings. Stir in cauliflorets and carrots. Cook covered over low heat for 10-15 minutes.
- Sprinkle half of cheese over bottom of pie shell. Spoon vegetable mixture over cheese.
- Combine eggs and milk. Pour over vegetables.
- Bake uncovered at 375 degrees for 15 minutes.
- Top with rest of cheese. Bake for 5-10 minutes or until set.

# EPICUREAN EGGPLANT

Serves 6-8

| | |
|---|---|
| 1 | large eggplant |
| 2 | Tbsp. flour |
| ½ | cup oil |
| 2 | eggs, lightly beaten |
| ½ | pound Mozzarella cheese, grated |
| ½ | cup bread crumbs |
| ½ | cup grated Parmesan cheese |
| ½ | tsp. salt |
| ¼ | tsp. pepper |
| ¼ | tsp. crushed dried basil |
| ½ | cup tomato sauce |
| ½ | cup beef bouillon |

- Pare and cut eggplant into ½-inch slices. Dip slices in flour. Fry on both sides in oil until lightly browned. Layer half of the eggplant in bottom of greased 3-quart casserole.
- Combine eggs and Mozzarella cheese. Add bread crumbs, half of Parmesan cheese, pepper, salt and basil. Top eggplant with mixture. Place remaining eggplant in casserole.
- Combine tomato sauce and bouillon. Pour over casserole.
- Sprinkle remaining Parmesan cheese over casserole.
- Bake at 400 degrees for 15 minutes.

# ITALIAN EGGPLANT

Serves 8

| | |
|---|---|
| 1 | eggplant, thinly sliced |
| 2 | summer or zucchini squash, thinly sliced |
| 1 | cup uncooked spaghetti in 1-inch pieces |
| 1 | cup sliced celery |
| 1 | green pepper, thinly sliced |
| 8 | ounces Mozzarella cheese, grated |
| 2 | 8-ounce cans tomato sauce |
| ¼ | cup water |
| 2 | tsp. Worcestershire sauce |
| ½ | tsp. salt |
| 1 | garlic clove, minced |
| | Pinch oregano |

- Combine tomato sauce, water, Worcestershire, salt, garlic and oregano.
- Layer half of vegetables, spaghetti, cheese and tomato mixture in greased 3-quart casserole in order listed. Repeat process.
- Bake, covered, at 350 degrees for 1½ hours.
- For a heartier dish, add a layer of browned ground beef.

# HERBED CARROTS

Serves 4

| | |
|---|---|
| 8 | medium carrots |
| 1 | Tbsp. sugar |
| 3 | Tbsp. butter |
| ¼ | tsp. onion salt |
| ¼ | tsp. celery salt |
| ¼ | tsp. crushed summer savory |
| ¼ | tsp. crushed basil or marjoram |
| ½ | cup hot water |

- Wash carrots, scrape and split. Parboil 10 minutes.
- Mix sugar, butter and seasonings in hot water.
- Place carrots in small casserole. Add liquid. Cover.
- Bake at 350 degrees for 25 minutes or until carrots are tender.

# VIRGINIA BEACH EGGPLANT

Serves 6-8

| | |
|---|---|
| 1 | large eggplant, peeled and sliced |
| | Salt and pepper |
| 1 | large onion, chopped |
| 1 | large green pepper, chopped |
| 4 | Tbsp. butter |
| 1 | cup chopped oysters with juice |
| 1 | cup grated sharp Cheddar cheese |
| 1 | cup cookod, peeled, and deveined small shrimp |
| 1 | Tbsp. flour |
| 1 | tsp. freshly ground pepper |
| 1 | tsp. seasoned salt |
| ¼ | tsp. celery seed |
| | Buttered bread crumbs |

- Parboil eggplant until tender. Drain well. Add salt and pepper.
- Sauté onion and pepper in butter until tender.
- Combine all ingredients except bread crumbs. Add a small amount of cream, if mixture seems dry.
- Pour into greased 3-quart casserole and top with crumbs.
- Bake at 350 degrees for 45 minutes.

*Casserole will freeze; however, leave out oysters and stir in gently when ready to bake.*

# ORANGE GLAZED CARROTS

Serves 6-8

| | |
|---|---|
| 10 | medium carrots |
| ½ | cup orange juice |
| ½ | cup sugar |
| 1 | Tbsp. grated orange rind |
| 1 | Tbsp. cornstarch |
| 1 | tsp. salt |
| 1 | Tbsp. butter |

- Wash carrots, scrape and split. Parboil 10 minutes.
- Place carrots in shallow buttered casserole dish.
- Combine all ingredients except butter and heat until cornstarch is dissolved. Pour over carrots. Dot with butter. Cover.
- Bake at 350 degrees for 30 minutes. Uncover and bake a few minutes longer, until some juice has evaporated.

# SPINACH BARS

Yields 30

| | |
|---|---|
| 1 | 10-ounce package frozen chopped spinach, thawed and drained |
| 4 | Tbsp. butter |
| 3 | eggs, beaten |
| 1 | cup milk |
| ¾ | cup flour |
| 1 | tsp. salt |
| 1 | tsp. baking powder |
| 12-16 | ounces sharp Cheddar cheese, finely grated |
| 1 | small onion, chopped |
| ½ | cup chopped fresh mushrooms |

- Preheat oven to 350 degrees.
- Melt butter in 13 x 9-inch pan.
- Mix remaining ingredients and spoon into pan.
- Bake at 350 degrees for 35 minutes or until lightly browned. Cool slightly and cut into squares.
- Serve hot or at room temperature.

*Good "finger food" for luncheon.*

# SPINACH SOUFFLÉ

Serves 4

| | |
|---|---|
| 1 | 10-ounce package frozen chopped spinach |
| 1 | tsp. grated onion |
| 2 | eggs, beaten |
| 1 | cup grated Parmesan cheese |
| ½ | cup sour cream |
| 1 | Tbsp. flour |
| 2 | Tbsp. butter, softened |
| | Salt and pepper to taste |

- Cook spinach and onion in small amount of water. Drain well.
- Combine eggs with spinach. Add other ingredients and pour into a greased 1-quart casserole.
- Bake at 350 degrees for 30 minutes or until center is set.

# SPINACH AND ARTICHOKES

Serves 8-10

3    **10-ounce packages frozen spinach, cooked and drained**
10    **ounces cream cheese, softened**
1    **Tbsp. butter**
½    **cup chopped onions, sautéed**
1    **tsp. salt**
½    **tsp. pepper**
2    **15-ounce cans artichoke hearts, cut into bite-size pieces**
1    **cup shredded Swiss cheese**
   **Grated Parmesan cheese**

- Combine spinach, cream cheese, butter, onions, salt and pepper.
- Place in a 13 x 9-inch casserole in alternating layers with artichoke hearts, starting with and ending with a layer of spinach. Top with cheeses.
- Bake at 350 degrees for 30 minutes or until bubbly.

# VEGETABLES VIRGINIA

Serves 12-16

2    **10-ounce packages frozen chopped spinach**
1    **10-ounce package frozen chopped broccoli**
1    **10-ounce package frozen artichoke hearts**
1    **10-ounce package frozen zucchini or yellow summer squash**
1    **cup grated Parmesan cheese**
½    **pound fresh mushrooms, sautéed**
   **Salt and pepper to taste**
   **Onion salt, oregano and garlic salt to taste**
9    **eggs, beaten**

- Cook vegetables only until defrosted; drain well.
- Add remaining ingredients except eggs. When ready to bake, mix eggs with vegetables; correct seasonings and place in a greased 13 x 9-inch baking dish.
- Bake uncovered at 350 degrees for 35-40 minutes.

# DILLED SQUASH

Serves 6-8

| | |
|---|---|
| 3 | pounds yellow squash, sliced |
| 2 | medium onions, diced |
| 3 | Tbsp. butter, melted |
| 1 | cup sour cream |
| 1½ | Tbsp. dill weed |
| 1 | Tbsp. cream |
| | Salt and pepper to taste |
| | Bread cubes |
| | Butter |

- Cook squash in a small amount of water with onion and salt. When tender, drain well, removing as much water as possible.
- Mash squash and onion to a pulp. Add butter, sour cream, dill weed, cream, salt and pepper.
- Pour into a 3-quart casserole; top with bread cubes which have been browned lightly in butter.
- Bake at 325 degrees for 20-30 minutes.

# CHEESY SQUASH

Serves 8

| | |
|---|---|
| 2 | pounds yellow squash, sliced and quartered |
| 2 | eggs, slightly beaten |
| ¼ | cup chopped green pepper |
| ¼ | cup chopped onion |
| 1 | cup mayonnaise |
| ½ | cup grated Cheddar cheese |
| ½ | cup grated Parmesan cheese |
| | Salt and pepper |
| | Buttered bread crumbs |

- Cook squash until tender; drain well. Add remaining ingredients. Taste for seasoning.
- Place in a greased 1½-quart casserole.
- Bake at 350 degrees for 20-30 minutes.
- When almost done, sprinkle with crumbs. Return to oven to complete baking.

# NEVER-FAIL HOLLANDAISE

Yields 1 cup

| | |
|---|---|
| 3 | large egg yolks |
| 1 | Tbsp. lemon juice |
| ¼ | pound butter, softened |
| ½ | tsp. salt |
| | Dash white pepper |
| ⅓ | cup boiling water |

- Mix all ingredients except water in blender or food processor until fairly smooth.
- With motor running, add the boiling water in a steady stream. Blend a few seconds longer.
- Pour in top of double boiler. Cook over low heat until thickened. May be reheated over hot water. Will not separate.

# POSH SQUASH

Serves 4-6

1    **cup sliced yellow squash**
1    **cup sliced zucchini**
1    **sliced onion**
2    **sliced tomatoes**
     **Butter**
     **Salt and pepper**
1    **cup grated Cheddar cheese**
     **Bread crumbs**

- Layer squash, zucchini, onion and tomatoes in casserole, beginning and ending with squash or zucchini, adding cheese in middle and on top.
- Dot with butter and salt and pepper. Sprinkle with bread crumbs.
- Bake at 350 degrees for 30-40 minutes.

# ZUCCHINI FRITTERS

Serves 6-8

2    **cups grated zucchini**
½    **medium onion, grated**
2    **eggs, beaten**
½    **cup grated Parmesan cheese**
¼    **tsp. pepper**
     **Chopped parsley**
     **Flour**
     **Oil**

- Combine ingredients, adding enough flour to hold shape when dropped by Tablespoons into hot, shallow oil.
- Brown on both sides; drain on paper towels. Serve immediately or reheat in oven.

# SPICY HOLLANDAISE

Yields 1½ cups

4    **egg yolks**
2    **Tbsp. lemon juice**
¼    **tsp. dry mustard**
     **Dash Tabasco sauce**
½    **pound butter**

- In a blender or food processor, mix first 4 ingredients by pulsing on and off quickly.
- Melt butter, bringing it to a bubbling hot stage.
- Remove blender or processor cover and add butter in a steady stream as sauce blends.
- Do not overblend. Sauce should be smooth and creamy.

*May be made ahead and gently reheated by placing container in warm water, stirring before serving. Serve over broccoli or asparagus.*

# ZUCCHINI SQUARES

Serves 12

| | |
|---|---|
| 1 | **cup buttermilk baking mix** |
| 4 | **eggs, beaten** |
| ½ | **cup vegetable oil** |
| ½ | **cup grated Parmesan cheese** |
| ½ | **cup chopped onion** |
| 2 | **Tbsp. chopped fresh parsley** |
| 1 | **garlic clove, minced** |
| ½ | **tsp. seasoned salt** |
| ½ | **tsp. dried, crushed oregano** |
| | **Dash of pepper** |
| 2 | **medium zucchini, thinly sliced** |

- Combine all ingredients except zucchini; beat well.
- Stir in zucchini. Pour into a greased 13 × 9-inch baking dish.
- Bake at 350 degrees for 35 minutes or until golden brown. Let stand 10 minutes before serving.

# MEXICAN MEDLEY

Serves 8

| | |
|---|---|
| 1 | **pound zucchini, cubed** |
| ¾ | **pound eggplant, cubed** |
| 1 | **cup thin onion strips** |
| ½ | **cup green pepper strips** |
| 1 | **8-ounce jar hot or mild picanté sauce** |
| 1 | **6-ounce can tomato paste** |
| 1¼ | **tsp. salt** |

- Combine first five ingredients. Bring to a boil, simmer covered 30 minutes, or until tender.
- Stir in tomato paste and salt. Reheat slowly to blend flavors. Serve hot, or chill and serve cold.

# TEMPTING TOMATOES

Serves 6

6   large tomatoes, peeled,
and sliced into ½-inch
slices
1   green pepper, chopped
½   tsp. Italian herbs
¼   tsp. salt
¼   tsp. black pepper
¼   tsp. cayenne pepper
1   Tbsp. brown sugar
3   spring onions, including
tops, chopped
1   cup Italian bread crumbs
¼   cup butter, melted
1   cup grated sharp Cheddar
cheese

- Place tomatoes in a 9-inch round casserole. Season while stacking with green pepper, herbs, salt and peppers.
- Sprinkle with sugar, onions and bread crumbs. Pour butter over all; top with grated cheese.
- Bake at 375 degrees for 25 minutes.

*Best in summer when tomatoes are in season.*

# TOMATO PIE

Serves 4-6

1   9-inch deep dish pie
shell, baked
2-3   large tomatoes, thickly
sliced and drained
2-3   green onions, chopped
Salt and pepper
Basil
Chives
1   cup mayonnaise
1   cup grated sharp cheese

- Fill cooled pie shell with alternating layers of tomatoes and onions, sprinkled with salt, pepper, basil and chives.
- Combine mayonnaise and cheese and spread over tomatoes.
- Bake at 350 degrees for 30 minutes.

# TANTALIZING TOMATOES AND ARTICHOKES Serves 6

| | |
|---|---|
| 1 | 28-ounce can whole pear-shaped tomatoes |
| 1 | 14-ounce can artichoke hearts |
| ½ | cup finely chopped onion |
| 2 | Tbsp. finely chopped shallots |
| ¼ | pound butter |
| ½ | tsp. basil |
| 2 | Tbsp. sugar |
| | Salt and pepper |

- Drain tomatoes and artichokes and quarter.
- Sauté onions and shallots in butter until tender. Add tomatoes, artichokes and basil; heat 2-3 minutes. Add sugar, salt and pepper. Place in 1½-quart casserole.
- Bake at 325 degrees for 15-20 minutes or until hot.

# BROILED TOMATO CUPS

Serves 10-12

| | |
|---|---|
| 5-6 | tomatoes |
| ½ | cup sour cream |
| ½ | cup mayonnaise |
| ¼ | cup grated Parmesan cheese |
| 1 | tsp. garlic salt |
| | Juice of 1 lemon |
| 1 | tsp. chopped parsley |
| 3 | green onions, chopped |

- Cut tomatoes in half, crosswise.
- Combine remaining ingredients, blending well.
- Top each tomato half with a small amount of mixture.
- Broil tomatoes until bubbly.

# CURRY SAUCE

Yields 1 cup

| | |
|---|---|
| ½ | cup mayonnaise |
| ½ | cup sour cream |
| ½ | tsp. curry powder |
| ½ | tsp. salt |
| | Dash seasoned salt |

- Blend all ingredients and refrigerate if not needed immediately.
- Excellent on vegetables.

# TOMATOES ROCKEFELLER

Serves 12

12    **thick tomato slices**
2    **10-ounce packages frozen chopped spinach, cooked and drained**
1    **cup soft bread crumbs**
1    **cup seasoned bread crumbs**
1    **cup finely chopped green onions**
6    **eggs, slightly beaten**
¾    **cup butter, melted**
½    **cup grated Parmesan cheese**
1    **tsp. thyme**
¾    **tsp. salt**
½    **tsp. minced garlic**

- Place tomato slices in a lightly greased 13 x 9-inch baking dish. Set aside.
- Squeeze excess water from spinach and combine with remaining ingredients.
- Mound mixture on tomato slices.
- Bake at 350 degrees for 15 minutes or until spinach mixture is set.

# SPINACH TOMATOES

Yields 8

8    **medium tomatoes**
   **Salt**
8    **slices bacon, crisply cooked and crumbled**
2    **10-ounce packages frozen chopped spinach**
¾    **cup soft bread crumbs**
   **Salt and pepper**
   **Pinch ground nutmeg**
   **Pinch garlic powder**
   **Melted butter**
   **Sour cream**

- With a sharp knife, cut a thin slice from top of each tomato. Scoop out pulp and discard. Sprinkle insides with salt; turn upside down to drain for about an hour.
- Cook spinach only until defrosted; drain well.
- Combine bacon, spinach, bread crumbs, salt, pepper, nutmeg, garlic powder and a little melted butter.
- Stuff tomatoes with mixture; place in a buttered baking dish. Drizzle a small amount of melted butter over tomatoes.
- Bake uncovered at 350 degrees for about 20 minutes, or until tender but still holding shape. Top with a dollop of sour cream.

# REGAL MUSHROOMS

Serves 4-6
Do ahead

| | |
|---|---|
| 1 | pound mushrooms, washed and halved |
| ½ | cup dry red wine |
| ¼ | cup teriyaki sauce |
| ¼ | cup butter |
| ¼ | cup chopped onion |
| ¼ | cup toasted almonds |

- Marinate mushrooms in wine and teriyaki sauce for 2-3 hours. Drain mushrooms, reserving marinade.
- Sauté mushrooms and onion in butter. Return marinade to mushrooms; add almonds. Simmer 5-10 minutes.

# SAVORY STUFFED MUSHROOMS

Serves 6-8

| | |
|---|---|
| 16 | large mushrooms, wiped clean and stemmed, stems chopped and reserved |
| ¼ | pound butter |
| 3 | Tbsp. finely chopped green pepper |
| 3 | Tbsp. finely chopped onion |
| 1 | cup herb stuffing mix |
| ½ | tsp. salt |
| ⅛ | tsp. pepper |
| | Dash cayenne pepper |
| 1 | tsp. Worcestershire sauce |

- Preheat oven to 350 degrees.
- Heat 3 Tablespoons butter in large skillet; add mushrooms, sautéeing only on bottom side 2-3 minutes.
- Remove and arrange top side down in shallow baking pan.
- Heat remaining butter in same skillet, sautéeing stems, peppers and onions until tender.
- Remove from heat and stir in stuffing mix and seasonings. Fill mushroom caps, mounding mixture high in center.
- Bake at 350 degrees for 15 minutes; serve immediately.

# PARMESAN ARTICHOKES ATLANTIC

Serves 12

| | |
|---|---|
| 3 | 14-ounce cans artichoke hearts, drained and halved |
| 6 | Tbsp. butter |
| 4 | Tbsp. flour |
| 1½ | cups milk |
| | Dash of Tabasco sauce |
| ½ | cup grated Gruyère cheese |
| ½ | cup heavy cream |
| | Salt and pepper |
| ½ | cup grated Parmesan cheese |

- Preheat oven to 400 degrees.
- Place artichoke hearts in shallow pan.
- Melt 4 Tablespoons butter, stir in flour; add milk, Tabasco sauce, Gruyère cheese, cream and seasonings to taste. Stir until thickened.
- Pour over artichoke hearts. Melt remaining butter, brush over top of dish and sprinkle with Parmesan cheese.
- Bake at 400 degrees for 10-12 minutes.

# CREOLE WATERCRESS FRITTERS

Makes 48

| | |
|---|---|
| 2½ | pounds watercress, ends trimmed and leaves washed |
| ¾ | cup water |
| 6 | eggs |
| 1 | large Spanish onion, chopped |
| 2 | Tbsp. shallots, chopped |
| 1 | large tomato, skinned, seeded and chopped |
| 1-1½ | Tbsp. creole seasoning to taste |
| 1 | 2½-ounce jar pimientos, drained and dried |
| | Olive or vegetable oil for cooking |

- Drop watercress into large pan in which water has come to boil. Cook 2-3 minutes; remove from heat and allow to sit for 2-3 minutes. Drain and set aside to cool.
- When cool, squeeze watercress between paper towels until all moisture is absorbed.
- Place cress in processor and pulse several times to chop. Do not purée.
- Add eggs, onion, shallots, tomato and creole seasoning. Pulse mixture several times. Add pimientos, pulsing only enough to mix. Batter should be coarse but not stringy.
- Heat oil in large frying pan over medium-low heat. Spoon rounded Tablespoons into pan, about 4 at a time, well separated. Gently sauté fritters on each side about 45 seconds.
- Remove and drain on paper towels.

*Cress, tomatoes and pimientos should be as dry as possible
so that fritters will not fall apart or oil foam up as you sauté.*

# CORN CASSEROLE

Serves 6-8

| | |
|---|---|
| 6 | slices bacon, cooked and crumbled |
| 2 | medium onions, sliced |
| 2 | 16-ounce cans whole kernel corn, drained |
| | Salt and pepper to taste |
| 1 | cup sour cream |

- Sauté onions in small amount of bacon drippings.
- Add salt and pepper to corn. Stir in onions, bacon drippings and sour cream.
- Spoon mixture into 1½-quart casserole. Top with bacon.
- Bake at 350 degrees just until mixture is thoroughly heated, 10-15 minutes.

# CORN PUDDING

Serves 6-8

| | |
|---|---|
| 6 | ears corn |
| ¼ | pound butter |
| 1½ | cups milk |
| 5 | eggs |
| | Pinch of salt |
| 2 | Tbsp. sugar |
| 1 | Tbsp. flour |

- Cut corn off cob. Scrape cob with knife to release juice into bowl.
- Melt butter in milk.
- Beat eggs with wire whisk. Mix all ingredients, adding eggs last.
- Bake in buttered 3-quart casserole at 375 degrees for 40 minutes or until brown.

# MAMIE'S CORN CAKES

Makes 16-20 thin cakes

| | |
|---|---|
| ¾ | cup milk |
| ½ | cup yellow corn meal |
| ¼ | cup flour |
| 1 | egg |
| 2 | Tbsp. sugar |
| 2 | Tbsp. butter, melted |
| 1 | tsp. salt |
| ½ | tsp. baking powder |

- Mix all ingredients. Mixture will be thin.
- Cook pancakes 3 inches in diameter on hot griddle (400 degrees). Turn as soon as pancakes are firm.
- Serve hot with butter.

*Serve as accompaniment with Smithfield Ham or fish.*

# CARRY ALONG BAKED BEANS

Serves 20

½     **pound bacon, cooked**
2     **Tbsp. bacon grease**
3     **medium onions, sliced**
2     **garlic cloves, chopped**
1     **cup brown sugar**
½     **cup vinegar**
¼     **tsp. dry mustard**
2     **15-ounce cans each of kidney, lima and northern white beans (or any combination), drained**

- Drain bacon on paper towels. Cook onions in grease, adding garlic.
- When onions are translucent, add brown sugar, vinegar and mustard. Simmer 20 minutes.
- While simmering, crumble bacon into mixture. Add beans; cover and simmer 1 hour.

# AU GRATIN POTATOES

Serves 6

5-6     **medium red potatoes**
1     **clove garlic, cut in half**
4     **Tbsp. butter**
1     **tsp. salt**
⅛     **tsp. pepper**
½     **cup grated sharp Cheddar cheese**
½     **cup grated Swiss cheese**
1     **cup boiling milk**

- Preheat oven to 425 degrees.
- Peel and thinly slice potatoes. Place in cold water until ready to cook.
- Rub a shallow 1½-quart baking dish with garlic. Use 1 Tablespoon of the butter to grease the dish.
- Drain potato slices and dry on paper towels. Spread half of the potatoes in the prepared baking dish. Divide the remaining butter, salt, pepper and cheese and sprinkle over potatoes. Repeat layers, ending with cheese. Pour milk over all.
- Bake at 425 degrees in the upper third of oven for 30-40 minutes until potatoes are tender, milk is absorbed and top is browned.

# POTATOES PIERRE

Serves 8

| | |
|---|---|
| 2½ | pounds potatoes, peeled and thinly sliced |
| 6 | Tbsp. butter |
| 2 | Tbsp. chopped parsley |
| 1 | tsp. salt |
| | Ground pepper to taste |
| 1 | small Spanish onion, thinly sliced |
| 1 | cup grated Gruyère cheese |
| ¼ | cup grated Parmesan cheese |
| 1¼ | cups beef broth, boiling |

- Preheat oven to 425 degrees.
- Butter inside of a 2-quart baking dish with 2 Tablespoons of the butter.
- Pat dry about half of the potatoes and overlap slices on the bottom of the baking dish to make the first layer. Sprinkle with half of the parsley, salt, pepper, onions and cheeses. Dot with 2 Tablespoons of butter. Repeat process for second layer.
- Pour in boiling broth.
- Bake at 425 degrees for 55-60 minutes until potatoes can be pierced with a fork, top is brown and broth absorbed.

*If there are any left, these are even better the second day!*

# GOLDEN STUFFED POTATOES

Serves 12

| | |
|---|---|
| 6 | large baking potatoes |
| 4 | Tbsp. butter |
| 2 | cups grated sharp Cheddar cheese |
| 1½ | cups sour cream |
| ⅓ | cup chopped green onions |
| 1 | tsp. salt |
| ¼ | tsp. pepper |
| 2 | Tbsp. butter |

- Bake potatoes at 400 degrees for 1 hour or until done.
- Meanwhile, in medium saucepan over low heat, combine the 4 Tablespoons butter and cheese, stirring occasionally, until almost melted. Remove from heat; blend in sour cream, onions, salt and pepper.
- Cut baked potatoes in half lengthwise and scoop out pulp. Place in large bowl and mash. Fold cheese mixture into potatoes.
- Stuff potato skins. Dot with butter and heat in 350 degree oven for 10 minutes.

# GERMAN POTATO PANCAKES

Makes 1-1½ dozen

| | |
|---|---|
| 5-6 | **medium potatoes, peeled and coarsely grated** |
| ½ | **medium onion, coarsely grated** |
| 1 | **egg** |
| 3-6 | **Tbsp. flour** |
| 6 | **Tbsp. milk** |
| ½ | **tsp. salt** |
| ⅛ | **tsp. pepper** |
| | **Vegetable oil or bacon grease** |

- Combine all ingredients except oil, mixing well and using enough flour to absorb moisture.
- Preheat about ¼ inch oil or bacon grease in a large skillet.
- When oil is hot but not smoking, add large spoonfuls of potato mixture, one at a time, flattening slightly into a pancake shape. Fry 3-4 minutes until browned; turn and continue to cook until other side is brown and crisp.
- Remove with slotted utensil to paper towels. Serve immediately or keep warm in a 200 degree oven until entire batch is done.

*A different twist to the usual potato dish.*

# SWEET POTATO PUFF

Serves 6-8

| | |
|---|---|
| 3 | **cups cooked and mashed sweet potatoes** |
| ¼ | **pound butter, melted** |
| 2 | **eggs** |
| 1 | **cup sugar** |
| 1 | **tsp. pumpkin pie spice** |
| 1 | **tsp. vanilla** |
| 1 | **cup crushed, drained pineapple** |
| ½ | **cup raisins** |

- Combine ingredients and place in flat baking dish.

**TOPPING**

| | |
|---|---|
| 1 | **cup brown sugar** |
| ⅓ | **cup butter, melted** |
| ⅓ | **cup flour** |
| 1 | **cup chopped pecans** |

- Combine ingredients. Sprinkle over casserole.
- Bake at 325 degrees for 30 minutes.

# SWEET POTATO AND CARROT PURÉE

Serves 6

| | |
|---|---|
| 4 | large sweet potatoes |
| 1 | pound carrots |
| 2½ | cups water |
| 1 | Tbsp. sugar |
| 12 | Tbsp. butter |
| | Salt and pepper to taste |
| ½ | cup sour cream |
| ½ | tsp. nutmeg |

- Scrub potatoes, cut small slit in each. Bake at 375 degrees for 1 hour or until tender.
- Peel and trim carrots into 1-inch lengths. Place in saucepan with water, sugar, 2 Tablespoons butter, salt and pepper. Bring to a boil over medium heat; cook uncovered until water has evaporated, about 30 minutes.
- Scrape out flesh of sweet potatoes, combine with carrots in food processor using steel blade. Add remaining butter and sour cream, processing until smooth. Add nutmeg, salt and pepper. Pour into serving dish and cover with foil.
- Bake at 325 degrees for 25 minutes.

# SHERRIED SWEET POTATOES

Serves 6-8

| | |
|---|---|
| 6-8 | sweet potatoes, baked |

**SAUCE**

| | |
|---|---|
| 6 | Tbsp. butter, melted |
| 2 | Tbsp. cornstarch |
| 1 | cup brown sugar |
| ⅓ | cup Sherry |
| 1 | tsp. salt |
| ½ | cup raisins |
| ½ | cup chopped walnuts |

- Peel and slice sweet potatoes; place in one layer in a 13 x 9-inch greased baking dish.

- Combine sauce ingredients except raisins and nuts in order given. Cook over medium heat until sauce thickens. Add raisins and nuts. Cool slightly and pour over sweet potatoes.
- Bake at 350 degrees for 20 minutes.

# SWEET POTATO AND APPLE SUPREME

Serves 6

| | |
|---|---|
| 3 | sweet potatoes, peeled, sliced and cut into pieces |
| 3 | tart apples, sliced |
| 1 | cup miniature marshmallows |
| ¼ | cup sugar |
| ¼ | cup brown sugar |
| 1 | tsp. salt |
| 1 | tsp. cinnamon |
| | Butter |
| | Additional marshmallows |

- Mix sugars, salt and cinnamon. Combine with potatoes, apples and marshmallows.
- Spread in greased 13 x 9-inch baking dish. Dot with butter. Cover tightly.
- Bake at 325 degrees for 45-60 minutes.
- Remove from oven; sprinkle extra marshmallows on top. Serve warm.

# LEMON-DILL RICE

Serves 8-10

| | |
|---|---|
| 1 | large onion, minced |
| 2 | cups uncooked rice |
| 3 | Tbsp. butter |
| 5 | cups water |
| 2 | tsp. salt |
| 2 | Tbsp. dill seed or dill weed |
| ¼ | cup fresh lemon juice |

- Preheat oven to 325 degrees.
- Brown onion and rice in butter. Add water and seasonings. Mix and bring to a boil.
- Transfer to a 2-quart casserole dish. Cover and bake at 325 degrees for 45-60 minutes.

# RICE PILAF

Serves 6-8

| | |
|---|---|
| 6 | **Tbsp. butter** |
| 1 | **medium onion, chopped** |
| ¼ | **cup finely chopped green pepper** |
| 2 | **stalks celery, finely chopped** |
| 1 | **cup uncooked rice** |
| ¼ | **tsp. crushed thyme leaves** |
| 1 | **10¾-ounce can chicken broth** |
| | **Water added to broth to equal 2 cups** |
| | **Salt and pepper to taste** |

- Preheat oven to 350 degrees.
- Heat half of butter in skillet; add onion, pepper and celery and sauté until golden. Remove vegetables and set aside.
- In same skillet, heat remaining butter; add rice and brown slightly, stirring, over low heat. Stir in vegetables and thyme.
- Meanwhile, heat broth/water mixture to boiling. Stir into rice mixture. Add salt and pepper. Transfer to 1½-quart casserole.
- Bake covered at 350 degrees for 30-40 minutes until liquid is absorbed and rice is tender.
- As a variation, add chopped fresh tomatoes after rice is cooked.

*Wonderful served with Hawaiian Chicken.*

# ROYAL RICE

Serves 6-8

| | |
|---|---|
| 1 | **12-ounce jar marinated artichoke hearts** |
| 1 | **cup uncooked rice** |
| 2 | **cups chicken broth** |
| ¼ | **tsp. salt** |
| | **Pinch thyme** |
| 4 | **scallions, chopped** |
| ½ | **green pepper, diced** |
| ⅓ | **cup mayonnaise** |
| ¾ | **tsp. curry powder** |

- Drain artichokes reserving liquid; set aside.
- Cook rice in broth in covered saucepan.
- When rice is done, add salt, thyme, scallions, artichokes and green pepper; mix well.
- Combine marinade from artichokes with mayonnaise and curry. Gently toss with rice mixture.
- Serve immediately as a warm side dish or chill and serve as luncheon salad.

# SOUR CREAM RICE

Serves 8-10

1    **cup uncooked rice**
2    **Tbsp. sugar, divided**
1    **pint sour cream, divided**
¾-1  **pound Cheddar cheese, grated and divided**
     **Coarsely ground black pepper**

- Preheat oven to 350 degrees.
- Cook rice according to package directions.
- Layer half of rice in a 1½-quart ungreased casserole. Sprinkle with 1 Tablespoon sugar. Spread half the sour cream over rice and spread half the cheese over sour cream. Sprinkle with pepper. Repeat layers.
- Bake uncovered at 350 degrees for 45-60 minutes or until hot and bubbly.

*Wonderful with roast beef.*

# RICE WITH CHEESE AND OLIVES

Serves 4-6

1    **cup uncooked rice**
⅔    **cup stuffed olives, sliced**
½    **cup oil**
1    **onion, diced**
2    **cups water**
1    **cup grated Cheddar cheese**
½    **tsp. salt**
¼    **tsp. pepper**

- Preheat oven to 325 degrees.
- Combine all ingredients. Transfer to a greased 1½-quart casserole dish.
- Bake at 325 degrees for ½ hour covered, then ½ hour uncovered. Serve piping hot.

## GRAPE-CHEESE PILAF

Serves 6

| | |
|---|---|
| 1 | 10¾-ounce can onion soup |
| 1 | soup can water |
| 1½ | tsp. mixed herbs |
| 1 | bay leaf |
| ¼ | tsp. salt |
| ¼ | tsp. pepper |
| 1 | cup rice |
| 1 | cup shredded Cheddar cheese |
| 2 | Tbsp. butter |
| 1½ | cups Tokay grapes, seeded and halved |

- In a medium saucepan, bring first 6 ingredients to a boil. Add rice, bringing back to a boil. Reduce heat to simmer and cook covered for 20 minutes.
- When rice is cooked, remove bay leaf, add cheese, butter and grapes.
- Serve immediately.

## PATIO PEAS AND RICE

Serves 6-8
Do ahead

| | |
|---|---|
| 4 | cups cooked rice |
| ½ | cup French dressing |
| 2 | 10-ounce packages frozen tiny peas |
| ½-1 | cup mayonnaise |
| 2 | Tbsp. minced onion |
| 1 | rounded tsp. curry powder or more to taste |
| ¾ | tsp. salt |
| ¼ | tsp. pepper |
| ½ | tsp. dry mustard |
| 1½ | cups diced celery |
| 1 | can sliced water chestnuts, drained |

- Toss warm rice with French dressing and allow to cool to room temperature.
- Cook peas for 1 minute; drain.
- Add peas and all other ingredients to rice. Toss, mixing well. Refrigerate overnight.
- Serve in a glass bowl or on lettuce and garnish with cherry tomatoes.

*Good for a summer buffet.*

# SAVORY RICE WITH SPINACH

Serves 6-8

| | |
|---|---|
| 1 | medium onion, diced |
| ¼ | cup olive oil |
| 1½ | cups uncooked rice |
| 6 | chicken bouillon cubes |
| 3 | cups boiling water |
| ½ | tsp. sage |
| 1 | 10-ounce package frozen spinach, partially thawed |

- Preheat oven to 375 degrees.
- Sauté onion in oil. Add rice. Sauté 2-3 minutes, stirring well. Transfer to a 1½-quart casserole.
- Dissolve bouillon cubes in water and add sage. Pour over rice.
- Place spinach on top of rice.
- Bake covered at 375 degrees for 45 minutes or until liquid is absorbed. When done, gently stir spinach into rice.

# HERBED LENTILS AND RICE

Serves 4

| | |
|---|---|
| 3½ | cups chicken broth |
| ¾ | cup dry lentils |
| ¾ | cup chopped onion |
| ½ | cup uncooked brown rice |
| ¼ | cup dry red wine |
| ½ | tsp. crushed dried basil |
| ¼ | tsp. salt |
| ¼ | tsp. oregano |
| ¼ | tsp. thyme |
| ⅛ | tsp. garlic powder |
| ⅛ | tsp. pepper |
| 4 | ounces Swiss cheese, shredded and divided in half |

- Preheat oven to 350 degrees.
- Combine all ingredients except ½ of Swiss cheese. Mix well and turn into an ungreased 2-quart casserole.
- Bake covered at 350 degrees for 1½-2 hours, or until rice and lentils are done, stirring twice during cooking.
- Uncover and sprinkle remaining cheese on top.
- Bake 2-3 minutes more until cheese melts.

*An inexpensive, healthful and delicious meatless dinner!*

# CHEESE GRITS

Serves 6

| | |
|---|---|
| 1 | quart milk |
| ½ | cup butter |
| 1 | cup regular grits, uncooked (not fast-cooking) |
| 1 | tsp. salt |
| ⅛ | tsp. pepper |
| 1 | cup grated Swiss cheese |
| ⅓ | cup grated Parmesan cheese |
| ⅓ | cup butter, melted |

- Preheat oven to 325 degrees.
- Bring milk to boil and add ½ cup butter.
- Stir in grits, salt, pepper and Swiss cheese. Resume boil and continue cooking, stirring frequently, until thickened. Remove from heat and let rest for 5 minutes.
- Beat 5 minutes with electric mixer. Pour into buttered 2-quart casserole, sprinkle Parmesan cheese and melted butter on top. Bake at 325 degrees uncovered for 25-30 minutes.
- Brown top under broiler if desired.

*Wonderful with Smithfield Ham and Cranberry Freeze.*

# BATTER BREAD

Serves 8

| | |
|---|---|
| 1 | cup plain corn meal |
| ¼ | cup sugar |
| 1 | tsp. salt |
| 4 | cups milk, warmed |
| ¼ | pound butter, melted |
| 1½ | tsp. baking powder |
| 4 | eggs, well beaten |

- Preheat oven to 350 degrees.
- In a saucepan, mix corn meal, sugar and salt together with a fork. Slowly pour warmed milk over mixture. Cook slowly until mixture thickens, stirring constantly. Remove from heat and add butter.
- Allow to cool slightly; stir in baking powder and beaten eggs.
- Bake in large casserole at 350 degrees for 40-50 minutes.

*Serve with Charcoaled Fish and Broiled Tomato Cups.*

# OYSTER BREAD

Serves 6

| | |
|---|---|
| 1 | quart fresh oysters with juice |
| ½ | cup yellow corn meal |
| ¼ | cup flour |
| 8 | slices bacon, cooked crisp and crumbled |
| ¾ | tsp. baking powder |
| ¼-½ | tsp. salt |
| ¼ | tsp. pepper |
| 3 | Tbsp. butter, melted |
| ½ | cup chopped parsley |

- Preheat oven to 400 degrees.
- Mix all ingredients, stirring until well mixed.
- Pour mixture into a greased shallow 2-quart baking dish.
- Bake at 400 degrees for 15 minutes. Raise temperature to 450 degrees and bake for 10 minutes. Raise temperature to 500 degrees and bake for 5-10 minutes, until slightly brown on top.

*Wonderful for oyster lovers, despite its "drab" look.*

# AUNT MARY'S ONION SHORTCAKE

Serves 6

| | |
|---|---|
| 2 | cups buttermilk baking mix |
| ⅔ | cup milk |
| 3 | large onions, sliced |
| 2 | Tbsp. butter |
| 2 | eggs |
| 1 | small can evaporated milk |
| ½ | tsp. salt |
| ¼ | tsp. pepper |

- Preheat oven to 350 degrees.
- Combine baking mix and milk until soft dough forms. Set aside.
- Steam onions in butter until iridescent.
- In a small bowl, beat eggs, evaporated milk, salt and pepper.
- Press dough into greased 11 x 7-inch casserole; top with onions. Pour egg mixture over all.
- Bake at 350 degrees for 30 minutes or until brown.

# APPLE-PECAN STUFFING

Serves 6-8

| | |
|---|---|
| 1 | cup chicken broth |
| ½ | cup chopped celery |
| ¼ | cup chopped onion |
| 4 | Tbsp. butter |
| ½ | tsp. salt |
| 4 | cups dry whole wheat bread cubes |
| 2 | medium apples, pared and chopped |
| ½ | cup chopped pecans |
| 1 | tsp. ground sage |
| ¼ | tsp. cinnamon |
| ⅛ | tsp. pepper |

- Combine the first 5 ingredients in saucepan and simmer for 5-10 minutes until tender.
- Combine remaining ingredients in bowl and pour broth mixture over all. Mix well.
- Stuff mixture loosely into bird or place in casserole.
- In casserole, bake at 350 degrees for 25-30 minutes.

# ROQUEFORT "FAIL-SAFE" SOUFFLÉ

Serves 6

| | |
|---|---|
| 6 | eggs |
| ½ | cup heavy cream |
| 1 | tsp. Worcestershire sauce |
| | Dash Tabasco sauce |
| ¼ | tsp. pepper |
| | Pinch salt |
| ½ | pound Roquefort or Blue cheese |
| 11 | ounces cream cheese |
| 1 | Tbsp. butter |

- Preheat oven to 375 degrees.
- Place first six ingredients in blender and blend until smooth.
- With blender running, break off pieces of Roquefort and cream cheese and add to the mixture. After all cheese is incorporated, blend at high speed for 5 seconds.
- Butter 6-cup soufflé dish or any deep baking dish, or use individual 1-cup baking dishes. Pour in batter and place in preheated oven.
- Bake at 375 degrees for 40-50 minutes. Individual soufflés bake 15-20 minutes.
- When done, the top should be nicely browned and center should jiggle a bit.
- Serve at once. If dish must be held, turn oven off and leave door partially open.

*May be prepared 1-2 hours ahead and set aside, covered, at room temperature until baking.*

# DESSERTS

# DESSERTS

## BARS

## COOKIES

## CONFECTIONS

## CAKES

## ICINGS

## PIES AND PIE CRUST

## CHEESECAKES

## REFRIGERATED DESSERTS

## FROZEN DESSERTS

## SWEET TEMPTATIONS

## SPECIAL SAUCES

# FUDGIES

Makes 36

| | |
|---|---|
| 4 | 1-ounce squares unsweetened chocolate |
| ½ | pound butter |
| 4 | eggs, beaten |
| 2 | cups sugar |
| ½ | cup flour |
| 1 | tsp. vanilla |
| | Confectioners sugar |

- Preheat oven to 375 degrees.
- Melt chocolate and butter over low heat.
- Beat eggs and sugar together. Add flour and vanilla. Add chocolate mixture and blend.
- Pour into greased 13 x 9-inch pan or two 8-inch square pans.
- Bake at 375 degrees for 20 minutes.
- Cool. Sprinkle with confectioners sugar.
- Cut into squares.

*Optional method to serve as pie:*
- Pour into two 9-inch pie pans.
- Bake at 350 degrees for 25-30 minutes.
- Cut into wedges and serve with fudge sauce and whipped cream.

# BLACK BOTTOM SQUARES

Makes 36-48

**FILLING**

| | |
|---|---|
| 8 | ounces cream cheese, softened |
| 1 | egg |
| ½ | cup sugar |
| ½ | tsp. salt |
| 6 | ounces semi-sweet chocolate chips |

- Preheat oven to 350 degrees.
- Mix first 4 ingredients for 4-5 minutes or until well blended.
- Add chips; blend. Set aside.

**BATTER**

| | |
|---|---|
| 1½ | cups flour |
| 1 | cup sugar |
| ¼ | cup cocoa |
| 1 | tsp. baking soda |
| ½ | tsp. salt |
| 1 | cup water |
| ⅓ | cup oil |
| 1 | Tbsp. vinegar |
| 1 | tsp. vanilla |

- Mix dry ingredients. Add all other ingredients and mix well.
- Pour into 13 x 9-inch pan. With a Tablespoon, drop filling on top of batter.
- Bake at 350 degrees for 30-35 minutes.
- Allow to cool for ½ hour before cutting into small pieces.
- As an alternative, divide batter into miniature muffin tins. Top with ½-1 teaspoon of filling.
- Bake at 350 degrees for 10-15 minutes.

# BLACK TIE BROWNIES

Makes 36-48

### BROWNIES

½    **pound butter, melted**
4    **Tbsp. cocoa**
1    **cup water**
2    **cups flour**
2    **cups sugar**
1    **tsp. baking soda**
½    **tsp. salt**
½    **cup buttermilk**
2    **eggs**
1    **tsp. vanilla**

- Preheat oven to 350 degrees.
- Add cocoa and water to butter. Bring to a boil.
- Sift together flour, sugar, soda and salt. Add boiling cocoa mixture. Stir until just blended.
- Add buttermilk, eggs and vanilla. Stir until smooth.
- Pour into greased jelly roll pan.
- Bake at 350 degrees for 15-20 minutes.

### FROSTING

¼    **pound butter, melted**
4    **Tbsp. cocoa**
6    **Tbsp. buttermilk**
1    **box confectioners sugar**
1    **tsp. vanilla**
1    **cup chopped nuts**

- Add cocoa and buttermilk to butter. Bring to boil.
- Add sugar and vanilla, stirring until smooth.
- Pour over warm brownies; sprinkle with nuts.

# FANFARE FUDGE

Makes 48
Do ahead

4½    **cups sugar**
1    **13-ounce can evaporated milk**
18    **ounces semi-sweet chocolate pieces**
½    **pound butter**
3    **tsp. vanilla**
2    **cups chopped pecans**

- Combine sugar and milk in saucepan. Bring to a boil and boil over medium heat for exactly 6 minutes, stirring constantly.
- Remove from heat, adding rest of ingredients. Stir.
- Spread evenly in greased 13 x 9-inch pan and allow to set up in a cool place for 6 hours before cutting.

# BEWITCHING FUDGE BARS

Makes 12-24

## BAR

| | |
|---|---|
| ¼ | pound butter |
| 1 | square unsweetened chocolate |
| 1 | cup flour |
| 1 | tsp. baking powder |
| 1 | cup sugar |
| 2 | eggs |
| 1 | tsp. vanilla |
| 1 | cup chopped nuts |

- Preheat oven to 350 degrees.
- Melt butter and chocolate over low heat.
- Sift together flour and baking powder.
- Add sugar to butter mixture, beating until thoroughly mixed. Mix in flour and eggs alternately, beating well after each addition.
- Add vanilla and fold in nuts.
- Spread in greased and floured 13 x 9-inch pan.

## FILLING

| | |
|---|---|
| 6 | ounces cream cheese |
| ½ | cup sugar |
| 2 | Tbsp. flour |
| 4 | Tbsp. butter, softened |
| 1 | egg |
| ½ | tsp. vanilla |
| ¼ | cup chopped nuts |
| 6 | ounces semi-sweet chocolate chips |
| 2 | cups miniature marshmallows |

- Combine first 6 ingredients, blending until smooth and fluffy.
- Stir in nuts.
- Spread over bar mixture in pan. Sprinkle with chips.
- Bake at 350 degrees for 25-30 minutes.
- Sprinkle with marshmallows and bake 2 minutes.
- While bars are baking, make frosting.

## FROSTING

| | |
|---|---|
| ¼ | cup butter, softened |
| 1 | square unsweetened chocolate |
| 2 | ounces cream cheese |
| ¼ | cup milk |
| 1 | pound confectioners sugar |
| 1 | tsp. vanilla |

- Heat first 4 ingredients over low heat. Stir until smooth.
- Stir in sugar and vanilla, mixing until smooth.
- Pour over hot baked bars and swirl to mix marshmallows.
- Allows bars to cool before cutting. Use a sharp knife dipped in hot water, if necessary.

*Cut into small pieces for a pick-up style dessert or cut into larger pieces and serve with vanilla ice cream.*

# EMERALD SQUARES

Makes 96-108
Do ahead

| | |
|---|---|
| 1¼ | cups butter |
| ½ | cup cocoa |
| 3½ | cups sifted confectioners sugar |
| 1 | egg, beaten |
| 1 | tsp. vanilla |
| 2 | cups graham cracker crumbs |
| ⅓ | cup green Crème de Menthe |
| 1½ | cups semi-sweet chocolate pieces |

- For bottom layer: combine ½ cup of butter and cocoa in saucepan over low heat. Stir until blended. Remove from heat, add ½ cup sugar, egg and vanilla. Stir in crumbs. Mix well and press into bottom of 13 x 9-inch pan.
- For middle layer: melt ½ cup butter. In small mixer bowl, combine butter and Crème de Menthe. On mixer's low speed, mix in 3 cups sugar until smooth. Spread over first layer. Chill 1 hour.
- For top layer: combine ¼ cup butter and chocolate pieces in a saucepan. Over low heat stir until melted. Spread over mint layer. Chill 1-2 hours.
- Cut into tiny squares. Store in refrigerator.

*Squares are almost like a candy.*

# TOFFEE BARS

Makes 84-96

| | |
|---|---|
| ½ | pound butter |
| ½ | cup brown sugar |
| ½ | cup sugar |
| 1 | egg yolk |
| 1 | tsp. vanilla |
| 1¾ | cups flour |
| 9 | ounces semi-sweet chocolate, chopped |
| ¾ | cup diced almonds |

- Preheat oven to 350 degrees.
- In a large bowl, cream butter and sugars. Mix in egg yolk and vanilla. Add flour and mix. Set aside.
- Roast diced almonds at 350 degrees for 5 minutes. Reserve.
- Spread batter evenly with fingertips in a greased jelly roll pan.
- Bake at 350 degrees for 20 minutes.
- Remove from oven and while still hot, top with broken pieces of chocolate. Spread evenly and sprinkle with almonds.

# YUM YUMS

Makes 48-60

|       | Graham crackers |
|-------|-----------------|
| ½     | pound butter, melted |
| 1     | egg |
| ½     | cup milk |
| 1     | cup sugar |
| 1     | cup nuts |
| 1     | cup semi-sweet chocolate chips |
| 1     | cup graham cracker crumbs |

- Line a 13 x 9-inch pan with whole crackers.
- Beat egg, milk and sugar together and add to melted butter; bring to a boil. Remove from heat and add remaining ingredients. Pour over crackers.
- Top with more whole crackers and frost with icing.

**ICING**

| ¼    | pound butter, softened |
|------|------------------------|
| 1    | box confectioners sugar |
| 2-3  | Tbsp. milk |
| 1    | tsp. vanilla |

- Combine all ingredients and beat until smooth. Add more milk if necessary, a teaspoon at a time, until icing reaches spreading consistency.
- Ice cookies and chill for 2 hours.
- Cut into small bars.

# CARMELITAS

Makes 24

| 32   | caramels |
|------|----------|
| 5    | Tbsp. cream |
| 1    | cup flour |
| 1    | cup quick oatmeal |
| ¾    | cup packed brown sugar |
| ½    | tsp. baking soda |
| ¼    | tsp. salt |
| ¾    | cup butter, melted |
| 8    | ounces semi-sweet chocolate chips |
| ½    | cup chopped pecans |

- Preheat oven to 350 degrees.
- Melt caramels and cream in double boiler. Set aside.
- Combine flour, oatmeal, sugar, soda, salt and butter. Press half of crumbs into 13 x 9-inch pan.
- Bake at 350 degrees for 10 minutes.
- Spread caramel mixture over crust, then chips and pecans. Sprinkle with rest of crumb mix.
- Bake another 15-20 minutes.
- Chill 1 hour. Cut into bars.

# GEORGE WASHINGTON BARS

Makes 36

**CRUST**

| | |
|---|---|
| 2 | cups flour |
| 1 | cup brown sugar |
| ½ | tsp. salt |
| ½ | pound butter |

- Preheat oven to 350 degrees.
- In a small bowl, combine flour, sugar and salt. Cut in butter until mixture is crumbly.
- Set aside 1 cup crumb mixture. Press remainder in bottom of ungreased 13 x 9-inch pan.
- Bake at 350 degrees for 15 minutes. Cool slightly.

**FILLING**

| | |
|---|---|
| ½ | cup sugar |
| 2 | Tbsp. cornstarch |
| 1 | 8-ounce can crushed pineapple, undrained |
| 2 | egg yolks, beaten |
| 1 | cup chopped maraschino cherries |

- In saucepan, combine sugar and cornstarch. Stir in undrained pineapple and egg yolks. Cook over medium heat, stirring constantly until mixture thickens.
- Remove from heat, stir in cherries. Spread evenly over baked layer. Sprinkle reserved crumb mixture over cherry layer.
- Bake at 350 degrees for 30 minutes. Cool before cutting in squares.

# BEST-EVER BUTTER COOKIES

Makes 36

| | |
|---|---|
| ½ | pound butter, softened |
| ¾ | cup cornstarch, sifted |
| ⅓ | cup confectioners sugar, sifted |
| 1 | cup flour |

- Preheat oven to 350 degrees.
- Mix all ingredients well. Batter will be stiff.
- Drop from teaspoon onto greased baking sheet.
- Bake at 350 degrees for 10-12 minutes.

**ICING**

| | |
|---|---|
| 3 | ounces cream cheese, softened |
| 1½ | cups confectioners sugar, sifted |
| 1 | tsp. vanilla |

- Mix cream cheese and sugar; add vanilla.
- Frost tops of cookies while still warm. Cookies are very fragile; handle carefully.

# SUNNY ISLAND BARS

Makes 24-36

**CRUST**

| | |
|---|---|
| ½ | **pound butter, softened** |
| 1 | **cup dark brown sugar** |
| 2 | **cups flour** |

- Preheat oven to 350 degrees.
- Cream butter and brown sugar. Add flour and mix well. Press into 13 x 9-inch pan.
- Bake at 350 degrees for 10-15 minutes.

**FILLING**

| | |
|---|---|
| 2 | **eggs, slightly beaten** |
| 1½ | **cups packed light brown sugar** |
| ½ | **cup coconut** |
| ¼ | **tsp. salt** |
| 1 | **tsp. vanilla** |
| 1 | **cup chopped pecans** |
| 2 | **Tbsp. flour** |
| ½ | **tsp. baking powder** |

- Beat eggs and brown sugar. Add remaining ingredients, mixing well.
- Spread over crust when it is removed from oven.
- Bake at 350 degrees for 20-25 minutes.

**GLAZE**

| | |
|---|---|
| 1¼ | **cups confectioners sugar** |
| | **Juice of 1 lemon** |

- Mix ingredients. If glaze is too thick, thin with a little more lemon juice until it becomes spreadable.
- Spread over baked batter while still warm.
- Cut into squares when cool.

# FRUIT DROP COOKIES

Makes 72

| | |
|---|---|
| 1⅓ | **cups butter** |
| 2 | **cups brown sugar** |
| 3 | **eggs, well beaten** |
| 4 | **cups flour** |
| 1 | **tsp. soda** |
| 1 | **tsp. salt** |
| 1⅓ | **cups chopped nuts** |
| 2⅔ | **cups crystallized fruit (1 pound)** |
| 3 | **Tbsp. Sherry** |
| | **Almond or pecan halves** |

- Cream butter and sugar. Add eggs; mix well.
- Sift together flour, soda and salt. Add fruit and nuts. Incorporate this and the Sherry into the butter mixture. Chill slightly.
- Drop batter from a teaspoon onto cookie sheet. Add an almond or pecan half to each.
- Bake at 350 degrees for 12-15 minutes.

# MOLASSES GINGER SNAPS

Makes 60

| | |
|---|---|
| 2 | cups sugar |
| 1 | cup shortening |
| 2 | eggs, beaten |
| ½ | cup light unsulphured molasses |
| 3½ | cups flour |
| 2 | tsp. baking soda |
| 2 | tsp. ground ginger |
| 1 | tsp. ground cloves |
| 1¼ | tsp. cinnamon |
| | Sugar to coat cookies |

- Preheat oven to 350 degrees.
- Cream sugar and shortening until fluffy. Add eggs and molasses, beating well.
- In a separate bowl, stir together all dry ingredients, adding to shortening mixture a small amount at a time.
- Form dough into 1-inch balls, rolling each in sugar. Place 2 inches apart on ungreased cookie sheet.
- Bake at 350 degrees for 15 minutes or until bottoms are lightly browned.

*Roll in colored sugar for holiday cookie.*

# COLOSSAL COOKIES

Makes 60

| | |
|---|---|
| ¼ | pound butter |
| 1½ | cups sugar |
| 1½ | cups brown sugar |
| 4 | eggs |
| 1 | tsp. vanilla |
| 1 | 18-ounce jar chunky peanut butter |
| 6 | cups uncooked oatmeal |
| 1 | 6-ounce package chocolate chips |
| 2½ | tsp. baking soda |

- Preheat oven to 350 degrees.
- In large bowl, cream butter and sugars. Blend in eggs and vanilla until smooth.
- Add peanut butter. Mix well.
- With wooden spoon, stir in oatmeal, chips and baking soda, mixing well.
- Drop by large spoonfuls onto cookie sheets. Flatten with fork.
- Bake at 350 degrees for 8-10 minutes. Cool 1 minute before moving to wire rack to cool completely.

# BAKED CARAMEL CORN

Makes 6 quarts

⅔  **cup butter**
2  **cups packed brown sugar**
½  **cup light corn syrup**
1  **tsp. salt**
½  **tsp. baking soda**
1  **tsp. vanilla**
6  **quarts popped corn**

- Preheat oven to 225 degrees.
- In a 1½-quart saucepan, melt butter; stir in brown sugar, syrup and salt. Bring mixture to a boil, stirring constantly. Boil over medium heat without stirring for 5 minutes.
- Remove from heat, stir in soda and vanilla. In a large bowl, gradually pour hot syrup over popped corn, mixing well.
- Turn coated corn into a very large buttered pan.
- Bake uncovered at 225 degrees for 30 minutes, stirring after 15 minutes.
- Remove from oven; let cool and break into pieces. Store in an airtight container.

*A cup of pecans or peanuts may be mixed with corn before syrup is added.*

# APPLESAUCE CAKE

Serves 24
Do ahead

½  **pound butter, softened**
2  **cups sugar**
2  **eggs**
4½  **cups flour**
2  **tsp. baking soda**
2  **tsp. cinnamon**
1  **tsp. salt**
1  **tsp. nutmeg**
2  **cups thick applesauce**
30  **ounces golden raisins**
1  **cup broken English walnuts**
½  **cup broken black walnuts**
1  **cup broken pecans**
1  **tsp. vanilla**

- Preheat oven to 300 degrees.
- Cream butter and sugar. Add eggs; mix well.
- Sift 4 cups of flour with soda, cinnamon, salt and nutmeg. Add flour mixture alternately with applesauce to butter mixture, blending after each addition.
- Coat nuts and raisins with remaining ½ cup flour. Add to above mixture.
- Add vanilla and mix well.
- Bake in greased and floured 10-inch tube pan at 300 degrees for 90-120 minutes or until cake tests done.
- This cake may be prepared a month or more in advance and stored in an airtight container without freezing.

*To keep cake moist, pour ¼ cup of sweet wine over thoroughly cooled cake.*
*Repeat every 2 weeks for up to 3 times.*

# APPLESAUCE FRUIT CAKE

Serves 24
Do ahead

| | |
|---|---|
| ½ | cup solid shortening |
| 2 | cups sugar |
| 2 | eggs, well beaten |
| 1½ | cups applesauce (thick canned or homemade) |
| 2½ | cups flour |
| ½ | tsp. salt |
| ½ | tsp. cinnamon |
| ½ | tsp. ground cloves |
| ½ | tsp. allspice |
| 3 | cups walnuts |
| ½ | cup red candied cherries |
| ½ | cup green candied cherries |
| ½ | cup candied mixed fruit |
| 1 | slice candied pineapple, chopped |
| ½ | cup currants |
| ½ | cup raisins |
| ½ | cup white raisins |
| 6 | chopped dates |
| 3 | chopped figs |
| 2 | tsp. baking soda |
| ½ | cup boiling water |

- Preheat oven to 350 degrees.
- Cream shortening, adding sugar gradually, until fluffy. Blend in eggs and applesauce.
- Sift flour, salt and spices together. Mix 2 Tablespoons of flour mixture with fruit and nuts.
- Dissolve soda in boiling water. Add sifted dry ingredients to creamed mixture alternately with soda water.
- Fold in fruit and nuts.
- Pour into greased and floured tube pan.
- Bake at 350 degrees for 1½ hours, turning cake 180 degrees after first 45 minutes. Test thoroughly before removing. If top browns too quickly, cover with foil.
- If desired, decorate top with extra fruit and nuts during final 15 minutes of baking.
- Wrap cake in wine-soaked cloth. Age at least one month, ideally 2-3 months, in a tightly sealed container, keeping cloth consistently damp.

# LACE COOKIES

Makes 50

| | |
|---|---|
| 2 | cups quick oatmeal |
| 2 | cups sugar |
| ½ | pound butter, melted |
| 6 | Tbsp. flour |
| ½ | tsp. salt |
| 1 | tsp. vanilla |
| 2 | eggs |
| ½ | tsp. baking powder |

- Preheat oven to 350 degrees.
- Mix ingredients well.
- Drop by the ½ teaspoon onto foil-lined cookie sheet 2 inches apart.
- Bake at 350 degrees for 8-10 minutes.
- Allow to cool thoroughly on foil. When cool, peel foil off back of cookies.

# OLD FASHIONED DATE LOAF

Makes 1 loaf

| 4 | eggs, separated |
| 1 | cup sugar |
| 1 | cup flour |
| 2 | heaping tsp. baking powder |
| 1 | tsp. salt |
| 1 | tsp. vanilla |
| ½ | cup Brandy |
| 1 | pound pecans, chopped and floured |
| 1 | pound dates, chopped and floured |

- Preheat oven to 225 degrees.
- Beat egg whites until stiff. Set aside.
- Cream egg yolks and sugar in a large bowl.
- Sift flour, baking powder and salt together; gradually add to egg yolk mixture.
- Add remaining ingredients, except egg whites. Mix well. Fold in whites.
- Pour into well greased and floured 8-cup loaf pan.
- Bake at 225 degrees for 3-4 hours.
- Store in Brandy-soaked cheesecloth in airtight container.

# DEEP DISH FRUIT CAKE

Serves 10-12

| ¼ | pound unsalted butter |
| ¼ | pound butter |
| 2 | cups flour |
| 2 | tsp. baking powder |
| 1 | tsp. salt |
| 2 | cups sugar |
| 2 | cups milk |
| 1 | tsp. vanilla |
| 2 | cups fresh or drained canned fruit |
| 2 | cups heavy cream, whipped |

- Preheat oven to 350 degrees.
- Melt butters in 13 x 9-inch baking dish in oven. Remove as soon as butter is melted.
- In a large bowl, mix dry ingredients. Beat in milk, then vanilla, but do not overbeat.
- Pour batter into baking dish. *Do not stir.* Drop fruit into batter evenly. Butter will be floating over portions of batter; this is normal.
- Bake at 350 degrees for 1 hour or until center of cake appears done.
- Serve warm with whipped cream and extra fruit if desired.

# PINEAPPLE CAKE WITH GINGER FROSTING   Serves 12

**CAKE**

| | |
|---|---|
| 2 | **eggs** |
| 1 | **20-ounce can crushed pineapple** |
| 2 | **cups flour** |
| 1 | **cup sugar** |
| 1 | **cup brown sugar** |
| 2 | **tsp. baking soda** |
| 1 | **cup chopped walnuts** |

- Preheat oven to 350 degrees.
- In a large bowl, beat eggs until fluffy. Add remaining ingredients except nuts. Mix well by hand. Add nuts.
- Pour batter into ungreased 13 x 9-inch pan.
- Bake at 350 degrees for 45-50 minutes.
- Allow cake to cool.

**GINGER FROSTING**

| | |
|---|---|
| 3 | **ounces cream cheese** |
| 4 | **Tbsp. butter** |
| 1 | **tsp. vanilla** |
| 2 | **cups confectioners sugar** |
| ½ | **tsp. ground ginger** |

- Cream cheese, butter and vanilla. Gradually add sugar and ginger, beating until smooth and creamy.
- Frost cooled cake. Refrigerate.

# RUM CAKE

Serves 12-15

| | |
|---|---|
| ½ | **pound butter, softened** |
| 1½ | **cups sugar** |
| 4 | **eggs, separated** |
| 1½ | **cups flour** |
| | **Pinch salt** |
| ¼ | **tsp. baking powder** |
| 1 | **tsp. vanilla extract** |
| 1 | **tsp. almond extract** |
| 3 | **Tbsp. dark Rum** |
| ½ | **cup ground pecans** |

- Preheat oven to 350 degrees.
- Cream butter, gradually adding sugar. Add yolks one at a time. Cream well.
- Add flour, salt and baking powder; blend well. Add extracts and Rum; mix thoroughly.
- Beat whites until stiff but not dry; fold into batter.
- Grease a 9-inch tube pan, cover bottom with wax paper and cover with pecans. Pour batter into pan.
- Bake at 350 degrees for 10 minutes.
- Reduce heat to 300 degrees and continue baking for 1 hour.

# PINEAPPLE TOTE CAKE

Serves 12-15

**CAKE**

| | |
|---|---|
| 1 | Tbsp. lemon juice |
| ¾ | cup milk |
| 2 | cups flour |
| 1½ | cups sugar |
| 1 | Tbsp. baking soda |
| 2 | tsp. cinnamon |
| ½ | tsp. salt |
| 3 | eggs |
| ½ | cup oil |
| 1 | tsp. vanilla |
| 1 | cup drained crushed pineapple |
| 2 | cups shredded carrots |
| 1 | cup flaked coconut |
| 1 | cup chopped almonds |

- Preheat oven to 350 degrees.
- Add lemon juice to milk. Set aside to sour.
- Sift together flour, sugar, soda, cinnamon and salt.
- Beat together eggs, oil, milk and vanilla. Add dry ingredients; mix well.
- Stir in pineapple, carrots, coconut and almonds. Pour batter into greased and floured 13 x 9-inch pan.
- Bake at 350 degrees for 30-40 minutes.
- Allow cake to rest in pan for 10 minutes; pour hot glaze over it.

**GLAZE**

| | |
|---|---|
| ⅓ | cup sugar |
| ¼ | tsp. baking soda |
| 1 | tsp. corn syrup |
| ¼ | cup milk |
| 4 | Tbsp. butter |
| ½ | tsp. vanilla |

- Bring combined ingredients, except vanilla, to a boil over medium heat; boil for 5 minutes. Add vanilla.
- Pour glaze over cake.

# STRAWBERRIES ROMANOFF

Serves 6

| | |
|---|---|
| 1 | quart fresh strawberries, washed and hulled |
| ½ | cup sugar |
| 1 | cup heavy cream |
| 4 | Tbsp. Brandy |

- Select 1 cup of imperfect berries for mashing. Mash and add sugar.
- Whip cream and add to mashed berries. Stir in Brandy. Refrigerate mixture and whole berries until needed.
- To serve, pour sauce over whole berries in individual bowls.

# ORANGE CHIFFON CAKE WITH WHITE CHOCOLATE ICING

Serves 16

| | |
|---|---|
| 6 | **extra large eggs, separated** |
| 1 | **cup sugar** |
| ⅓ | **cup fresh orange juice** |
| | **Grated zest of 1 orange** |
| 1 | **cup plus 2 Tbsp. flour, sifted** |
| | **Pinch salt** |
| | **Pinch cream of tartar** |

- Preheat oven to 350 degrees.
- Beat yolks until foamy. Slowly add sugar a Tablespoon at a time. Beat until very pale and thick. Mixture should form a thick ribbon when beater is lifted from bowl and no sugar granules should be present to the touch.
- Gently mix in orange juice. Add flour gradually, mixing at low speed. Do not overbeat.
- Stir in orange zest. Set aside.
- Beat whites until foamy; add salt and cream of tartar and whip until stiff but not dry.
- Stir ¼ of whites into batter. Gently fold in rest of whites, a quarter at a time.
- Turn the batter into 10-inch ungreased 2-piece tube pan. Smooth top.
- Bake at 350 degrees for 50 minutes or until top springs back when lightly touched and cake begins to pull away from side of the pan.
- Remove from oven, inverting cake immediately over the neck of a Worcestershire sauce bottle. Allow to hang until cool.
- Gently remove cake from pan by running a thin, sharp knife around edges.

## WHITE CHOCOLATE ICING

| | |
|---|---|
| 10 | **ounces Lindt Blancor white chocolate** |
| ½ | **pound unsalted butter, softened** |
| 1 | **egg yolk** |
| 1½-2 | **cups confectioners sugar, sifted** |
| 1½ | **tsp. vanilla** |

- Melt chocolate gently in a double boiler (do not heat long enough for toffee to melt). Remove from heat. Beat in butter.
- Add yolk, mixing well.
- Add confectioners sugar to taste, mixing until smooth. Add vanilla and spread over cake.

*Use fresh sliced peaches or raspberries as an alternative to frosting this ultra-light cake.*

# PUMPKIN CHIFFON CAKE

Serves 16

| | |
|---|---|
| 2 | cups flour, sifted |
| 1½ | cups sugar |
| 3 | tsp. baking powder |
| 1 | tsp. salt |
| 1 | tsp. cinnamon |
| ½ | tsp. ground cloves |
| ½ | tsp. nutmeg |
| ¼ | tsp. ground ginger |
| 7 | eggs, separated |
| ¾ | cup canned pumpkin |
| ½ | cup salad oil |
| ½ | cup water |
| ½ | tsp. cream of tartar |

- Preheat oven to 325 degrees.
- Sift first 8 ingredients together in a large bowl. Make a well in center of mixture. Set aside.
- In a small bowl combine yolks with pumpkin, oil and water.
- Add liquids all at once to dry ingredients. Blend until smooth.
- Beat whites until foamy; add cream of tartar and beat until stiff. Fold into pumpkin batter.
- Turn into a 10-inch ungreased tube pan. Bake 55 minutes at 325 degrees. Raise temperature to 350 degrees and bake 15 minutes longer.
- Invert pan onto Worcestershire bottle to hang until cool. With a thin-bladed knife, release cake from pan and turn onto a serving plate.

### MAPLE-WALNUT FROSTING

| | |
|---|---|
| ¼ | cup butter, softened |
| 1 | pound box confectioners sugar |
| ⅓ | cup evaporated milk |
| ½ | tsp. maple extract |
| 1½ | cups chopped pecans |

- Cream butter. Blend in half of sugar, mixing until light and fluffy. Blend in milk, then remaining sugar. Add extract.
- Spread on cake while frosting is still moist. Immediately press pecans into icing.
- Use serrated blade to cut cake.

# SNOWBALLS

Makes 30

| | |
|---|---|
| 6 | ounces semi-sweet chocolate pieces |
| ⅓ | cup evaporated milk |
| 1¼ | cups confectioners sugar, sifted |
| ¾ | cup chopped walnuts |
| 3½ | ounces flaked coconut |

- Stir chocolate and milk in saucepan over low heat until chocolate melts. Remove from heat and stir in sugar and nuts.
- Chill for a few minutes then roll into 1-inch balls.
- Roll in coconut.

*Easy enough for children to make.*

# BLACK CHOCOLATE CAKE

Serves 12

**CAKE**

| | |
|---|---|
| ¼ | pound butter, softened |
| 2 | cups packed dark brown sugar |
| 3½ | ounces unsweetened chocolate |
| 4 | eggs |
| ¾ | cup milk |
| 1 | tsp. baking soda |
| 2 | cups flour |

- Preheat oven to 350 degrees.
- Cream butter and sugar. Melt chocolate and add to mixture.
- Gradually add eggs, one at a time. Mix well.
- Dissolve soda in milk. Add alternately with the flour, beginning and ending with dry ingredients.
- Pour into 2 greased and floured 9-inch round cake pans.
- Bake at 350 degrees for 25-30 minutes.
- Cool 10 minutes before removing from pans. Cool completely before icing.

**MOCHA ICING**

| | |
|---|---|
| 4 | Tbsp. butter, softened |
| ⅔ | cup unsweetened cocoa |
| 1 | pound confectioners sugar |
| 4 | Tbsp. strong coffee |
| 1 | tsp. vanilla |
| 1¼ | Tbsp. water, if needed |

- Cream butter until fluffy. Add cocoa; blend well.
- Gradually add sugar alternately with coffee. Add vanilla and beat to spreading consistency. Add water, a few drops at a time, only if icing is too thick to spread.

# CHOCOLATE VELVET

Frosts 1 cake

| | |
|---|---|
| 6 | ounces semi-sweet chocolate pieces |
| 4 | Tbsp. butter |
| ½ | cup sour cream |
| 1 | tsp. vanilla |
| ¼ | tsp. salt |
| 2½ | cups confectioners sugar, sifted |

- Melt chocolate and butter over low heat in double boiler. Pour mixture into mixing bowl.
- Add remaining ingredients and mix well. Ice cake.

# CHOCOLATE TWEED LAYER CAKE

Serves 12

### CAKE

| | |
|---|---|
| ¼ | pound plus 2 Tbsp. butter, softened |
| 1 | cup sugar |
| 3 | eggs, separated |
| 1 | tsp. vanilla |
| 2 | cups sifted flour |
| 3 | tsp. baking powder |
| ⅛ | tsp. salt |
| 1 | cup buttermilk |
| 3 | squares unsweetened chocolate, grated |

- Preheat oven to 350 degrees.
- In large mixing bowl, cream butter and sugar. Add egg yolks one at a time. Beat in vanilla.
- Sift together flour, baking powder and salt. Add to creamed mixture alternately with buttermilk, beginning and ending with dry ingredients, beating well after each addition.
- Stir chocolate into batter.
- Beat egg whites until foamy; gently fold into batter.
- Turn into 3 8-inch or 2 9-inch round cake pans, greased and lined with wax paper.
- Bake at 350 degrees for 20-25 minutes. Cool in pans for 5 minutes; turn onto wire racks to cool.

### GOLDEN BUTTER CREAM FROSTING

| | |
|---|---|
| 1 | egg yolk |
| ¾ | cup butter, softened |
| 2¼ | cups confectioners sugar |

- Beat together yolk and butter, gradually adding sugar, beating until smooth.
- Spread between layers and frost cake.

### CHOCOLATE SHADOW

| | |
|---|---|
| ½ | cup semi-sweet chocolate pieces |
| 2 | Tbsp. warm water |

- Melt chocolate slowly in a small saucepan over low heat.
- Add water to chocolate, stirring until smooth.
- Drizzle mixture over cake, allowing some to run down sides of cake.

# CHOCOLATE SHELL

Yields 1 cup

| | |
|---|---|
| 5 | ounces semi-sweet chocolate |
| 1 | ounce unsweetened chocolate |
| ¼ | pound butter |
| ½ | cup finely chopped walnuts |

- In top of double boiler over simmering water, slowly melt first 3 ingredients. Stir gently to blend thoroughly. Do *not* cover double boiler.
- Add walnuts, stir to blend. Pour over ice cream; sauce will harden.

*May be prepared in afternoon and gently reheated.*

# APRICOT BRANDY POUND CAKE

Serves 15-20

| | |
|---|---|
| ½ | pound butter, softened |
| 3 | cups sugar |
| 6 | eggs |
| 3 | cups flour |
| ½ | tsp. salt |
| ¼ | tsp. baking soda |
| 1 | cup sour cream |
| 1 | tsp. orange extract |
| 1 | tsp. vanilla extract |
| ½ | tsp. lemon extract |
| ½ | tsp. rum extract |
| ¼ | tsp. almond extract |
| ½ | cup apricot Brandy |
| | Confectioners sugar |

- Preheat oven to 325 degrees.
- Cream butter and sugar. Add eggs one at a time, beating well after each addition.
- Sift together flour, salt and soda.
- Combine sour cream, flavorings and Brandy. Alternately add flour and sour cream to butter mixture; blend well.
- Pour into greased and lightly floured large tube pan.
- Bake at 325 degrees for 80-90 minutes.
- Dust cooled cake with confectioners sugar.

*Cake is better after 3-4 days.*

# CHOCOLATE CHIP CAKE

Serves 12

| | |
|---|---|
| 1 | cup chocolate chips |
| ½ | cup graham cracker crumbs |
| ⅓ | cup butter, melted |
| ½ | cup chopped nuts |
| 2 | cups flour |
| 1 | tsp. baking soda |
| 1 | tsp. salt |
| ½ | cup butter |
| 1½ | cups sugar |
| 2 | eggs |
| 1 | tsp. vanilla |
| 1¼ | cups buttermilk |
| 2 | cups heavy cream |
| 2 | Tbsp. sugar |

- Preheat oven to 375 degrees.
- Melt ⅓ cup of chocolate chips. Set aside.
- In a small bowl, combine crumbs and melted butter. Stir in nuts and remaining chocolate chips. Set aside.
- Sift together flour, soda and salt.
- Cream butter in large bowl. Gradually add 1½ cups sugar, creaming until light and fluffy. Add eggs, one at a time, beating well after each addition.
- Blend in melted chocolate and vanilla. Add dry ingredients alternating with buttermilk, beginning and ending with dry ingredients.
- Pour into 2 greased and floured 9-inch round cake pans and sprinkle with crumb mixture.
- Bake at 375 degrees for 30-40 minutes.
- When cake is cool, add 2 Tablespoons sugar to cream and whip until stiff. Spread whipped cream between layers and on top. Refrigerate.

# POPPY SEED CAKE

Serves 12-15

## CAKE

| | |
|---|---|
| 2 | Tbsp. poppy seeds |
| ¼ | cup milk |
| 6 | eggs, separated |
| 1 | cup shortening |
| 3 | cups sugar |
| 1 | cup buttermilk |
| ¼ | tsp. baking soda |
| ¼ | tsp. almond extract |
| 1 | tsp. lemon extract |
| 1 | tsp. butter flavoring |
| ¼ | tsp. salt |
| 3 | cups flour |

- Preheat oven to 350 degrees.
- Soak poppy seeds in milk for 30 minutes.
- Cream yolks and shortening. Add sugar, beat well. Add poppy seed mixture.
- Add buttermilk with baking soda dissolved in it, then add extracts, butter flavoring, salt, and flour.
- Beat egg whites until stiff. Fold into batter.
- Gently pour into greased bundt or tube pan. Bake at 350 degrees for 75 minutes.
- While cake is warm, pour on glaze.

## GLAZE

| | |
|---|---|
| 1⅓ | cup confectioners sugar |
| 1 | Tbsp. orange marmalade |
| ⅓ | cup fresh or frozen orange juice |
| 1 | tsp. butter flavoring |
| 1 | tsp. almond extract |
| 1 | tsp. orange extract |

- Gently heat all ingredients, blending.
- Cool slightly.

# CHOCOLATE SUNDAE SAUCE

Yield 1½ cup

| | |
|---|---|
| 2 | squares unsweetened chocolate |
| ½ | cup water |
| 1 | cup sugar |
| 1 | Tbsp. flour |
| ¼ | tsp. vanilla |
| ⅛ | tsp. salt |
| 1 | tsp. butter |

- In heavy saucepan, melt chocolate in water.
- Combine sugar and flour. Stir into chocolate. Bring sauce to light boil, stirring constantly. Cook 5 minutes.
- Remove from heat and stir in vanilla, salt and butter.
- Let stand to thicken and cool. Store in covered glass jar in refrigerator. Sauce may need to be heated in pan of water if it is too stiff.

*Keeps indefinitely.*

# GINGERBREAD

Serves 16

| | |
|---|---|
| 2 | eggs, beaten |
| ¾ | cup brown sugar |
| ¾ | cup molasses |
| ¾ | cup vegetable oil |
| 2½ | cups flour |
| 2 | tsp. baking soda |
| 2 | tsp. ginger |
| 1½ | tsp. cinnamon |
| ½ | tsp. cloves |
| ½ | tsp. nutmeg |
| ½ | tsp. baking powder |
| 1 | cup boiling water |
| 2 | cups heavy cream, whipped |
| 2 | Tbsp. sugar |

- Preheat oven to 350 degrees.
- Mix first 4 ingredients. Sift dry ingredients and add to egg mixture.
- Stir in boiling water.
- Pour into greased 13 x 9-inch pan.
- Bake at 350 degrees for 25 minutes or until cake is springy to touch.
- While still warm, serve with sweetened whipped cream or Brandied Gingerbread Sauce.

# NEVER-FAIL CUPCAKES

Makes 16

| | |
|---|---|
| 1 | egg |
| ½ | cup cocoa |
| ½ | cup butter |
| 1½ | cups flour |
| ½ | cup buttermilk |
| 1 | tsp. vanilla |
| 1 | tsp. baking soda |
| 1 | cup sugar |
| ½ | cup hot water |

- Preheat oven to 350 degrees.
- Put ingredients in bowl in order given. Do not mix until last ingredient has been added, then beat well. Pour into greased muffin tins.
- Bake at 350 degrees for 20 minutes.
- Frost as desired.

# CHOCOLATE FLUFF

Frosts 1 cake

| | |
|---|---|
| 6 | ounces semi-sweet chocolate pieces |
| ½ | cup milk |
| 16 | large marshmallows |
| 1 | cup heavy cream, whipped |

- Melt first 3 ingredients together. Chill until thick but not set.
- Fold in whipped cream. Ice cake and refrigerate.

# PEACHES AND CREAM KUCHEN

Makes 2 pies

| | |
|---|---|
| 2 | cups flour |
| ¼ | tsp. baking powder |
| ½ | tsp. salt |
| 1 | cup sugar |
| ¼ | pound butter |
| 14 | peach halves, fresh, frozen or canned |
| 1 | tsp. cinnamon |
| 2 | egg yolks, beaten |
| 1 | cup sour cream |

- Preheat oven to 400 degrees.
- Combine first 3 ingredients plus 1 Tablespoon sugar. Work in butter until mixture resembles corn meal. Heap into two 9-inch pie pans and pat evenly over bottom and sides.
- Place peach halves over pastry; sprinkle mixture of cinnamon and remaining sugar.
- Bake at 400 degrees for 15 minutes.
- Mix egg yolks and sour cream and pour over peaches.
- Bake 30 minutes more. Serve warm. (May be reheated.)

*Ice cream is the perfect topping.*

# DEVONSHIRE APPLE PIE

Serves 6-8

**PIE**

| | |
|---|---|
| ¾ | cup sugar |
| ¼ | cup packed brown sugar |
| 1 | Tbsp. flour |
| ½ | tsp. cinnamon |
| ½ | tsp. nutmeg |
| 1 | tsp. lemon juice |
| ⅛ | tsp. salt |
| ½ | cup sour cream |
| 4 | medium apples, pared and sliced |
| 1 | 9-inch unbaked pie shell |

- Preheat oven to 350 degrees.
- Mix first 7 ingredients in large bowl. Stir in sour cream and apples.
- Spoon into shell. Add topping.

**STREUSEL TOPPING**

| | |
|---|---|
| ½ | cup flour |
| ½ | cup packed brown sugar |
| 4 | Tbsp. cold butter |

- Mix flour and sugar; cut in butter until mixture is crumbly. Sprinkle on pie.
- Bake at 350 degrees for 40 minutes or until topping is golden.

# LA TARTE DE MADAME TATIN

Serves 8

| | |
|---|---|
| 3-4 | **cooking apples, cored and peeled** |
| 3-5 | **Tbsp. sugar, depending on tartness of apples** |
| | **Cinnamon to taste** |
| 1 | **tsp. vanilla** |
| | **Pastry crust for *top* of 9-inch pie** |
| | **Heavy cream, whipped** |

- Preheat oven to 425 degrees.
- Slice apples thinly and uniformly.
- Spread sugar evenly over bottom of 9-inch metal pie pan buttered on bottom and sides. Sprinkle cinnamon over sugar and vanilla over all.
- Arrange apples in attractive layer over sugar mixture. Pile remaining apple slices on top.
- Cover apples *loosely* with thin pastry crust, not attaching it to sides of pan but tucking it under fruit.
- Bake at 425 degrees for 20-25 minutes or until crust is brown and crisp.
- Remove pie from oven and place pan directly on burner over medium heat. Brown until sugar caramelizes, 3 minutes or longer, depending on thickness of pan.
- Immediately invert tarte onto serving dish so that crust is on bottom. Top with whipped cream and serve warm.

*May be baked ahead and caramelized on stove immediately before serving.*

# BLUEBERRY SPECIAL

Serves 6-8
Do ahead

| | |
|---|---|
| 1 | **cup sour cream** |
| 2 | **Tbsp. flour** |
| ¾ | **cup sugar** |
| 1 | **egg, beaten** |
| 1 | **pint fresh blueberries** |
| 1 | **Butter Flavored pie crust** |
| 3 | **Tbsp. flour** |
| 2 | **Tbsp. butter** |
| ¼ | **cup chopped pecans** |

- Preheat oven to 400 degrees.
- Mix first 4 ingredients until smooth.
- Fold in blueberries and pour mixture into prepared pie crust.
- Bake at 400 degrees for 25 minutes. Remove from oven.
- Combine rest of ingredients and sprinkle on top of pie. Bake another 10 minutes.
- Chill before serving.

# TANGY LEMON PIE

3    Tbsp. flour
1    cup sugar
     Grated zest and juice of
     1½ lemons
3    Tbsp. butter, softened
2    egg yolks
     Pinch of salt
1    cup milk
2    egg whites
1    9-inch unbaked pie shell

- Preheat oven to 350 degrees.
- Mix flour and sugar well; add lemon, butter, egg yolks and salt, blending well. Add milk and stir.
- Beat egg whites until stiff but not dry. Fold into lemon mixture.
- Pour into shell and bake at 350 degrees for 45 minutes.

# LEMON CHESS PIE

2    cups sugar
     Pinch of salt
1    Tbsp. yellow corn meal
1    Tbsp. flour
2    Tbsp. butter, melted
¼    cup milk
     Grated zest and juice of
     2 lemons
4    eggs
1    9-inch unbaked pie shell

- Preheat oven to 350 degrees.
- Mix first 4 ingredients in bowl. Add butter and milk. Add lemon zest and juice.
- Beat in eggs and pour into pie shell.
- Bake at 350 degrees for 40 minutes. Take care not to overbake. After 30 minutes, check to see that delicate crust that forms on top of filling is becoming tan. Center should be just barely firm.
- Serve at room temperature.

*Mixture may also be put into 10-12 small tart shells. Bake for 20-30 minutes.*

# BUTTERSCOTCH SAUCE

2    cups brown sugar
⅔    cup light corn syrup
4    Tbsp. butter
½    cup light cream
1    tsp. vanilla

- Bring first 3 ingredients to a boil, boiling for exactly 5 minutes.
- Add cream and vanilla, stirring until blended.
- Allow to cool, then refrigerate.
- Serve warm or cold over ice cream or cake.

# RUM PIE

Serves 6-8

| | |
|---|---|
| 6 | **egg yolks** |
| 1 | **cup sugar** |
| ½ | **cup dark Rum** |
| 1½ | **packages unflavored gelatin** |
| ½ | **cup cold water** |
| 1 | **pint heavy cream** |
| 1 | **9-inch graham cracker crust** |
| | **Chocolate curls or pistachio nuts** |

- Beat egg yolks until light; add sugar and Rum.
- Soak gelatin in water. Cook over low heat, bringing to a boil. Slowly pour into egg mixture, whisking constantly. Chill until mixture starts to set.
- Whip cream until stiff; thoroughly fold into egg mixture. Refrigerate until mixture again begins to set. Pour into pie shell. Chill until firm.
- Sprinkle with chocolate curls or pistachio nuts. Serve cold.

# SOUR CREAM-RAISIN PIE

Serves 6-8

**FILLING**

| | |
|---|---|
| 3 | **egg yolks, whites reserved** |
| 1 | **cup sour cream** |
| 1 | **cup sugar** |
| 1 | **cup dark raisins** |
| ¼ | **tsp. cloves or nutmeg** |
| 1 | **9-inch baked pie shell** |

- Preheat oven to 325 degrees.
- Beat egg yolks, adding remaining filling ingredients; mix well.
- Bring to a boil in heavy pan, stirring constantly, then cook slowly at least 2 minutes. Let cool.

**TOPPING**

| | |
|---|---|
| 3 | **egg whites** |
| 1 | **tsp. water** |
| ¼ | **tsp. cream of tartar** |
| ½ | **cup sugar** |
| | **Nutmeg** |

- Beat first 3 ingredients until whites are partially stiff. Slowly add sugar, beating constantly until whites hold nice peaks.
- Pour cooled custard mixture into baked shell. Apply meringue, sealing edges. Sprinkle nutmeg on top.
- Brown in 325 degree oven for 10 minutes.

# TOFFEE ICE CREAM PIE

Serves 8
Do ahead

| | |
|---|---|
| 18 | vanilla wafers |
| ½ | gallon vanilla ice cream, softened |
| 1 | cup chopped Heath bars |

- Line bottom and sides of buttered 9-inch pie pan with wafers. Spoon ice cream into wafer shell, sprinkling ½ cup of chopped candy between ice cream layers. Freeze for at least 2 hours.

**SAUCE**

| | |
|---|---|
| 1 | cup sugar |
| 1 | cup evaporated milk |
| 4 | Tbsp. butter |
| ¼ | cup light corn syrup |
| | Dash of salt |

- Combine all ingredients and bring to boil over low heat. Boil 1 minute.
- Remove from heat and stir in remaining chopped candy. Cool, stirring occasionally.
- Serve sauce over pie wedges.

# CHOCOLATE PIE FANTASTIC

Serves 8-12
Do ahead

| | |
|---|---|
| 12 | ounces semi-sweet chocolate pieces |
| ¾ | cup unsalted butter |
| 4 | egg yolks |
| ½ | cup sugar |
| 4 | egg whites, room temperature |
| | Whipped cream to decorate |
| | Shaved chocolate curls |

- Slowly melt chocolate and butter in top of double boiler. Remove from heat, stirring until smooth and allow to cool.
- Beat egg yolks and sugar together, adding sugar a little at a time. Correct consistency has been reached when a pinch of mixture rubbed between thumb and index finger does not feel grainy and a ribbon forms when beaters are lifted from bowl. Mixture will be very pale.
- Beat the two mixtures together.
- Beat whites until stiff but not dry. Before adding whites to chocolate, make sure chocolate is cool. Very gently fold in whites.
- Turn into a buttered pie pan and freeze overnight.
- Decorate with whipped cream and chocolate curls or top with whole fresh strawberries.

# BLACK BOTTOM ICE CREAM PIE

Serves 8
Do ahead

| 18 | chocolate wafer cookies, crushed |
| 1/3 | cup butter, melted |
| 6 | ounces semi-sweet chocolate pieces |
| 1/2 | cup heavy cream |
| 1/2 | tsp. vanilla |
| 1/2 | pint chocolate ice cream, slightly softened |
| 1-1/2 | quarts vanilla ice cream |

- Combine crumbs and butter; pat into buttered 9-inch pie pan. Freeze while preparing filling.
- Melt chocolate in cream over low heat; stir occasionally. When melted and thoroughly blended, remove from heat. Add vanilla and chill until thickened.
- Spoon chocolate ice cream into pie crust and smooth with back of spoon. Refreeze 30-40 minutes. Spread 3/4 of sauce over ice cream. Freeze until quite firm.
- Place large scoops of vanilla ice cream over sauce. Drizzle remaining sauce over top of pie. Freeze.
- Remove from freezer 15 minutes before serving.

*Coffee ice cream is a good substitute for the vanilla.*

# CHOCOLATE PIES FOR A CROWD

Makes 4 pies

| 1/4 | pound butter |
| 4 | cups sugar |
| 5 | large eggs, well beaten |
| 1/2 | cup cocoa |
| 1 | 13-ounce can evaporated milk |
| 1 | cup chopped pecans |
| 1 | cup flaked coconut |
| 4 | unbaked pie shells |

- Preheat oven to 350 degrees.
- Cream butter and sugar until light.
- Beat in remaining ingredients and pour into pie shells.
- Bake at 350 degrees for 45-50 minutes.
- Serve with whipped cream or ice cream.

*Pies freeze well; great for bazaars and school carnivals.*

# SOUTHERN PECAN PIE

Serves 6-8

## CRUST

| | |
|---|---|
| 1½ | cups flour |
| ½ | tsp. salt |
| ½ | cup solid shortening |
| 4-5 | Tbsp. ice water |

- Preheat oven to 400 degrees.
- Sift flour and salt together. Cut in shortening until dough mixture is size of small peas.
- Sprinkle water over dough, 1 Tablespoon at a time, tossing mixture after each addition. Form into ball.
- Flatten on lightly floured surface and roll into circle. Place in a 9-inch pie pan.

## FILLING

| | |
|---|---|
| 3 | eggs, beaten |
| ½ | cup sugar |
| ½ | cup light corn syrup |
| ½ | cup dark corn syrup |
| 4 | Tbsp. butter, melted |
| 1 | tsp. vanilla or dark Rum |
| 1 | cup pecan halves |
| | Heavy cream, whipped |

- Add remaining ingredients to eggs.
- Pour into pie shell; nuts will rise to top.
- Bake at 400 degrees for 10 minutes; reduce heat to 350 degrees and bake for 35-40 minutes.
- Serve warm with whipped cream.

# EASY PIE CRUST

Makes 2 crusts

| | |
|---|---|
| 2½ | cups sifted flour |
| 1 | heaping Tbsp. sugar |
| 1 | tsp. salt |
| 1 | cup shortening |
| 1 | egg yolk |
| | Milk |

- Combine flour, sugar and salt. Cut shortening into flour mixture.
- Put egg yolk into a measuring cup and add enough milk to make ⅔ cup liquid. Add to flour mixture; mix lightly until ball forms.
- Divide dough into 2 parts. Refrigerate. When ready to use, roll out, fill and bake according to pie recipe.

# NEVER-FAIL PIE CRUST

Makes 3 crusts

| | |
|---|---|
| 1 | egg |
| ⅓ | cup cold water |
| 1 | Tbsp. vinegar |
| 3 | cups flour |
| 1 | tsp. salt |
| 1 | cup plus 1 Tbsp. solid shortening |

- In small bowl, mix liquid ingredients. Set aside.
- Mix dry ingredients with pastry blender until crumbs form.
- Add liquid to crumb mixture. Mix well and refrigerate if not needed immediately.
- Yields three 8-inch pie shells.

*Dough will keep up to a week refrigerated.*

# CABAÑA CHEESECAKE

Serves 12
Do ahead

| | |
|---|---|
| | Graham cracker crumbs |
| 16 | ounces small curd cream-style cottage cheese |
| 16 | ounces cream cheese, softened |
| 1½ | cups sugar |
| 4 | eggs, slightly beaten |
| ⅓ | cup corn starch |
| 2 | Tbsp. lemon juice |
| 1 | tsp. vanilla |
| ¼ | pound butter, melted |
| 2 | cups sour cream |

- Preheat oven to 325 degrees.
- Grease 9-inch springform pan and dust with crumbs.
- Sieve cottage cheese into large mixing bowl. Add cream cheese, beating at high speed until well blended and creamy.
- Continuing on high, blend in sugar, then eggs.
- At low speed, add corn starch, lemon juice and vanilla. Beat until blended. Add remaining ingredients; blend well.
- Pour into pan, bake at 325 degrees for 70 minutes or until firm around edges. Do not open oven while baking.
- Turn off oven; let cake stand in oven for 2 hours. Remove and cool completely.
- Glaze with fruit preserves or top with fresh fruit if desired.

*Use as dry a cottage cheese as possible.*

# CELEBRATION CHEESECAKE

Serves 12-16
Do ahead

## CRUST

| | |
|---|---|
| 1½ | cups graham cracker crumbs |
| 4 | Tbsp. sugar |
| 4 | Tbsp. butter |

- Preheat oven to 300 degrees.
- Mix all ingredients well and press onto bottom of 9-inch greased springform pan.

## FILLING

| | |
|---|---|
| 24 | ounces cream cheese, softened |
| 5 | eggs |
| 1 | cup sugar |
| 2 | tsp. vanilla |
| 1 | tsp. almond extract |

- Blend all filling ingredients well; pour into prepared pan.
- Bake at 300 degrees for 1 hour or until set.

## TOPPING

| | |
|---|---|
| 2 | cups sour cream |
| ½ | cup sugar |
| 1-2 | tsp. almond extract |

- Blend topping ingredients. Pour over cake and return to oven for 15 minutes.
- Remove from oven and allow to cool uncovered overnight on wire rack.
- Loosen, then remove sides of pan; cover cake loosely and refrigerate.

# BRANDIED GINGERBREAD SAUCE

Yields 1 cup

| | |
|---|---|
| 3 | egg yolks, beaten |
| 1 | cup confectioners sugar |
| 1 | cup heavy cream, whipped |
| 3 | Tbsp. Brandy or Sherry |

- Beat yolks with sugar until very light and creamy.
- Fold in whipped cream. Stir in Brandy.
- Refrigerate until needed. Serve very cold.

*Good on fruitcake or warm gingerbread.*

# CHOCOLATE CHEESECAKE

Serves 12-16
Do ahead

**CRUST**

| | |
|---|---|
| 1 | **8½-ounce box chocolate wafers, crushed** |
| ¼ | **tsp. cinnamon** |
| ¼ | **pound butter, melted** |

- Preheat oven to 350 degrees.
- Combine ingredients and blend to make crust. Pat into 12-inch springform pan and chill.

**FILLING**

| | |
|---|---|
| 32 | **ounces cream cheese, softened** |
| 4 | **eggs** |
| 2 | **cups sugar** |
| 1 | **Tbsp. cocoa** |
| 1 | **Tbsp. vanilla** |
| 12 | **ounces semi-sweet chocolate pieces, melted** |
| 2 | **cups sour cream** |

- Beat cream cheese until fluffy. Add eggs, one at a time, alternating with sugar.
- Mix in cocoa and vanilla. Fold in melted chocolate. Stir in sour cream. Pour into crust.
- Bake at 350 degrees for 70-80 minutes.
- Cool; run knife around sides of pan to loosen.
- When ready to serve, remove springform sides and garnish with chocolate curls. May be frozen and defrosted before serving.

*Bake any excess filling in a small ramekin for a shorter time.*

# SINFUL CHOCOLATES

Makes 40-50

**BALLS**

| | |
|---|---|
| 1 | **cup peanut butter** |
| 1 | **cup confectioners sugar** |
| 1 | **cup chopped nuts** |
| 1 | **cup chopped dates** |
| 1 | **Tbsp. butter, softened** |

- Mix all ingredients. Shape into balls the size of a teaspoon.

**COATING**

| | |
|---|---|
| 2 | **ounces unsweetened chocolate, chopped** |
| 6 | **ounces semi-sweet chocolate pieces** |
| 1½ | **inch square paraffin** |

- Melt ingredients in top of double boiler.
- Dip balls into mixture. Place on cookie sheet and refrigerate until firm. Toothpicks facilitate the dipping process.

# RUM CHEESECAKE

Serves 12-16
Do ahead

## BOTTOM CRUST

| | |
|---|---|
| 1 | cup graham cracker crumbs |
| ½ | cup well-chopped pecans |
| 6 | Tbsp. butter, melted |

- Preheat oven to 300 degrees.
- Mix all ingredients and pat into bottom of 9-inch springform pan. Set aside.

## MIDDLE LAYER

| | |
|---|---|
| 24 | ounces cream cheese, softened |
| ¾ | cup brown sugar |
| 5 | eggs, room temperature |
| 1 | tsp. vanilla extract |
| 1 | tsp. rum extract |
| 1½ | Tbsp. Myers's Rum |
| ⅓ | cup finely chopped pecans |

- Beat softened cream cheese. When fluffy, add sugar; mix well. Add eggs one at a time, beating well after each addition. Beat in remaining ingredients.
- Pour mixture into prepared pan.
- Bake at 300 degrees for 50-60 minutes, until top is firm and set. Do not overbake.

## TOP LAYER

| | |
|---|---|
| 2 | cups sour cream |
| ¼ | cup sugar |
| 1 | tsp. vanilla extract |

- Allow cheesecake to stand for 20 minutes; mix all ingredients. Pour over top of cheesecake.
- Return to 325 degree oven for 5 minutes.
- Cool. Chill in refrigerator overnight.

# PRALINE PARFAIT SAUCE

Yields 3 cups

| | |
|---|---|
| 2 | cups dark corn syrup |
| ⅓ | cup sugar |
| ⅓ | cup boiling water |
| 1 | cup chopped pecans |

- Combine all ingredients in a medium saucepan and bring to boil over medium heat. Remove immediately and let cool.
- Store in a tightly covered jar.
- To make a parfait, alternate layers of vanilla ice cream with sauce, ending with sauce. Garnish with whipped cream and pecan halves.

# PUMPKIN CHEESECAKE

Serves 10-12
Do ahead

### CRUST

⅓    **cup butter, softened**
⅓    **cup sugar**
1    **egg**
1¼    **cups flour**

- Preheat oven to 400 degrees.
- Cream butter and sugar until light and fluffy; blend in egg. Add flour, mixing well.
- Spread dough on bottom and 2 inches up sides of 9-inch springform pan.
- Bake at 400 degrees for 5 minutes. Remove from oven and lower oven temperature to 350 degrees.

### BATTER

16    **ounces cream cheese, softened**
¾    **cup sugar**
2    **cups cooked, mashed pumpkin**
1    **tsp. cinnamon**
¼    **tsp. ginger**
¼    **tsp. nutmeg**
     **Dash salt**
2    **eggs**
     **Whipped cream**

- Combine cream cheese and sugar. Beat until smooth. Blend in pumpkin, spices and salt.
- Add eggs, one at a time; beat well after each addition. Pour into baked crust.
- Bake at 350 degrees for 50 minutes.
- Loosen cake from sides of pan. Cool. Remove rim of pan; chill. Garnish with whipped cream.

# CHOCOLATE PECAN PIE

Serves 8

2    **ounces unsweetened chocolate**
3    **Tbsp. butter**
1    **cup light corn syrup**
¾    **cup sugar**
½    **tsp. salt**
3    **eggs, slightly beaten**
1    **tsp. vanilla**
1    **cup chopped pecans**
1    **9-inch unbaked pie shell**
     **Heavy cream, whipped**

- Preheat oven to 375 degrees.
- In double boiler, melt chocolate and butter.
- In a separate pan, simmer syrup and sugar for 2 minutes. Add chocolate mixture and cool slightly.
- Add salt to eggs. Slowly dribble chocolate mixture into eggs, stirring constantly. Blend in vanilla and nuts.
- Pour into shell and bake at 375 degrees for 35 minutes.
- Serve with whipped cream.

# STRAWBERRIES IMPERIAL

Serves 6
Do ahead

**BERRIES**

| | |
|---|---|
| 2 | **pints strawberries, washed and hulled** |
| ½ | **cup confectioners sugar** |
| 1½ | **ounces Vodka** |
| 1½ | **ounces Triple Sec** |
| 1½ | **ounces Rum** |

- Toss strawberries with sugar in large bowl. Pour liquor over berries and chill several hours.
- May be served over Imperial Mousse.

**IMPERIAL MOUSSE**

| | |
|---|---|
| 1 | **Tbsp. unflavored gelatin** |
| ⅓ | **cup cold water** |
| ⅓ | **cup boiling water** |
| 1 | **cup heavy cream** |
| 1 | **cup sour cream** |
| ½ | **cup sugar** |

- Soften gelatin in cold water. Add boiling water and stir until gelatin is dissolved.
- Blend in heavy cream, sour cream and sugar.
- Pour into a 1-quart ring mold. Chill until firm (about 3 hours).
- Unmold and serve with berries.

# WASHINGTON FAMILY CHOCOLATE PUDDING

Serves 4-6

| | |
|---|---|
| 3 | **ounces semi-sweet chocolate** |
| 2 | **cups milk, divided** |
| 2 | **eggs** |
| ¾ | **cup stale bread crumbs** |

- Melt chocolate in 1 cup milk in top of double boiler.
- Beat eggs until thick and foamy. Add remaining cup of milk and bread crumbs; stir well.
- Slowly pour melted chocolate mixture into egg mixture, blending thoroughly.
- Pour into buttered 1½-quart baking dish and bake at 350 degrees for 30-40 minutes until set.
- Serve warm with sauce.

**SAUCE**

| | |
|---|---|
| ½ | **cup brown sugar** |
| ⅓ | **cup butter** |
| 2 | **Tbsp. boiling water** |

- Cream sugar and butter. Add boiling water and beat well. Serve immediately.

*A very old fashioned recipe handed down from the Mt. Vernon Washingtons.*
*An appropriate choice for Virginia, the "Mother of Presidents."*

# STRAWBERRY CLOUD SOUFFLÉ WITH CHOCOLATE BERRY GARNISH

Serves 6-8
Do ahead

## SOUFFLÉ

| | |
|---|---|
| 2 | **pints strawberries, hulled** |
| 2 | **envelopes unflavored gelatin** |
| ¾ | **cup cold water** |
| ¼ | **cup Kirsch** |
| 2 | **Tbsp. sugar** |
| 1 | **Tbsp. fresh lemon juice** |
| 4 | **egg whites, room temperature** |
| ¼ | **tsp. salt** |
| ¼ | **cup sugar** |
| 1 | **cup heavy cream, whipped** |

- Purée strawberries in processor or blender; set aside.
- In a small saucepan, sprinkle gelatin over water, stirring over low heat until dissolved. Allow to cool slightly. Pour into strawberries. Stir in Kirsch, 2 Tablespoons sugar and lemon juice. Chill until slightly thickened but not set.
- Beat whites and salt to soft peaks. Gradually beat in ¼ cup sugar. Continue beating until stiff but not dry.
- Fold strawberry mixture into whites, then fold in whipped cream.
- Pour into prepared 1-quart soufflé dish which has a lightly-buttered foil collar extending 2 inches over dish rim. For best results, collar should be 3 layers thick. Collared individual soufflé dishes may also be used. Chill several hours.

## GARNISH

| | |
|---|---|
| 1 | **pint strawberries, rinsed and, if desired, hulled** |
| 6 | **ounces semi-sweet chocolate, melted** |

- Insert bamboo skewers into stem end of dry berries. Swirl in chocolate to cover ⅔ of berry.
- Stand skewers in drinking glass until chocolate has hardened, about 1 hour. Remove from skewers.
- Place on soufflé or present alone on decorative tray.

*For optimum success in coating berries, they should be unblemished and dry before being dipped.*

# STRAWBERRY FORGOTTEN TORTE

Serves 8-10
Do ahead

| | |
|---|---|
| 8 | **egg whites, room temperature** |
| ¼ | **tsp. salt** |
| ½ | **tsp. cream of tartar** |
| 1¾ | **cups sugar** |
| 1¼ | **tsp. vanilla** |
| 2 | **cups heavy cream** |
| ½ | **cup confectioners sugar, sifted** |
| | **Fresh strawberries, sliced and sweetened** |

- Preheat oven to 450 degrees.
- Beat whites and salt until foamy; add cream of tartar and beat until stiff but not dry.
- Gradually beat in sugar. Add vanilla. Turn into well greased 2-piece angel food cake pan.
- Put in oven, closing door quickly. Turn off oven immediately, leaving meringue overnight. Do not open door.
- In morning, remove torte from oven. Loosen edges and bottom with thin-bladed knife and place on plate.
- Beat cream until stiff, folding in confectioners sugar. Frost cake.
- Refrigerate until serving time. Slice with serrated knife and serve with strawberries or other fruit.

*Must be baked in an electric oven.*

# STRAWBERRY NUTCRACKER

Serves 8-10

| | |
|---|---|
| 3 | **egg whites, room temperature** |
| 1 | **cup sugar** |
| 1 | **tsp. vanilla** |
| ½ | **tsp. baking powder** |
| 14 | **Ritz crackers, crushed** |
| ¾ | **cup chopped nuts** |

- Preheat oven to 325 degrees.
- Beat egg whites until soft peaks form, gradually adding sugar.
- Combine remaining ingredients. Fold into egg whites. Spoon evenly into well greased 9-inch square pan.
- Bake at 325 degrees for 45 minutes.

**TOPPING**

| | |
|---|---|
| 1 | **10-ounce package frozen strawberries, thawed** |
| 1 | **cup heavy cream, whipped** |
| 1 | **Tbsp. cornstarch** |

- Drain strawberries; reserve juice. Fold fruit into cream. Spread over crust and chill 1 hour.
- Bring juice to boil and thicken with cornstarch.
- Spoon juice onto each piece as it is served.

*Pan may be lined with buttered foil to ease removal.*

# FRUIT SPECTACULAR

Serves 12-16
Do ahead

**CRUST**

| | |
|---|---|
| ¼ | **pound butter** |
| ¼ | **cup confectioners sugar** |
| 1 | **cup flour** |

- Preheat oven to 350 degrees.
- In a food processor, mix ingredients until dough ball forms. Pat into a 12-inch pizza or tart pan.
- Bake at 350 degrees for 15-20 minutes. Cool.

**FILLING**

| | |
|---|---|
| 16 | **ounces cream cheese, softened** |
| ½ | **cup brown sugar** |
| | **Assorted fresh fruits, sliced and patted dry** |
| 1 | **cup marmalade** |
| ¼ | **cup water** |

- Beat first 2 ingredients until fluffy. Spread over cooled crust.
- When cool, arrange fruit over top in a decorative pattern.
- Melt marmalade and water in a saucepan. Drizzle over pizza. Cool.

*May also be put in oblong pan and cut
into small squares for a buffet finger food*

# CHILLED LEMON SOUFFLÉ

Serves 8-10
Do ahead

| | |
|---|---|
| 3 | **egg yolks, beaten** |
| 1 | **cup sugar** |
| ⅓ | **cup lemon juice** |
| 1 | **envelope unflavored gelatin** |
| ¼ | **cup cold water** |
| 4 | **egg whites** |
| 2 | **cups heavy cream** |

- Mix yolks with sugar and lemon juice.
- Stir gelatin and water together. Place gelatin mixture in small pan of hot water, allowing to melt. Cool slightly and mix with egg yolks.
- In a large bowl, beat egg whites until stiff.
- In another large bowl, beat cream until stiff.
- Fold all ingredients together gently. Pour into soufflé dish or crystal bowl. Cover with plastic wrap and chill for 2 hours.
- Decorate with additional whipped cream and grated lemon rind if desired.

# HEAVENLY SNOW SQUARES

Serves 9
Do ahead

**SNOW LAYER**

|   |   |
|---|---|
|   | Graham cracker crumbs |
| 1 | envelope plain gelatin |
| 4 | Tbsp. cold water |
| 1 | cup boiling water |
| ⅔ | cup sugar |
| 3 | egg whites (reserve yolks) |
| ¼ | tsp. salt |
| 1 | tsp. vanilla |

- Press crumbs in bottom of greased 9-inch square pan. Chill.
- Soak gelatin in cold water. Add boiling water and sugar. Cool.
- Beat egg whites well; stir into gelatin mixture. Add salt and vanilla. Beat until very thick. Pour into pan and chill.

**BUTTER SAUCE**

|   |   |
|---|---|
| 3 | egg yolks |
| 7 | Tbsp. sugar |
| 7 | Tbsp. butter, melted |
| 2 | Tbsp. grated lemon rind |
| 3 | Tbsp. lemon juice |
| ⅔ | cup heavy cream, whipped |

- Beat first 5 ingredients until thick.
- Fold in whipped cream. Refrigerate.
- When ready to serve, cut snow layer into squares and top with butter sauce.

# CHOCOLATE MOUSSE

Serves 8
Do ahead

|   |   |
|---|---|
| 12 | ounces semi-sweet chocolate pieces |
| 1½ | tsp. vanilla |
|   | Pinch of salt |
| 1½ | cups heavy cream (heated to boiling point) |
| 6 | egg yolks |
| 2 | egg whites |
|   | Heavy cream for topping, whipped |

- Combine first 3 ingredients in processor, mixing 30 seconds. Add heated cream and mix 30 seconds more or until chocolate is melted. Add yolks and mix for 5 seconds.
- Transfer mixture to bowl and allow to cool.
- Beat whites, forming stiff peaks; fold into chocolate mixture.
- Place mixture in serving bowl or small individual soufflé dishes. Cover with plastic wrap and chill for several hours.
- Top with whipped cream before serving.

# CHOCOLATE MOUSSE CAKE

Serves 12
Do ahead

**CAKE LAYERS**

| | |
|---|---|
| 5 | **egg whites, room temperature** |
| ¼ | **tsp. cream of tartar** |
| ¾ | **cup sugar** |
| 1¾ | **cup confectioners sugar** |
| ⅓ | **cup unsweetened cocoa** |

- Preheat oven to 300 degrees.
- Beat first 2 ingredients in a large bowl until soft peaks form. Beat in sugar, 2 Tablespoons at a time, until stiff peaks form.
- Sift sugar and cocoa together. Fold into meringue.
- Cut three 8-inch square pieces of parchment paper, anchoring them to baking pans with a dab of meringue on bottom of each square.
- Divide meringue among squares, spreading evenly to edges.
- Bake at 300 degrees for 75 minutes.
- Gently peel off paper and cool on racks.

**FILLING**

| | |
|---|---|
| 13 | **ounces semi-sweet chocolate, chopped** |
| 7 | **egg whites** |
| ¼ | **tsp. cream of tartar** |
| 3 | **cups heavy cream** |
| 1½ | **tsp. vanilla** |

- Melt chocolate in double boiler set over hot water. Stir until smooth. Let cool.
- Beat whites with cream of tartar until stiff peaks form.
- In another large bowl, beat cream with vanilla until stiff.
- Fold chocolate into whites; fold in cream.
- Frost meringues with filling as with a layer cake. Cover lightly and chill at least 4 hours or overnight.
- To serve, cut with serrated knife.

# HARD SAUCE

Yields 1½ cups

| | |
|---|---|
| 6 | **ounces butter, softened** |
| 1¼ | **cups confectioners sugar, sifted** |
| 3-4 | **Tbsp. Brandy** |
| ⅛ | **tsp. nutmeg** |

- Beat butter until fluffy. Gradually beat in powdered sugar until well blended.
- Add Brandy and nutmeg. Mix well and chill.
- Serve over plum pudding or gingerbread.

*Keeps 3-4 weeks in refrigerator, tightly capped.*

# COFFEE-ALMOND TORTONI

Serves 8
Do ahead

| | |
|---|---|
| 1 | cup heavy cream |
| ½ | cup sugar, divided |
| 1 | tsp. vanilla extract |
| ¼ | tsp. almond extract |
| 2 | egg whites, room temperature |
| ¼ | cup finely chopped almonds, toasted |
| ¼ | cup flaked coconut, toasted |
| 1 | tsp. instant coffee powder |

- Combine cream, ¼ cup sugar, vanilla and almond extracts. Beat until soft peaks form.
- Beat egg whites until foamy. Gradually add remaining sugar, beating until soft peaks form.
- Fold in whipped cream mixture and half of the almonds and coconut. Spoon half of the mixture into 8 paper-lined muffin tins.
- Stir coffee into reserved portion of tortoni. Spoon over whipped cream mixture. Sprinkle with remaining almonds and coconut. Cover and freeze.
- Cups may be removed from tins and stored in freezer bags.

# MOCHA FREEZE

Serves 8
Do ahead

| | |
|---|---|
| 1⅓ | cups finely crushed vanilla wafers |
| 4 | Tbsp. butter, melted |
| 1 | quart coffee ice cream, softened |
| ½ | cup butter |
| 2 | ounces unsweetened chocolate |
| 3 | egg yolks, well beaten |
| 1½ | cups confectioners sugar, sifted |
| ¾ | cup chopped pecans |
| 1 | tsp. vanilla |
| 3 | egg whites |

- Mix crumbs and melted butter. Reserve ¼ cup of mixture; press remainder into 9-inch square pan. Spread with softened ice cream. Freeze.
- Melt ½ cup butter with chocolate over low heat. Slowly stir into egg yolks which have been mixed with confectioners sugar, pecans and vanilla. Cool thoroughly.
- Beat whites until stiff peaks form, then beat chocolate mixture until smooth. Fold in egg whites.
- Spread chocolate mixture over ice cream. Top with reserved crumbs. Freeze.
- Remove from freezer just before serving.

## INDIVIDUAL BAKED ALASKAS

Serves 4

| | |
|---|---|
| 4 | dessert sponge cups |
| 4 | scoops ice cream (any flavor) |
| 4 | jiggers liqueur |
| 3 | egg whites |
| 6 | Tbsp. sugar |

- Preheat oven to 500 degrees.
- Arrange sponge cups on layer of foil on a cookie sheet. Sprinkle a teaspoon of liqueur on each sponge cup, if desired. Place a medium size scoop of ice cream in each cup. With your thumb, make a small depression in each scoop and fill with liqueur. Freeze.
- Beat whites until soft peaks form; gradually add sugar, beating until stiff and glossy. Cover ice cream and cake completely with meringue, sealing all around bottoms. Alaskas may be frozen at this point if being held for later use.
- Bake Alaskas about 2 minutes, until meringue is lightly browned.
- Serve at once, flaming with additional liqueur if desired.

## MOUSSE GRAND MARNIER WITH BERRY BERRY SAUCE

Serves 4-6
Do ahead

**MOUSSE**

| | |
|---|---|
| 2 | egg whites, room temperature |
| | Pinch of salt |
| 6 | Tbsp. sugar |
| 1 | cup heavy cream |
| ¼ | cup Grand Marnier |

- Beat whites with salt until softly peaked. Whip in 3 Tablespoons sugar until whites are stiff.
- Using same beaters, whip cream until stiff, adding 3 remaining Tablespoons sugar. Blend in Grand Marnier, then fold in whites.

**SAUCE**

| | |
|---|---|
| 1 | 10-ounce package frozen strawberries |
| 1 | 10-ounce package frozen raspberries |
| | Grand Marnier to taste |

- Purée fruit with Grand Marnier.
- In parfait glasses, alternate mousse and sauce layers. Freeze for at least 4 hours.

# LUSCIOUS LEMON DESSERT

Serves 12
Do ahead

| | |
|---|---|
| 1 | cup vanilla wafer crumbs |
| 4 | Tbsp. butter |
| 2 | Tbsp. sugar |
| 3 | eggs, separated |
| ½ | cup sugar |
| 1 | cup heavy cream, whipped |
| ¼ | cup lemon juice |
| | Grated zest of 1 lemon |
| | Additional whipped cream |
| | Lemon peel slivers |

- Combine first 3 ingredients in processor and blend. Press into bottom of 9-inch spring-form pan, reserving 2 Tablespoons to sprinkle over dessert.
- Beat egg whites until frothy. Gradually add sugar, beating until soft peaks form. Add yolks one at a time and beat well.
- Fold in whipped cream, lemon juice and zest.
- Pour into prepared crust. Sprinkle with reserved crumbs. Cover and freeze overnight.
- Before serving, garnish with additional whipped cream and lemon peel slivers.

*Light, lemony and refreshing.*

# SHERRY ICE CREAM CAKE

Serves 10-12
Do ahead

| | |
|---|---|
| 1 | angel food cake |
| 1 | quart vanilla ice cream, softened |

**SAUCE**

| | |
|---|---|
| 1 | cup sugar |
| ¼ | pound butter |
| 2 | egg yolks, beaten |
| 1 | cup Sherry |

- Early in day, split cake in half horizontally, packing well with ice cream. Fill in hole with ice cream also. Freeze.
- Cream butter and sugar well. Melt slowly over low heat. Add yolks a little at a time, stirring constantly.
- In a thin stream add Sherry. Continue stirring over lowest heat until sauce is well blended and thick. Cool.
- At beginning of meal, remove cake from freezer, placing in refrigerator.
- To serve, pour sauce over cake, as much as it will absorb. Slice and serve.
- Remaining sauce may be served with cake.

*For extra moistness, ½-1 cup of Sherry may be poured over bottom half of cake before filling with ice cream.*

# KIR SORBET

Serves 6
Do ahead

| ¼ | cup sugar |
| 1 | cup water |
| 1-2 | Tbsp. Crème de Cassis or black currant syrup |
| 1⅞ | cups dry white wine |

- Bring sugar and water to boil. Remove from heat and allow to cool thoroughly.
- Add remaining ingredients. Pour into bowl; put in freezer.
- Stir a few times after mixture has begun to freeze.
- Remove from freezer 10-15 minutes before needed. Spoon into parfait glasses.

**CHAMPAGNE SORBET OPTION**

| ⅓ | cup sugar |
| 1 | cup water |
| 1-1½ | tsp. grated lemon rind |
| | Juice of ½ lemon |
| 2 | cups Champagne |

*A perfect between-course palate cleanser or light dessert, served with fruit.*

# LEMON ICE CREAM

Serves 12

| 4 | cups milk |
| 1 | cup cream |
| 1½ | cups sugar |
| 1 | tsp. vanilla |
| | Zest of 1 lemon, grated |
| | Juice of 3 lemons |

- Combine ingredients; mix well and follow ice cream churn instructions to freeze.

# EASY CHOCOLATE FROSTING

Frosts 1 cake

| 12 | ounces semi-sweet chocolate pieces |
| ⅛ | tsp. salt |
| 1 | cup sour cream |

- Melt chocolate over low heat; cool slightly. Add sour cream and salt.
- Allow to cool slightly before icing cake.

# PICK-OF-THE-PEACH ICE CREAM

Makes 3-4 quarts

| | |
|---|---|
| 8 | cups milk |
| 2 | cups sugar |
| 1 | Tbsp. flour |
| ¼ | tsp. salt |
| 6 | eggs, beaten |
| 1 | 14-ounce can condensed milk |
| 4 | cups mashed peaches or other seasonal fruit |
| 1 | Tbsp. vanilla |

- Pour milk into large saucepan placed in frypan of water. Heat milk by boiling the water.
- Add sugar, flour and salt to milk, stirring well.
- Pour some of hot mixture into eggs, whisking constantly. Blend eggs into rest of mixture.
- Continue cooking, stirring constantly, until custard coats spoon. Cool. Store in refrigerator until ready to freeze in automatic ice cream maker.
- Before freezing, add remaining ingredients.

# EASY FRENCH CHOCOLATE ICE CREAM

Serves 4
Do ahead

| | |
|---|---|
| ¼ | cup sugar |
| ⅓ | cup water |
| 6 | ounces chocolate chips |
| 3 | egg yolks |
| 1½ | cups heavy cream, whipped |

- Combine sugar and water. Bring to a boil and boil 5 minutes.
- Add hot syrup to chocolate chips In a processor or blender, blending at high speed for 20-30 seconds or until sauce is smooth.
- Add yolks, blending 10 seconds more.
- Fold this mixture into whipped cream and spoon into freezer tray. Cover with wax paper. Freeze for 2-3 hours.

*Wonderful light dessert after heavy meal.*

# PRALINE PECAN PIE

Makes 2 pies

| | |
|---|---|
| 2 | 9-inch unbaked pie shells |
| 4 | eggs |
| 1 | pound light brown sugar |
| ¼ | pound butter, melted |
| 2 | scant Tbsp. corn meal |
| 2 | Tbsp. water |
| 1 | Tbsp. vanilla |
| | Pinch of salt |
| 2 | cups chopped pecans |

- Preheat oven to 325 degrees.
- Beat eggs until frothy. Add remaining ingredients and mix well.
- Pour into pie shells and bake at 325 degrees for 40-45 minutes.

# APPLE GALETTE PASTRY

Serves 6-8

### PÂTÉ BRISÉE

| | |
|---|---|
| 1⅓ | **cups flour** |
| ¼ | **pound *cold* butter, cut up** |
| 1 | **tsp. salt** |
| ¼ | **cup ice water** |

- Preheat oven to 400 degrees.
- In processor, combine flour, butter and salt. Process for several seconds and, with machine still running and pieces of butter still visible, slowly add water until pastry forms a ball.
- Place pastry in refrigerator to cool.

### FILLING

| | |
|---|---|
| 5-8 | **apples, peeled and cored (Golden Delicious are best)** |
| 3 | **Tbsp. sugar** |
| | **Dash cinnamon** |
| | **Grated lemon rind to taste** |
| 2 | **Tbsp. butter** |

- Chop ½ an apple into tiny pieces and set aside. Cut remaining apples in half and slice in ¼-inch slices.
- On an open-sided cookie sheet roll out pâté brisée into a circle. Crust should be rolled very thin.
- Place chopped apple in center of crust. Beginning 1½ inches from edge of crust, arrange sliced apples in circles all the way to the apples in the center. It will look like a flower.
- Bring up sides of pastry to the apples. Patch any rips which occur.
- Sprinkle sugar, cinnamon and grated lemon rind over apples. Cut up butter and place on top of spices.
- Bake at 400 degrees for 60-70 minutes or until *very crusty*.

### GLAZE

| | |
|---|---|
| 4 | **Tbsp. apricot preserves** |
| 1 | **Tbsp. Cognac** |

- Combine preserves and Cognac and spread over top of cooked galette.

# GERMAN APPLE DANDY

Serves 8
Do ahead

**PUFF PASTRY**

| | |
|---|---|
| 1¼ | cups flour |
| ¼ | pound butter, softened |
| ½ | tsp. salt |
| 4-5 | Tbsp. water |

- Mix flour and salt. Cut in butter. Add water 1 teaspoon at a time. Mix until elastic, then form into a ball and chill one hour or longer.

**APPLES**

| | |
|---|---|
| 3-4 | apples, peeled and sliced |
| | Lemon juice |
| | Dash cinnamon |
| | Dash nutmeg |
| | Dash salt |
| 1 | cup sugar |
| 1 | Tbsp. whiskey |

- Place apples in bowl and sprinkle with only enough lemon juice to keep slices from turning brown.
- Mix remaining ingredients and pour over apples. Combine.

**TOPPING**

| | |
|---|---|
| ¼ | pound butter, softened |
| ½ | cup sugar |
| ½ | cup flour |

- Mix ingredients until crumbly.
- Pat chilled dough into a 13 x 9-inch pan. Spread apples over dough. Sprinkle topping over apples.
- Bake at 350 degrees for 30 minutes.

# BANANAS FLAMBÉ

Serves 8-10

| | |
|---|---|
| 6-8 | firm, ripe bananas |
| ½ | cup butter |
| ½ | cup brown sugar |
| ⅔ | tsp. cinnamon |
| 2 | Tbsp. lemon juice |
| 2 | Tbsp. Crème de Cacao |
| ⅔ | cup Rum |
| | Vanilla ice cream |

- Peel and slice bananas in half lengthwise and horizontally.
- In a chafing dish, melt butter. Add sugar. Stir until blended. Add cinnamon.
- Add bananas. Turn in butter mixture until golden brown.
- Add lemon juice and Crème de Cacao.
- Just before serving, heat Rum and pour over bananas. Flame and serve over vanilla ice cream.

# DEEP DISH PEACH COBBLER

Serves 6-8

**FILLING**

| | |
|---|---|
| 6 | cups peaches, peeled and sliced |
| 1½ | cups sugar |
| 1½ | tsp. grated lemon rind |
| 2 | tsp. lemon juice |
| 3 | tsp. flour |
| 1 | Tbsp. butter |

- Preheat oven to 450 degrees.
- Combine ingredients; stir until coated.
- Pour into a 4-inch tall casserole and dot with butter. Set aside.

**PÂTÉ BRISÉE**

| | |
|---|---|
| ¼ | pound cold butter |
| 1⅓ | cups flour |
| 1 | tsp. salt |
| ¼ | cup ice water |

- Cut stick of butter in quarters and place in processor. Add flour and salt. While running, add water very slowly until dough forms a ball.
- On floured surface, roll out dough to fit inside of casserole. Fit over mixture and prick dough.
- Bake at 450 degrees for 10 minutes; turn heat to 350 degrees and bake for 40 minutes. Let stand 15 minutes to cool.

*Whipped cream or ice cream may be served with cobbler.*

# FONDUE AU CHOCOLAT

Serves 4-6

| | |
|---|---|
| 9 | ounces German chocolate |
| ½ | cup heavy cream |
| 2 | Tbsp. Kirsch, Brandy or Cointreau |
| ¼ | tsp. cinnamon |
| 1 | tsp. vanilla |

- Combine chocolate and cream in pan over low heat, stirring occasionally until chocolate is melted.
- Add remaining ingredients. Pour into fondue pot surrounded by platters of fresh fruit, marshmallows, cubes of angel food cake and pound cake. Provide skewers for dipping.

*Best if prepared immediately before serving, but may be done ahead, refrigerated and reheated.*

# ELEGANT CREAM PUFFS

Makes 12 puffs

## PUFF PASTRY

| | |
|---|---|
| ¾ | cup water |
| 6 | Tbsp. butter |
| ¾ | cup flour |
| 3 | eggs |

- Preheat oven to 425 degrees.
- Boil water and add butter. Continue to boil until butter is melted.
- Add flour all at once while water is hot, beating with wooden spoon until mixture forms a ball. Remove from heat and cool 5-10 minutes.
- Add eggs one at a time, beating after each addition until dough forms a ball again. Roll dough into 12 balls, placing on greased cookie sheet.
- Bake at 425 degrees for 20 minutes, then at 325 degrees for 30 minutes. Remove from oven; place on wire rack and cool completely. Cut open, spooning out any moist interior dough; fill with filling.

## FILLING

| | |
|---|---|
| 1½ | cups scalded milk |
| ½ | cup sugar |
| ¼ | cup flour |
| 2 | eggs plus 2 egg yolks |
| 1 | tsp. vanilla |

- Use heavy saucepan for scalding milk.
- Beat sugar, flour and egg mixture over low heat in a double boiler.
- Add milk gradually, stirring constantly until custard mixture begins to thicken. Filling is thick enough when you can lift spoon from mixture, run a finger down middle of spoon's bowl and have a clean line left.
- Remove from heat and add vanilla, cooling custard before filling puffs.

## TOPPING

| | |
|---|---|
| 2 | squares unsweetened chocolate |
| 2 | Tbsp. butter |
| 1½ | cups confectioners sugar, sifted |
| 3 | Tbsp. milk |

- Melt chocolate and butter over low heat, stirring constantly.
- Remove from heat and stir in sugar and milk until smooth. Spread quickly on puffs.

# HOT RUM FONDUE

Yields 2¾ cups

| | |
|---|---|
| 1 | **cup light brown sugar, firmly packed** |
| 1 | **cup light corn syrup** |
| ⅛ | **tsp. salt** |
| 4 | **Tbsp. butter** |
| ¾ | **cup light cream** |
| ¼ | **cup Rum** |

- Put sugar and syrup in fondue pot over low heat. Stir for 5 minutes or until sugar has completely melted and mixture is smooth.
- Add salt and butter. Stir until butter is melted. Stirring constantly, gradually add cream. Stir for 3 minutes more or until fondue coats spoon.
- Turn off heat; allow fondue to cool until it stops bubbling. Add Rum, mix well. Serve while still warm for dipping skewered fresh fruit, angel food cake, marshmallows, or whole pecan halves.

# CHOCOLATE ON A CLOUD

Serves 12-16
Do ahead

| | |
|---|---|
| 1 | **13-ounce can evaporated milk** |
| 1 | **10½-ounce package miniature marshmallows** |
| 6 | **ounces semi-sweet chocolate pieces** |
| ¼ | **pound butter** |
| 1 | **3½-ounce can flaked coconut** |
| 2 | **cups graham cracker crumbs** |
| ½ | **gallon vanilla ice cream** |
| 1 | **cup chopped pecans or walnuts** |
| | **Whipped cream** |

- Combine first 3 ingredients in top of double boiler set over boiling water. Reduce heat, cooking until mixture is melted and smooth. Set aside to cool.
- Cook butter and coconut over medium heat, stirring until coconut is lightly browned. Remove from heat and stir in graham cracker crumbs.
- Press ¾ of crumb mixture into a 13 x 9-inch pan.
- Cut ice cream crosswise into ½-inch-thick slices. Arrange half of slices over crust. Pour half of chocolate mixture over ice cream. Repeat layers.
- Combine remaining crumb mixture and pecans; sprinkle over top of dessert. Cover and freeze until firm.
- Let stand at room temperature 5 minutes before serving. To serve, cut into squares and place each square on a "cloud" of whipped cream.

*May be divided into 2 9-inch square pans—serve one, save one.*

# CONDIMENTS

# CONDIMENTS

# ARTICHOKE RELISH

| | |
|---|---|
| 1 | quart plus 1 cup white vinegar |
| 2 | Tbsp. mustard seed |
| ¼ | cup prepared mustard |
| 3 | cups sugar |
| 1 | tsp. salt |
| 2 | tsp. turmeric |
| ½ | tsp. black pepper |
| 1 | tsp. crushed dried red pepper |
| 1½ | quarts scrubbed, peeled and thinly sliced Jerusalem artichokes |
| 4 | cups thinly sliced onions |
| 5 | large red and green sweet peppers, sliced |

- Combine first 8 ingredients in a large saucepan and bring to a boil.
- Add artichokes, onions and peppers and boil gently for 30 minutes.
- Ladle into hot jars, seal and process in boiling water bath canner for 5 minutes.
- Let flavors marry for several weeks before trying.

# CORN RELISH

| | |
|---|---|
| | Corn on the cob, enough to yield 2 quarts cut corn |
| 1 | quart cabbage, shredded |
| 1 | cup chopped green pepper |
| 1 | cup chopped red pepper |
| 2 | large onions, chopped |
| 1 | cup sugar |
| 2 | Tbsp. dry mustard |
| 1 | Tbsp. salt |
| 1 | Tbsp. mustard seed |
| 1 | Tbsp. celery seed |
| 1 | quart vinegar |
| 1 | cup water |

- Cook corn for 5 minutes; immerse in cold water. Cut from cob.
- Combine remaining ingredients and add to corn. Cook 20 minutes.
- Ladle into hot jars and process in boiling water bath canner for 10 minutes.
- If a thicker relish is desired, use half the liquid.

# TOMATO RELISH

Yields 4-5 quarts

| | |
|---|---|
| 12-16 | pounds tomatoes, peeled, cored and chopped |
| 6 | medium onions, chopped |
| ½ | cup salt |
| 2 | pounds brown sugar |
| 2 | Tbsp. cinnamon |
| 4 | Tbsp. white mustard seed |
| 3-4 | red peppers, chopped |
| 3 | pints vinegar |

- Mix all ingredients. Place in jars; refrigerate.
- Serve on top of cabbage, collard greens, etc.

# ZUCCHINI RELISH

Yields 7 pints

| | |
|---|---|
| 5 | pounds zucchini |
| 4 | large onions |
| 4 | large green peppers |
| 4 | large red peppers |
| ½ | cup salt |
| 2½ | cups cider vinegar |
| 4 | cups sugar |
| 2 | Tbsp. cornstarch |
| 1 | Tbsp. turmeric |
| 1 | tsp. nutmeg |
| 2 | tsp. celery seed |
| ¼ | tsp. pepper |

- Put zucchini, onions and peppers through food grinder using a medium blade. Sprinkle with salt; let stand overnight.
- Drain and rinse well with cold water.
- Combine remaining ingredients in a large pot and bring to a boil.
- Add the vegetables and simmer 30 minutes.
- Ladle into hot jars, leaving ½-inch headspace. Process in boiling water bath canner for 5 minutes.

# ITALIAN SEASONING

Yields ¼ cup

| | |
|---|---|
| 1 | Tbsp. dried oregano |
| 1 | Tbsp. dried marjoram |
| 1 | Tbsp. dried basil |
| 2 | tsp. dried savory |
| 1 | tsp. dried rosemary |
| 1 | tsp. dried sage |

- Mix herbs thoroughly and store in airtight container.
- Use in Italian dishes, soups and stews.

# CRANBERRY-WALNUT RELISH

*Yields 5-6 cups*

1  **pound fresh cranberries**
2  **cups sugar**
1  **cup chopped English walnuts**
1  **cup orange marmalade**
   **Juice of 1 lemon or lime**

- Wash and drain cranberries. Mix with sugar and place in shallow baking dish.
- Cover dish and bake at 350 degrees for one hour.
- Toast walnuts in oven for 12 minutes.
- Add marmalade and lemon juice to cranberry mixture. Stir in nuts. Mix well and pour into container. Chill before serving.

*Great for Thanksgiving or Christmas dinner.*

# FRESH CRANBERRY RELISH

*Yields 3 cups*

2    **cups fresh cranberries**
1    **cup brown sugar**
½    **cup raisins**
¼    **cup orange juice**
1    **orange peel, grated**
1½   **tsp. grated lemon peel**
1    **Tbsp. lemon juice**
¼    **tsp. each cinnamon, allspice, cloves**
¼    **cup broken pecans**

- Chop all ingredients, except nuts, in grinder or food processor. Do not use blender.
- Add nuts and mix well. Store in covered container in refrigerator. Keeps for weeks.

# BRANDIED CRANBERRIES

*Yields 1½-pints*

1     **pound cranberries**
2¼    **cups sugar**
¼     **cup Brandy**

- Preheat oven to 350 degrees.
- Place cranberries in single layer in shallow baking pan.
- Sprinkle with 2 cups of the sugar. Cover tightly with foil.
- Bake at 350 degrees for 1 hour. Remove and sprinkle with remaining sugar and Brandy.
- Place in jars and refrigerate.

# EASY REFRIGERATOR PICKLES

Yields 2 quarts

| | |
|---|---|
| 7 | **cups sliced cucumbers** |
| 1 | **cup sliced onions** |
| 1 | **Tbsp. salt** |
| 1 | **cup cider vinegar** |
| 1¾ | **cup sugar** |
| 1 | **tsp. celery seed** |
| 1 | **tsp. mustard seed** |

- In a large bowl combine cucumbers and onions. Sprinkle salt over mixture and let stand 20 minutes.
- Combine remaining ingredients and pour over cucumbers.
- Ladle into jars and refrigerate.

# BEST-EVER BREAD AND BUTTER PICKLES

Yields 6 pints

| | |
|---|---|
| 4 | **quarts sliced cucumbers** |
| 6 | **medium onions, sliced** |
| 2 | **green peppers, sliced** |
| ½ | **cup uniodized salt** |
| 2 | **whole cloves of garlic** |
| 2 | **trays ice cubes** |
| 2 | **cups sugar** |
| 1½ | **tsp. turmeric** |
| 2 | **Tbsp. mustard seed** |
| 3 | **cups cider vinegar** |

- Place cucumbers, onions and green peppers in a large pot.
- Add salt, garlic and ice; mix well. Let stand 3 hours. Drain well 10-15 minutes. Return to pot.
- Combine sugar, turmeric, mustard seed and vinegar. Pour over drained ingredients. Bring to a boil.
- Ladle into hot jars, leaving ½-inch headspace. Process in boiling water bath canner 5 minutes. When cool invert jars for 20 minutes.

# 24-HOUR PICKLES

Yields 10 pints

| | |
|---|---|
| 7 | **pounds cucumbers, thinly sliced** |
| 2 | **cups pickling lime** |
| 1 | **cup salt** |
| ½ | **cup alum** |
| 4-6 | **cups sugar** |
| ½ | **box pickling spices** |
| 2 | **quarts vinegar** |

- Soak cucumbers in lime and enough water to cover for 14 hours or overnight. Drain.
- Wash and soak in salt water to cover for 4 hours. Drain. Soak in cold water to cover for 2 hours. Drain.
- Add alum and enough water to cover; bring to a boil. Drain and rinse.
- Add sugar, spices and vinegar to cucumbers; cook 30 minutes.
- Ladle into hot jars, seal and process in boiling water bath canner for 5 minutes.

# DILL PICKLES

Yields 7 quarts

| | |
|---|---|
| 17-18 | **pounds pickling cucumbers, washed** |
| 1½ | **cups salt** |
| 2 | **gallons water** |
| 6 | **cups vinegar** |
| ¾ | **cup salt** |
| ¼ | **cup sugar** |
| 9 | **cups water** |
| 2 | **Tbsp. whole pickling spice** |
| 2 | **Tbsp. dried dill weed per jar** |
| 1 | **Tbsp. whole mustard seed per jar** |

- Combine first 3 ingredients; let stand overnight. Drain well.
- Combine vinegar, salt, sugar, and water along with pickling spice tied loosely in a cloth bag. Heat to boiling.
- Pack cucumbers into hot jars.
- Add dill weed and mustard to each jar.
- Pour boiling vinegar mixture (spice bag removed) over cucumbers to within ½-inch headspace. Seal jars and process in boiling water bath canner for 20 minutes.

*Cucumbers may be cut lengthwise in half or quartered.*

# GREEN TOMATO PICKLES

Yields 10-12 quarts

| | |
|---|---|
| 20 | **pounds green tomatoes, cored and sliced ¼-inch thick** |
| 12 | **large onions, sliced** |
| 4 | **pounds light brown sugar** |
| 2 | **quarts cider vinegar** |
| 1 | **Tbsp. black pepper** |
| 2 | **Tbsp. dry mustard** |
| 2 | **Tbsp. ground allspice** |
| 2 | **Tbsp. ground cloves** |
| 2 | **Tbsp. ground turmeric** |

- Soak tomatoes and onions overnight in salt water. Drain well.
- Make syrup of sugar and vinegar in a 12-quart pan; bring to a boil.
- Add tomatoes and onions to syrup. Bring back to a boil and simmer 1 hour, stirring occasionally.
- Add spices and cook 1 hour. Ladle into jars, seal and process in boiling water bath canner for 5 minutes.

*Make in October when lots of green tomatoes are available; delicious with hamburgers.*

# PICKLED BEETS

Yields 4 ½-pints

| | |
|---|---|
| 2 | pounds beets |
| 1½ | cups cider vinegar |
| 1½ | Tbsp. dry mustard |
| ½ | tsp. salt |
| 1½ | cups sugar |
| 2 | medium onions, sliced |
| 2 | tsp. celery seed |

- Cook whole beets in enough water to cover, until tender.
- Drain, reserving one cup of liquid.
- Slip off skins and slice ¼-inch thick. Set aside.
- Add vinegar to reserved liquid and boil.
- Mix mustard, salt and sugar. Add to vinegar mixture and boil.
- Arrange onions and beets alternately in jars.
- Add celery seed to hot liquid and pour into jars, leaving ½-inch headspace. Seal and process in boiling water bath canner for 30 minutes.

*May be stored in refrigerator without processing.*

# OLD CHURCH WATERMELON RIND PICKLES

Yields 5-6 pints

| | |
|---|---|
| | Rind of 1 watermelon, pared and cubed, thick rind preferred |
| 1 | cup pickling lime to 1 gallon of water |
| 10 | cups sugar |
| 5 | cups white vinegar |
| 1 | box whole cloves |
| 1 | box cinnamon sticks |

- Soak watermelon rind overnight in lime water. Rinse.
- Bring rind to boil 3 times in fresh water, draining each time.
- Make syrup of sugar and vinegar. Add spices tied loosely in cheesecloth bag.
- Cook rind in syrup 1 hour. Ladle into jars, leaving ½-inch headspace. Process in boiling water bath canner for 5 minutes.

*If using thin rind, cook mixture no longer than 45 minutes.*

# SWEET PICKLED FIGS

Yields 6-8 pints

| | |
|---|---|
| 4 | pounds figs, stem attached |
| 1 | Tbsp. baking soda |
| 4 | pounds sugar |
| 2 | cups vinegar |
| 3 | Tbsp. pickling spices, tied in cheesecloth bag |

- Place figs in large pot, sprinkle with soda. Cover with boiling water; let stand 5 minutes.
- Pour figs into colander; wash lightly with cold water.
- Return figs to pot, add remaining ingredients. Let sugar dissolve on low temperature; raise temperature and boil for 15 minutes. Set aside.
- Next day, drain liquid into another pot and boil. Pour over figs. Repeat procedure for 2 more days.
- On fourth day, boil all together for 15 minutes.
- Ladle into jars, seal, process in boiling water bath canner for 10 minutes.

# SUNSHINE GRANOLA

Makes 12 cups

| | |
|---|---|
| 3 | cups regular oatmeal, uncooked |
| 1 | 1½-ounce package sesame seeds |
| 1 | cup sunflower seeds |
| 1 | cup wheat germ |
| ½ | cup vegetable oil |
| ½ | cup honey |
| 1 | cup golden seedless raisins |
| 1 | cup diced dried apricots |
| 1 | cup chopped dates |
| 1 | cup flaked coconut |
| 1 | cup sliced almonds |

- Preheat oven to 250 degrees.
- Combine first 4 ingredients in large bowl.
- Stir oil and honey together and pour over dry mixture, stirring well.
- Spread mixture on a lightly greased cookie sheet and bake at 250 degrees for 45 minutes. Allow mixture to cool and then break into large pieces.
- Combine pieces with remaining ingredients; store in an airtight container.

*Kids love to make—and eat—and it's good for them.*

# DILLED OKRA

Yields 9 pints

| | |
|---|---|
| 3 | **pounds young okra, uncut** |
| 2-3 | **celery leaves per jar** |
| 1 | **garlic clove per jar** |
| ½ | **tsp. dill seed per jar** |
| ½ | **tsp. red pepper flakes per jar** |
| 1 | **quart water** |
| 1 | **pint vinegar** |
| ½ | **cup salt** |

- Wash and pack okra into hot jars. Add celery leaves, garlic clove, dill seed, and red pepper.
- Heat water, vinegar and salt to boiling.
- Pour over okra, leaving ½-inch headspace. Seal and process in boiling water bath canner for 5 minutes.
- Let stand 3-4 weeks.

*Wonderful as an hors d'oeuvre.*

# APRICOT JAM

Yields 5 ½-pints

| | |
|---|---|
| 11 | **ounces dried apricots** |
| 1 | **small can crushed pineapple, drained** |
| 3 | **cups water** |
| 3 | **cups sugar** |
| ¼ | **cup lemon juice** |
| | **Rind of 1 lemon, grated** |

- Soak fruits overnight in water, reserving liquid.
- Next day, chop apricots and return to water along with remaining ingredients.
- Cook over medium heat until thickened.
- Ladle into jars, leaving ¼-inch headspace. Seal and process in boiling water bath for 5 minutes.

# BLUEBERRY JAM

Yields 8 ½-pints

| | |
|---|---|
| 3 | **pints blueberries, rinsed, stems removed** |
| 7 | **cups sugar** |
| 2 | **Tbsp. lemon juice** |
| 2 | **pouches fruit pectin (liquid)** |

- In a large saucepan combine blueberries, sugar and lemon juice. Bring to a boil mashing fruit occasionally. Bring to a full rolling boil (one that cannot be stirred down) for 1 minute.
- Remove from heat. Stir in pectin. Skim off foam.
- Ladle into hot jars leaving ¼-inch headspace, seal and process in boiling water bath canner for 5 minutes.

# BLUEBERRY BUTTER

Yields 8 pints

2  quarts fresh blueberries, rinsed and drained
8  large green cooking apples, peeled, cored and sliced
8  cups sugar
1  tsp. ground allspice
1  tsp. ground mace
1  tsp. ground nutmeg

- Combine ingredients in a large saucepan.
- Bring to a boil, lower heat and simmer 1 hour, stirring occasionally. Cook until mixture thickens slightly.
- Ladle into hot jars, leaving ¼-inch headspace, seal and process in boiling water bath canner for 5 minutes.

# DELICIOUS FRUIT MARMALADE

Yields 7 ½-pints

3  oranges
1  lemon
2  cups drained crushed pineapple
6¾  cups sugar
½  cup hot water
1  6-ounce jar maraschino cherries, drained and chopped

- Wash oranges and lemon; cut in half crosswise. Remove seeds and membrane in center of each. Cut fruit into quarters; grind unpeeled fruit in meat grinder or food processor.
- Combine ground fruit, pineapple, sugar and water in Dutch oven; bring to boil over high heat. Reduce heat and boil 30 minutes, stirring often. Remove from heat; stir in cherries.
- Pour into hot half-pint jars, leaving ¼-inch headspace. Seal and process in boiling water bath canner for 10 minutes.

# DILLY BEANS

Yields 4-5 pints

3  pounds green beans
1  clove garlic per jar
   Fresh dill or 2 tsp. dried dill per jar
½  tsp. mustard seed per jar
2½  cups water
2½  cups vinegar
¼  cup salt

- Clean beans and blanch for 3 minutes. Pack beans into jars; add garlic, dill and mustard seed.
- Heat vinegar, water and salt to boiling.
- Pour over beans, leaving ½-inch headspace. Seal and process in boiling water bath canner for 15 minutes.

# CHRISTMAS SHERRY JELLY

Yields 4 ½-pints

| | |
|---|---|
| 2 | **cups inexpensive sweet Sherry** |
| 3 | **cups sugar** |
| ½ | **bottle Certo** |
| 1-1½ | **tsp. red food coloring** |

- Heat Sherry and sugar until sugar is dissolved and mixture is very hot.
- Remove from heat and add Certo and food coloring until desired shade is reached.
- Ladle into jars leaving ¼-inch headspace. Seal and process in boiling water bath canner for 5 minutes.
- Serve with cream cheese and crackers or on English muffins.

*A lovely addition to a Christmas basket.*

# OLD FASHIONED MINT SAUCE

Yields 4 ½-pints

| | |
|---|---|
| 3 | **cups finely chopped mint leaves** |
| 3 | **cups vinegar** |
| 6 | **cups sugar** |

- Sterilize 4 ½-pint jars.
- Fill each jar one-fourth (or more) full of mint leaves.
- Boil vinegar and sugar mixture until it is as syrupy as pancake syrup. Pour over mint leaves and seal the jars.
- Serve heated over lamb or peas.

# TOMATO SAUCE

| | |
|---|---|
| ½ | **bushel fresh garden tomatoes** |
| 1 | **tsp. celery salt** |
| 1 | **tsp. salt** |
| ½ | **tsp. paprika** |
| ¼ | **tsp. thyme** |
| 2 | **tsp. Worcestershire sauce** |

- Wash and quarter unpeeled tomatoes. Boil until soft enough to go through sieve.
- Put through sieve and for each 2 quarts juice and pulp, add dry seasonings listed.
- Boil 8 minutes and add Worcestershire sauce.
- Pour into hot sterile jars and cool. Freeze if keeping longer. Use as tomato sauce or as a thick tomato juice cocktail.

*May be frozen in paper cups, then transferred to freezer bags.*
*Wonderful flavor addition to soups or stews during winter.*

Our sincere appreciation to the members of the Junior League of Norfolk-Virginia Beach, Inc., and their friends and relatives who graciously contributed over 2,000 recipes which were then triple-tested for quality and edited for clarity. Similarity of content and space limitations prevented us from including all recipes.

Mrs. Charles T. Abeles
Joann Moore Ackerman
Virginia Ann Ames
Peggy Jo Marable Arnold
Mary Lewis Webb Ash
Mary Cary Willcox Atkinson
Ann Rodman Avery
Lee Ann Curtis Avery
Nancy Black Baillio
Elizabeth Finnell Bain
Mary Scott Whitehead Baker
Carolyn Kennett Barry
Elizabeth Smith Bartee
Margaret R. Beale
Nancy Gregory Beebe
Susan Jackson Beers
Andrea Harkness Bell
Jeanne Yates Bell
Jeanne Marie Grell Bellis
Betsy Fitch Benton
Susan Terjen Bernard
Diane Bowles Berry
Kathy Nowlin Bethea
Joan Ward Birdsong
Nellie Taylor Bishop
Sarah Morin Bishop
Olivia Smith Bissell
Sandra Spratley Bond
Rosalind Redfearn Boothby
Donna Foster Bortell
Jean Gregg Blair Bowerman
Eloise Wigg Bradley
Marian Gates Breeden
Sheila Rukas Breeden
Amory Paulsen Brewster
Atwood Abbitt Brewton
Pauline Campbell Brickman
Candy Spier Brown
Margaret Rogers Brown
Susan Upshur Brown
Kimberley Brown-Bailey
Jeanne Ball Burger
Ann Stall Burke
Hunter Joyce Burt
Perry Wise Bussard
Marie Callahan
Nettie Callahan
Ann Hanbury Callis
Margaret Graham Campbell
Marie Mercer Campbell
Mary Louis Stack Campbell
Martha Gartrell Capshaw
Maryse Casanova

Gail Sherwood Cervarich
Eloise Clyde Chandler
Lisa Smith Chandler
Jackie Cheshire
Susan Fawcett Chewning
Shirley Edmonson Clare
Missy Flanigan Clark
Price Mears Clarke
Kirkland Tucker Clarkson
Peter Davis Coe
Susan Gross Coe
Mary Payne Jett Cole
Barbara Beaver Conaway
Mary Jane Connor
Sharon Callahan Connor
Eileen Farley Cooper
Susan Barnes Cotten
Rachel Koser Cottrell
Sigrid Clark Couch
Susanne Boothby Councill
Virginia Phillips Counselman
Linda Carroll Coupland
Betty Wade Wyatt Coyle
Catherine Connell Craft
Susan Szymczyk Craig
Ann Kiley Crenshaw
Jane Treadwell Crenshaw
Noel Williamson Crisler
Mary Ann Horton Crocker
Susan Curtis
Ann Wray Cutchins
Charlie Wilbourne Davey
Cathy Ann Davis
Donna Hoover Davis
Dorothy Mixon Davis
Geraldine Hempel Davis
Joyce Bullock Davis
Katherine Mixon Davis
Gaye Mitchell Deal
Mary Ludwig Denny
Nanette Allen Derkac
Laura Penzold Derrickson
Joyce Lindkens Dickerson
Marianne Monette Dickerson
Elizabeth Brichter DiPeppe
Ann Seay Duncan
Mary Barrett Easton
Ann Weart Ege
Micheal Hartgen Eisenbeiss
Mary Douglas Enghause
Margaret Addison Enright
Martha Lee Erwin
Diane Abrigg Estes

Edward R. Estes, III
Brenda L. Exum
Ann Reeves Farley
Madeline Anderson Finney
Mary Margaret Penzold Fooks
P.J. Hughes Forbes
Gayle Blackstone Fox
Elizabeth Peer Fraim
Pamela G. Fulghum
Pat Turney Garris
Susan Hathaway Gentry
Marietta Norris Gibbs
Sue Grandy Gibson
Judith Tucker Gilbert
Ann Wagner Gill
Martha Jacobs Goodman
Sarah Robinson Graham
Loretta Councill Grant
Constance Weiser Gregg
Virginia Gregory
Patricia Sullivan Grell
Anne Dowding Groth
Patricia Briggs Grulke
Clara Boll Gurkin
Elizabeth Conklin Guy
Pamela Coverdale Haarmann
Patricia Hamlin Hall
Carole Lee Hoffman Hancock
Judith Kendall Harden
Jean Jennings Hardy
Emily Symington Harkins
Jackie Harkness
Anne Reed Harper
Eleanor Magruder Harris
Nancy Rhodenhizer Henderson
Margaret Curtis Herron
Cecilia Taylor Hickerson
Nancy Brower Hicks
Sue Trant Hill
Linda Fore Hinnant
Elizabeth Wallin Hoey
Janice Reece Holmes
Toy Shreeves Holmes
Molly Williams Holt
Paige Somers Hood
Candace Stecker Hubbard
Nancy Norman Huber
Sarah Booth Huber
Lida Kepner Hudson
Jean Davis Hughes
Jane Wade Humphrey
Leigh Seward Huston
Cindy Hart Hutton

Patricia Simpson Hylton
Robin Woody Ingram
Margaret Ray Jenkins
Patricia Smyle Johnson
Debra Neuschel Jones
Meeta Lawrence Jones
Constance Phillips Kellam
Kirkland Molloy Kelley
Marietta Simpkins Kelly
Carolyn Annas Kelsey
Mary Grissom Keogh
Hays Leeper Kiefner
Sally Old Kitchin
Katherine Brown Knight
Catherine Taylor Koch
Catherine Palmer Laird
Pamela Hodgman Laird
Carolyn Miller Lammers
Margaret Dalton Land
Nancy Townsend Larmore
Sally James Laster
Susan Elizabeth Laster
Sandra Dougan Laudenslager
Julia Williams Layfield
Lucy Cunningham Lee
Mary Stuart Leming
Mary Jean Redon Levin
Eleanor Adams Lewis
Lois Prime Liles
Mary Locknane
Vivian Cabe Lollar
Harriet Ringstaff Long
Judith Hayman Long
Sarah J. Longstreth
Nancy Loughridge Lowe
Harriet Henry Maresh
Joan Ellingston Marshall
Frances Suber Martin
Harriet Martin
Heather Laird Martin
Alice Craddock Massey
Melissa Kinsey Mathews
Sarah Coles McBrayer
Julie M. McCollum
Mary Helen McCoy
Glenda Goodman McKinnon
Virginia Garrett McKinnon
Lillian Reeves McLemore
Kathy Farrell McNaughton
Mary Lou Dacier McPhaul
Shaune Wittie Meredith
Susan Toro Meredith
Anne Rhett Taylor Merrill
Elisabeth Fuqua Miles
Diane Millar
Deborah Lawrence Miller
Page McRae Miller

Emily Gill Mills
Emily Minges Mitchell
Barbara Bull Monahan
Diane Burrell Morris
Jane Miller Moss
Alice Milton Mountjoy
Myrtle Brown Muehlenbeck
Elizabeth Dalton Neale
Jean Fuller Neuschel
Karen Oetjen O'Brien
Margaret Thrift Oates
Nancy Lawson Oelrich
Elizabeth Kernan Old
Jean Curtis Old
Susan Hodges Oldfield
Mary Mayhew Owens
Linda Bruce Palmer
Beverly Muhlsteff Parker
Beth Blanchard Pennington
Linda Anderson Peterson
Laura Wall Phillips
Marbury Taylor Plant
Mary Barclay Porter
Kathleen Black Powell
Ellen Wallenborn Procejus
Suzanne Pearce Prueher
Ann Robinson Quarterman
Judy Ann Hallam Rachels
Mary McCoy Ramsey
Kathleen Lawrence Redfern
Caroline Green Reeves
Robin Neuschel Reeves
Jean Gray Schenck Rice
Casey Lambert Rice
Kay Smith Richardson
Margaret Alley Richardson
Franklynn Williamson Ring
Paige Gannon Romig
Jane Rathbone Sanders
Frances Holcombe Saul
Carol Smith Schaefer
Lesley Brown Schless
Katherine Morris Schoew
Page Camp Schoew
Marjorie Rooke Schwab
Leeanne Dupree Sears
Betsey Blades Selig
Wanda Buie Sellers
Betty Howe Shannon
Rebecca Whitfield Sherwood
Marian Langley Shuttleworth
Ann-Meade Baskervill Simpson
Particia Carr Slaughter
Priscilla Hubbard Small
Eleanor Bradshaw Smith
Janice Book Smith
Prentiss Davies Smith

Rebecca Beach Smith
Sallie Spence Smith
Sharon Smith Smith
Marcia Ames Spence
Katherine Anderson Spindle
Ann Blakeslee Stables
Linda Ward Starr
Dorothy Manss Stedfast
Debra Rubin Steiger
Elaine Smith Stephens
Jarrett Michael Stephens
Carol Roberts Straeten
Lynda Gomez Strickler
Nancy Willis Tatterson
Cecelia Ashton Taylor
Kaye McPherson Taylor
Lydia Calvert Taylor
Suzanne McCoy Taylor
Carol Forney Temple
Betsy Ames Terry
Nancy Upton Thiemeyer
Ann Ailor Thornton
Margaret Rose Thornton
Jeanne Froment Tiedemann
Mary Devine Timberlake
Josephine Jenks Trant
Suzanne Moore Trapani
Priscilla Dunn Trinder
Jane Ruffin Tucker
Barbara Barrow Turner
Samuel D. Turner, Jr.
Cecilia Driesell Vail
Mita Vail
Christiane Ellis Valone
Ann Waddell Vance
Virginia Buck Van de Water
Patricia Laughbaum Wallace
Nonie White Waller
Maureen Hampton Warman
Janet McConnell Warner
Martha Miller Watson
Mary Lou Callis Weaver
Jane Claytor Webster
Connie Simpson Wehmann
Janette Ownby Wells
Peggy Bullard Whitfield
Kate de Rosset Wilkinson
Elizabeth Ferguson Willcox
Elizabeth Plunkett Williams
Virginia Hanbury Williams
Widget Farley Williams
Blair Robertson Willis
Doris MacDougall Winn
Clara Mitchell Wolcott
Lauren Vance Wolcott
Joyce Jackson Wood
Scott Young

# TIDEWATER ON THE HALF SHELL

The Junior League of Norfolk-Virginia Beach, Inc.
P.O. Box 956
Norfolk, Virginia 23501
(804) 627-3033

Please send _____ copies of **TIDEWATER ON THE HALF SHELL** .......... @ 16.95 each _____
Add postage and handling.............................................................. @ 3.00 each _____
Add gift wrap*........................................................................... @ 1.00 each _____
Virginia residents add 4.5% sales tax........................................... @ .76 each _____
Total _____

☐ Check or money order enclosed. Make checks payable to **TIDEWATER ON THE HALF SHELL**
Please charge to: ☐ Mastercard    ☐ Visa
Card Number: ☐☐☐☐ ☐☐☐☐ ☐☐☐☐ ☐☐☐☐
Expiration date:_____Signature of card holder:_____

From:                                          Ship To:
Name:_____          Name:_____
Address:_____          Address:_____
City:_____State:_____Zip:_____     City:_____State:_____Zip:_____
*If gift, enclosure card to read_____

---

# TIDEWATER ON THE HALF SHELL

The Junior League of Norfolk-Virginia Beach, Inc.
P.O. Box 956
Norfolk, Virginia 23501
(804) 627-3033

Please send _____ copies of **TIDEWATER ON THE HALF SHELL** .......... @ 16.95 each _____
Add postage and handling.............................................................. @ 3.00 each _____
Add gift wrap*........................................................................... @ 1.00 each _____
Virginia residents add 4.5% sales tax........................................... @ .76 each _____
Total _____

☐ Check or money order enclosed. Make checks payable to **TIDEWATER ON THE HALF SHELL**
Please charge to: ☐ Mastercard    ☐ Visa
Card Number: ☐☐☐☐ ☐☐☐☐ ☐☐☐☐ ☐☐☐☐
Expiration date:_____Signature of card holder:_____

From:                                          Ship To:
Name:_____          Name:_____
Address:_____          Address:_____
City:_____State:_____Zip:_____     City:_____State:_____Zip:_____
*If gift, enclosure card to read_____

I would like to see **TIDEWATER ON THE HALF SHELL** in the following stores in my area:

Store Name: _____

Address: _____

City: _____ State: _____ Zip: _____


Store Name: _____

Address: _____

City: _____ State: _____ Zip: _____

---

I would like to see **TIDEWATER ON THE HALF SHELL** in the following stores in my area:

Store Name: _____

Address: _____

City: _____ State: _____ Zip: _____


Store Name: _____

Address: _____

City: _____ State: _____ Zip: _____